Economic Policy in Covid-19 Times

Economic Policy in Covid-19 Times

Edited by

P. G. BABU

Orient BlackSwan

ECONOMIC POLICY IN COVID-19 TIMES

ORIENT BLACKSWAN PRIVATE LIMITED

Registered Office
3-6-752 Himayatnagar, Hyderabad 500 029, Telangana, India
e-mail: centraloffice@orientblackswan.com

Other Offices
Bengaluru, Chennai, Guwahati, Hyderabad, Kolkata,
Mumbai, New Delhi, Noida, Patna, Visakhapatnam

First published by Orient Blackswan Private Limited 2022

ISBN 978-93-5442-290-4

Typeset in
Adobe Jenson Pro 11/13
by Le Studio Graphique, Gurgaon 122 007

Printed in India at
Yash Printographics, Greater Noida 201 310

Published by
Orient Blackswan Private Limited
3-6-752 Himayatnagar, Hyderabad 500 029, Telangana, India
e-mail: info@orientblackswan.com

For

Professor K. L. Krishna

Chairperson, MIDS (1 August 2013 to 31 July 2020)

50 years
mids
Madras
Institute of
Development
Studies

Contents

Section III—Environmental Markets and Policy

Section IV—Trade and Industry

Section V—Labour

Section VI—Infrastructure Development

Section VII—Local Governance and Social Development

Tables, Figures and Boxes

Tables

Figures

Boxes

Preface

We are in the midst of a pandemic shock as well as a deep economic recession. It necessitates extraordinary policy action. However, we do not have the luxury of time to carry out a new research plan. The situation calls for immediate reflection and action, based on available data. In this volume entitled *Economic Policy in Covid-19 Times*, the authors, primarily Madras Institute of Development Studies (MIDS) faculty and their collaborators from elsewhere, contemplate on diverse issues of importance, contextualise their work to the contemporary challenge, draw attention to linkages with interrelated sectors and issues, and suggest short- to medium-term policy measures. This volume would be a useful input in the design of Tamil Nadu's post-pandemic socio-economic policy and is also a part of MIDS Golden Jubilee celebrations.

Special thanks go to three Vs of MIDS—Venkatachalam, Venkatachalapathy, and Vijayabaskar—for their support, continuous input, and unobtrusive advice all through this process during truly trying times. All the authors and their co-authors met a tight schedule and demands for revisions quite promptly, often with a smile. I am thankful to Ashok R. Chandran (copy-editing), M. R. Prasanna (overall coordination and final round of copy-editing), A. Arivazhagan (initial typesetting), R. Dharumaperumal (electronically distributing the material to MIDS networks), and Rengaiah Murugan (disseminating the work in print and online forums in English and Tamil) for their timely and tireless efforts.

Reaching the target audience and going beyond to common people was made easy by the wholehearted faith, effort, and support to this line of MIDS work by Bharathi Puthakalayam's *bookday.co.in*, *Kalvi Today*, Puthiya Thalaimurai, *The Hindu* (Tamil and English editions), *The New Indian Express*, and Vikatan Publications.

MIDS has been fortunate to have had Professor K. L. Krishna as its chairman for the past seven years. Economists revere him as the quintessential Teacher's Teacher. The only way to acknowledge and say 'Thank You' to such a great scholar is through academic work. This volume is dedicated to Professor Krishna as a small token of appreciation of his commitment and great work as the chairperson of MIDS Governing Council and the Board of Trustees for the past seven years, in the MIDS prelude run towards its golden jubilee in 2021. Thank you very much Professor Krishna, for your erudite scholarship, wisdom, and subtle guidance.

P. G. Babu
Director, MIDS

Publishers' Acknowledgements

The publishers would like to thank the following for granting permission to reproduce the below-mentioned copyrighted material used in this volume.

'Protecting Livelihood, Health, and Decency of Work: Paid Domestic Workers in the Time of Covid-19' by S. Anandhi and E. Deepa has been reproduced with permission of Informa UK Limited through PLSclear. It was first published in Hans, A., K. Kannabiran, M. Mohanty, and Pushpendra (eds), *Migration, Workers, and Fundamental Freedoms: Pandemic Vulnerabilities and States of Exception in India*, London, Routledge India, 2021.

'Covid-19 Pandemic and Social Protection in Tamil Nadu: Need to Strengthen a Life-Cycle Approach' by Gayathri Balagopal and M. Vijayabaskar has been reproduced with permission of Mr Anil Nair, Founder and Editor, *Policy Circle*, where it had been published under the title, 'Social protection in Tamil Nadu: Covid-19 highlights need for universal coverage' on 3 August 2020.

'Affordable Housing in Chennai and Some Notes on Post-Pandemic Prospects' by Karen Coelho and A. Srivathsan has been reproduced with permission of *India Housing Report*, an online archive by the Centre for Policy Research, New Delhi.

Abbreviations

AEP	Assembled End Products
ANM	Auxiliary Nurse Midwives
APMC	Agricultural Produce Market Committee
AWC	Anganwadi Centres
BAPASI	Booksellers and Publishers Association of South India
BLC	Beneficiary-Led Construction
CAA	Citizenship Amendment Act
CAC	Command-and-Control Approach
CHC	Community Health Centres
CLSS	Credit Linked Subsidy Scheme
CMA	Chennai Metropolitan Area
CMGCPS	Chief Minister's Girl Child Protection Scheme
CMIE	Centre for Monitoring Indian Economy
CMWSSB	Chennai Metropolitan Water Supply and Sewerage Board
CPI	Consumer Price Index
CPHS	Consumer Pyramids Household Survey
CWSN	Children with Special Needs
DCR	Development Control Regulations
DES	Department of Economics and Statistics of the Government of Tamil Nadu
DPC	District Planning Committees
DPL	Directorate of Public Libraries, Tamil Nadu
DTP	Desktop Publishing
EAS	Environmental Accounting System
EDE	Environmental Defensive Expenditure
EME	Emerging Market Economy
EPZ	Export Processing Zones
EWS	Economically Weaker Section
EU	European Union

FAO	Food and Agriculture Organization of the United Nations
FIMSUL	Fisheries Management for Sustainable Livelihoods
FRBM	Fiscal Responsibility and Budget Management Act
FSI	Floor Space Index
GCC	Greater Corporation of Chennai
GDP	Gross Domestic Product
GKRA	Garib Kalyan Rojgar Abhiyaan
GIM	Global Investors' Summit
GPDP	Gram Panchayat Development Plans
GSDP	Gross State Domestic Product
GST	Goods and Services Tax
GVC	Global Value Chain
IAMWARM	Irrigated Agriculture Modernisation and Water-Bodies Restoration and Management
ICDS	Integrated Child Development Services
IIPS	International Institute for Population Sciences
ILO	International Labour Organization
IMF	International Monetary Fund
IMFL	Indian-made foreign liquor
IT	Information Technology/Income Tax
J&K	Jammu and Kashmir
LBS	Lead Bank Scheme
LIG	Low-income Group
LPR	Labour Participation Rate
LPVR	Least Present Value of Revenue
LTRO	long-term repo operation
MGNREGA	Mahatma Gandhi National Rural Employment Guarantee Act
MGNREGS	Mahatma Gandhi National Rural Employment Guarantee Scheme
MIDS	Madras Institute of Development Studies
MIG	Middle-income Group
MMF	Man-made Fibre
MNE	Multinational Enterprises
MRMBS	Muthulakshmi Reddy Maternity Benefit Scheme
MSME	Micro, Small and Medium Enterprises

MSP	Minimum Support Price
NABARD	National Bank for Agriculture and Rural Development
NIA	Net Irrigated Area
NP	Network Product
NRC	National Register of Citizens
NSA	Net Sown Area
NSSO	National Sample Survey Office
OECD	Organisation for Economic Co-operation and Development
O&M	Operations & Maintenance
ONOC	One Nation, One Card
P&C	Parts and Components
PDS	Public Distribution System
PES	Payment for Ecosystem Services
PHC	Primary Health Centres
PIP	Participatory Identification of the Poor
PLFS	Periodic Labour Force Survey
PMAY	Pradhan Mantri Awas Yojana
POD	Print on Demand
PPP	Public–Private Partnership
PRI	Panchayati Raj Institution
PSE	Preschool Education
PSL	Priority Sector Lending
PT MGR NMP	Puratchi Thalaivar M. G. Ramachandran Nutritious Meal Programme
PWD	Public Works Department
PWES	Payment for Water Ecosystem Services
RBB	River-basin Board
RBI	Reserve Bank of India
RDA	Recommended Dietary Allowance
RIDF	Rural Infrastructure Development Fund
R&D	Research and Development
SACON	Salim Ali Centre for Ornithology and Natural History
SARS	Severe Acute Respiratory Syndrome
SDGs	Sustainable Development Goals

SEZ	Special Economic Zone
SGDP	State Gross Domestic Product
SHG	Self-Help Group
SITC	Standard International Trade Classification
SLBC	State Level Bankers' Committee
SPS	Sanitary and Phytosanitary
SRC	Survey Research Center of the University of Michigan's Institute for Social Research
TNAU	Tamil Nadu Agricultural University
TNFMIS	Tamil Nadu Farmers' Management of Irrigation Systems Act
TNHB	Tamil Nadu Housing Board
TNPCB	Tamil Nadu Pollution Control Board
TNSCB	Tamil Nadu Slum Clearance Board
TPDS	Targeted Public Distribution System
TTDC	Tamil Nadu Tourism Development Corporation
TWR	Tradable Water Rights
UER	Unemployment Rate
UPDS	Universal Public Distribution System
UT	Union Territory
VP	Village Panchayat
WFP	World Food Programmes
WHO	World Health Organization
WUA	Water Users' Association

1

Introduction

Economic Policy in Covid-19 Times

P. G. Babu

It was in February 2020, during short visits to Erasmus University at Rotterdam in the Netherlands and Chiang Mai University in Thailand, that I had the first inkling of the pandemic. In the Netherlands, colleagues lamented a sudden spurt in paranoia about people of Chinese origin, and at Bangkok airport, I felt as if I were playing a part in a movie about a virus outbreak that Hollywood periodically churns out—everyone, me included, was walking around wearing face masks. Little did I know then that in a few weeks, 'Corona' as it then was called, would engulf the world, including India, and hurtle us down a path that would be worse than the Great Depression. Now that we are in the midst of Covid-19 (as it has now been officially christened), this book attempts to make sense of its immediate effects on lives, livelihoods, and policy across the economy as well as contemplate short- and medium-term mitigating measures that policymakers could potentially take.

Pre–Covid-19: World, India, and Tamil Nadu[1]

Let me pause for a moment and begin with a quick overview of world economic trends before Covid-19. The annual growth in global trade in goods and services had slumped to just over 3 per cent since 2012, which is less than half the average rate of growth seen during the previous thirty-year period. A deceleration in global demand for goods and services, along with increasing protectionist tendencies, and a peaked-out growth in global supply chains might have possibly contributed to this slowdown. The growth rate of investment slowed down from 12 per cent during the 2000s to about 3 per cent in 2015, and again steadily decelerated over the past five years,[2] pointing to a steady decline.

Compared to the 1940s, when 90 per cent of 30-year-olds were earning more than their parents, now only approximately 50 per cent are earning more than their parents. One keeps hearing about different estimates of the impact of increasing automation on employment and income. For example, Jim Yong Kim, the then president of the World Bank, in a speech at Washington D.C.,[3] on 3 October 2016 noted that 69 per cent of jobs in India and around 77 per cent in China were under threat from automation. All of this points to a considerable slowing down of the world economy since 2016.

India has not been an exception. Many of the states have been showing a consistent decline in the labour force participation rate (LPR) since January 2016. Shocks such as demonetisation and the introduction of the Goods and Services Tax (GST), have accentuated the slowing international trend in the Indian context.

Tamil Nadu appears as a touchstone in the pandemic context. Along with Maharashtra and Gujarat, it is among the states most affected by Covid-19. Urban Tamil Nadu looks similar to states such as Maharashtra and Gujarat and like them, it boasts of a large manufacturing base. It also ranks among the best in terms of sustainable development indicators such as literacy and gender. While it also ranks among the new economy hubs such as Karnataka, Haryana, and Telangana, a sharp decline of LPR in Tamil Nadu sets it apart from the other states. Hence, it is useful to think about India through the prism of a representative state such as Tamil Nadu.

Tamil Nadu is predominantly rural, with 53 per cent of households living in rural areas (as per 2011 Census). The gender divide is very small, with 51 per cent males and 49 per cent females in the total population of the state. Tamil Nadu has a huge demographic dividend with 70 per cent of the population in the age group of up-to-45-years. The percentage of people above 60 years of age is 11 per cent.

The literacy rate has improved to 86 per cent in 2018. The female literacy rate too has increased, up to 80 per cent in 2018. Fifteen per cent of the population have completed a bachelor's degree or above. Four per cent have a diploma degree. Two-thirds of the population are either pursuing or have completed education up to high-school level.

Tamil Nadu's unemployment rate is around 3 per cent; while 45 per cent of the population are employed, 52 per cent are not in the workforce (a category which includes retired persons, homemakers, students, and those not seeking employment). However, if we exclude students in the 'not in the workforce' category and analyse only the rest of the working age population (15 years and above), then the unemployment rate increases to 4 per cent. At the same time, the percentage of people who are employed also increases to 57 per cent, and people 'not in the workforce' reduces to 39 per cent. Of all employed, 63 per cent of males and 27 per cent of females are employed. The unemployment rate is 2 per cent for females, and 4 per cent for males. Most males who are currently not working are students whereas most females in this category are homemakers, followed by students. Private sector salaried employment has emerged as the major work type, with 21 per cent of population involved in salaried private sector employment, followed by 'casual labour (agriculture)' at 19 per cent and 'self-employment (non-agriculture)' at 14 per cent. In rural areas, almost one third of the population is involved in 'casual labour (agriculture)'.

The mean household income in the financial year 2017–2018 was Rs. 25,420; in urban areas it was Rs. 99,629, and in rural areas it was Rs. 92,765. Mean income was highest from salaried work (Rs. 2,05,250), followed by self-employment (Rs. 1,32,545). Household per capita income in the financial year 2017–2018 was Rs. 36,973. Rural per capita income was Rs. 24,157, and urban per capita income was Rs. 51,388. Fifty per cent of households in the state expected their income to increase in the next five years. Urban households were more optimistic than rural households about the increase in their future income.

Against this background of slowing international and Indian trends and somewhat positive trends in the state of Tamil Nadu, prior to the Covid-19–imposed lockdowns, let us juxtapose the current happenings.

Covid-19: A Few General Pointers

While thinking about the impacts of the Covid-19 lockdown, the general equilibrium effects are important. We need to keep intersectoral linkages, synergies, and complementarities in mind. For example, the general sense is that the garment industry in Tamil Nadu is suffering from high rental and land costs. On the other hand, the construction industry is going through a slump. There is also a realisation that migrant labour working in these factories need to be better housed so as to achieve the social distancing norms that have emerged. Perhaps all these issues could be resolved by building housing projects for these migrant labourers through Public–Private Partnership (PPP), which would help both the garment and the construction sectors while addressing the issue of the welfare of the migrant labourers. Another example of these intersectoral linkages is that the Tiruppur garment industry is characterised by machinery of low sophistication. The engineering sector in nearby Coimbatore, with a bit of help from public investment in research and development (R&D), might be able to produce better quality machinery.

There would certainly be an effect of the fear of 'contagion', resulting in significant changes in precautionary behaviour of consumers. This has to be seen in the light of the nature of consumption today, compared to, say, last century. Today's consumption, a large part of it, has a high 'social' aspect and can therefore be easily postponed or abandoned altogether. As a result, modern economies may be more vulnerable to a decline in economic activity. Hence, precautionary changes in consumption patterns are likely to result in huge economic losses.

To elaborate, economic impact is determined by the desire of people to reduce their public interaction, say, travel, leisure, and tourism. This delineates the importance of accurate portrayal of the correct picture of the risk posed by the pandemic to the population. The role of the media in this correct depiction of reality versus rhetoric is absolutely essential. Communication from the government and media play a crucial role in characterising the risk perceptions of the pandemic. One cannot help but compare the neutral government-sponsored communication, both in terms of quality and intensity, during the 'Green Revolution' and the paucity of such 'neutral' information throughout the 'Bt Cotton' saga.

Death and absenteeism, particularly when healthy workers stay away for the fear of disease, could have serious effects. Lack of 'trust' will heavily affect migrant labour, and those who go home are unlikely to return soon. The usual annual trips to home states might get extended. Assuming that overcrowding of public transport would recur as in normal days, it is futile to assume that bus conductors would be able to maintain order and social distancing norms. Hence, anticipating this, the office hours of various establishments could be staggered to minimise peak-hour traffic, and think in a way which would eliminate the very idea of peak hours.

In all this, group behaviour is likely to be very different from individual behaviour. A group could potentially get into an irrational frenzy, for example, with burials. However, individuals may choose to shop for necessities irrespective of overcrowding, forgetting altogether about the possibility of Covid-19 infection.

In the case of Covid-19, the World Health Organization (WHO) is not ruling out the possibility of once-infected people getting infected again. Hence, these affected people are likely to consume fewer goods, such as food, travel, and services. As has been said earlier, healthy unaffected people too are likely to be influenced by 'precautionary behaviour', which is likely to be further accentuated by the presence of affected people within the family or in the neighbourhood. 'Consumption smoothing' may not be efficient in partially correcting these shocks, as more people are likely to become 'credit constrained'. Hence, policy in response to the pandemic will be as important, if not more, than the pandemic itself.

Organisation of this Book

This book, comprising 18 essays besides this Introduction, undertakes such a policy analysis in the midst of the crisis. It is organised under seven broad sections: Macroeconomic Scenario, Agriculture Policy Reforms, Environmental Markets and Policy, Trade and Industry, Labour, Infrastructure Development, and Local Governance and Social Development.

Macroeconomic Scenario

In 'Pre– and Post–Covid-19 Macroeconomic Scenarios for India', Shesadri Banerjee offers a recap of the state of the Indian economy before Covid-19 struck, with a careful look at sectoral growth rates of production, capacity utilisation, and aggregate demand both at the national and subnational levels. Having highlighted that the economy was not healthy in the pre–Covid-19 period, Banerjee traces the phases of pandemic-induced lockdowns and their additional effects on output loss. He delineates the additional constraints imposed by low fiscal space and the predominantly informal nature of Indian labour markets during such trying times. Due to frictions in the financial markets, monetary policy is expected to have lesser impact on the economy and therefore, Banerjee prescribes expansionary fiscal policies to increase the effective demand.

In 'Employment and Covid-19: Trends and Issues in Tamil Nadu', Babu, Vikas Kumar, and Poonam Singh use Centre for Monitoring Indian Economy monthly data on states of India to show that there has been a steady decline in Tamil Nadu's LPR since January 2016. Demonetisation did not significantly impact either rural or urban LPR. The introduction of GST, on the other hand, had a significant negative effect on urban LPR. The immediate effect of the nationwide Covid-19 lockdown is visible through a significant decline in LPR in both the rural and urban sectors. They show comparisons with other comparable states and trace challenges facing major industries in Tamil Nadu, with a brief note on the way forward that includes promoting self-reliant domestic industry and supply chains.

Agriculture Policy Reforms

In 'Reforms in the Agriculture Sector in the Post-Covid-19 Era', L. Venkatachalam outlines reforms that could unearth the fortune at the bottom of the agriculture pyramid through medium- to long-term measures, such as market reforms, contract farming, demand-based agriculture to stabilise prices of agricultural commodities, payment for ecosystem services for promoting sustainable agriculture, focusing on more value-added products that would benefit both agriculture and MSME (Micro, Small & Medium Enterprises) sectors, and promoting medicinal plants for crop diversification, apart from process-based short-term measures, such as faster and direct procurement, storage facilities, and flexible crop loans.

Prosperity in agriculture depends, in large part, on irrigation resources available to enable better cropping pattern. In 'Irrigation in Tamil Nadu: Pre– and Post–Covid-19 Eras', K. Sivasubramaniyan undertakes a precise analysis of tank and canal irrigation in Tamil Nadu and outlines the impact of Covid-19 on farm activities. He emphasises the part played by the World Bank IAMWARM (Irrigated Agriculture Modernization and Water-Bodies Restoration and Management) project's idea of more income per drop of water, role of Mahatma Gandhi National Rural Employment Guarantee Act (MGNREGA) in possibly stopping and reversing the rising input cost of cultivation, the contribution of the State Level Bankers' Committee in preparing Covid-19 special credit plans, and a Covid-19–related revamp of the Rural Infrastructure Development Fund, and lists several short-term measures.

In 'Reforms in the Farm Acts: Agriculture Markets', Babu, Ganesh-Kumar, and Chandan Kumar analyse three farm acts passed by the Government of India (now withdrawn) and possible reform measures arising out of them. New market opportunities, institutional structures and the regulatory framework necessary for such markets, information intermediaries, contract farming, environment, and food safety are outlined. Important policy prescriptions, such as reforming the Minimum Support Price (MSP) mechanism, encouraging farmers' markets to bring producers and consumers closer, and promoting competitive agricultural markets through Special Economic Zones are discussed in the way ahead.

Environmental Markets and Policy

In 'Environmental Reforms in Tamil Nadu after Covid-19', P. Durairasu and L. Venkatachalam begin with India's poor rank in the global Environmental Performance Index, and the trade-off between economy and environment which resulted in the improvement of the latter under lockdown. They emphasise the role of Green GDP and Environmental Accounting System and argue for the inclusion of biodiversity in the latter. Keeping with their argument for a movement away from the command-and-control system towards market-based economic instruments for environmental management, their policy prescription includes economic valuation of and payment for ecosystem services, the introduction of tradable water rights for efficient water allocation, the introduction of tradable pollution permits, and creation of environmental databases.

In 'Covid-19 and Tamil Nadu's Marine Fisheries Sector', Ajit Menon and Maarten Bavinck look at the adverse impact of the Covid-19 pandemic on Tamil Nadu's marine fisheries sector, which in 2019 became the top producer in the country. After a careful summary of the status of this important sector, they precisely discuss the pandemic impacts. This is followed by short- and medium-term policy measures, such as credit cards for fishers and centralised insurance schemes. They also contemplate policy measures to increase the resilience of this sector, by pointing out the challenges that are external and internal to the fisheries sector.

Trade and Industry

In 'Why Assemble in Tamil Nadu? Ideas from Trends in Global Trade', C. Veeramani and Babu argue that in the current context, with everyone's focus inward, time is perhaps ripe for 'Assemble in Tamil Nadu for the World'. Which industries should Tamil Nadu focus on? First, there exists a significant unexploited export potential in state's traditional, unskilled labour-intensive industries, such as textiles, clothing, footwear, and toys. The Global Value Chains (GVCs) in these industries are controlled by 'buyer-driven' networks. Second, Tamil Nadu has a huge potential to emerge as a major hub for final assembly in a range of products, referred to as 'network products' (NPs). The GVCs in these industries are controlled by leading multinational enterprises within 'producer-driven' networks. To give an idea of the market size, NP accounts for about 42 per cent of global manufactured exports.

M. Vijayabaskar looks at the garment MSME cluster in Tamil Nadu in 'Sustaining Industrial Clusters in Tamil Nadu for Employment Generation: Some Policy Lessons from Tiruppur'. He starts by pointing out that India's share in the global garment trade is 4.2 per cent whereas that of China is 37 per cent. A movement towards more value-added segments, as well as an increase in market share are likely to result in higher employment. The policy consequence of 'small-scale' sector is high levels of subcontracting and the resultant failure to exploit scale economies. Vijayabaskar argues that the sector could be upgraded by bypassing intermediaries, direct retailing or creation of brands, moving into Man-Made Fibre (MMF), blends and technical textiles, improving quality and productivity through R&D, and backward induction into spinning and garment manufacture. Lack of design studio and/or failures to run one is emphasised. The use of relatively unsophisticated machinery has also been found to hamper the industry. He points out that there is higher duty on MMF and high rental as well as land costs that needs to be addressed.

A. R. Venkatachalapathy takes a passionate look at the precarious state of the Tamil publishing industry in 'The Tamil Book-Publishing Industry and the Impact of Covid-19 Pandemic: A Note'. This is an MSME which is facing grim prospects owing to the pandemic. In the historical introduction where we learn that Tamil was the first non-European language to deploy moveable type, he traces the evolution of this industry. Various aspects, such as organisation, production, distribution, and sales apart from precarious demand are carefully outlined. Venkatachalapathy then goes on to capture the impact of Covid-19 on the publishing industry in the state and flags possible measures, to be undertaken largely by the government, to mitigate negative impacts.

In 'Measures to Revive the Tourism Sector in Tamil Nadu After the Covid-19 Pandemic', Krishanu Pradhan follows with a study on another industry that has been badly affected by the pandemic. He starts with the importance of the tourism sector and summarises the pre– and post–Covid-19 scenarios of Tamil Nadu tourism and the impact of the pandemic. Pradhan explores the need for credit support, ways to increase footfall, and regeneration of tourism demand through various measures, such as promotion of pilgrim tourism, ecotourism and medical tourism, efficient information dissemination about opportunities in the sector and the participation of private players in maintaining the tourism-related logistics and infrastructure, with a plea to create a better database.

Labour

In 'Covid-19 and Migration: The Experience of Tamil Nadu', K. Jafar and A. Kalaiyarasan provide valuable insight into the dynamics of pre–Covid-19 migration trends in India, and Tamil Nadu in particular. They then trace the causes and consequences of post–Covid-19 reverse migration. They highlight various short-term and medium-term policy measures, such as affordable housing, portability of access to universal basic services, more efficient functioning of relevant welfare boards (such as the Tamil Nadu Construction Workers Welfare Board) and MGNREGA, and development of a better database are highlighted by them.

In 'Protecting Livelihood, Health, and Decency of Work: Paid Domestic Workers in the Time of Covid-19', S. Anandhi and E. Deepa outline the plight of paid domestic workers. They undertake a careful analysis of the challenges, such as low pay, liquidity crunch, consumption smoothing issues, and the welfare crisis induced by Covid-19 lockdowns on this vulnerable set of workers. The challenges faced by these workers while returning to work post-lockdown, such as the perception that they are virus carriers, and the need for coordinated health and social policy for their welfare are carefully documented. They offer valuable insights into how the institutional contours of the Tamil Nadu Domestic Workers Welfare Board can be reimagined and redesigned.

Infrastructure Development

To overcome the recessionary mode of the economy due to the Covid-19 pandemic, Tamil Nadu may immediately focus on restarting construction in the infrastructure sector. In 'Infrastructure Development Post Covid-19: PPP Contracts and Design Issues', Babu and Chandan Kumar caution that such reliance on private investment for infrastructure development through the PPP model has its own challenges. Such a PPP model would need a supportive institutional system and must balance various aspects, such as risk sharing, selection of suitable partners, risk pricing or risk premium, government guarantees, incomplete contracts, governance and regulation, and contract renegotiations. They illustrate these issues with carefully chosen lessons from Indian highways development contracts and suggest possible alternative PPP bidding methods.

In 'Affordable Housing in Chennai and Some Notes on Post-Pandemic Prospects', Karen Coelho and A. Srivathsan use their study of Chennai's affordable housing to illustrate possible impacts of Covid-19 and policy measures to contain them. They look at housing demand, shortage, and more importantly, affordability and their interplay with housing supply in the context of Chennai. They then analyse the challenges faced by the private sector in providing affordable housing and outline what an evidence-based housing policymaking would require. They end with a careful summary of prospects for affordable housing in a post-pandemic scenario.

Local Governance and Social Development

Kripa Ananthpur points out in 'Role of Panchayati Raj Institutions in Dealing with the Covid-19 Crisis' that a pandemic situation requires a decentralised approach to contain and mitigate it. Focusing on local governments (village panchayats), she traces the evolution of decentralised governance in Tamil Nadu and presents a succinct account of the current status. Various feasible sectoral interventions by the panchayats in sectors such as health, education, employment and livelihood, water management, agriculture and public markets, ways to increase tax collection, and local-level planning in the context of Covid-19 are presented in both short-and long-term perspectives. All these policy analyses are linked to an overall adherence to sustainable development goals.

In a pandemic, social protection plays an all-important mitigating role. In 'Covid-19 Pandemic and Social Protection in Tamil Nadu: Need to Strengthen a Life-Cycle Approach', Gayathri Balagopal and M. Vijayabaskar undertake a careful evaluation of Tamil Nadu's current social protection system from a life-cycle perspective so as to achieve sustainable development goals. They break the life cycle into various stages and look at the impacts of the pandemic on prenatal and early childhood, school age and adolescence, working age and old age. They touch upon health, sanitation, and food security issues. Various policy suggestions, such as maternity benefits, girl-child protection, access to education, nutrition and social security pensions, and public health system staffing are presented. They conclude by arguing for a movement away from disaster relief to disaster protection systems.

In the final essay, 'Food Security in the Covid-19 Era', Umanath Malaiarasan undertakes a careful analysis of food security issues during Covid-19. After identifying the most vulnerable in this context, and delineating the food supply chain, dietary pattern, and malnutrition, he takes up a careful scrutiny of various food safety measures by central and state governments, such as the Targeted Public Distribution System (TPDS), Integrated Child Development Services (ICDS), Tamil Nadu's Mid-day Meal Scheme (PT MGR NMP), Pradhan Mantri Matru Vandana Yojana, POSHAN Abhiyaan, and the recent National Food Security Act of 2013. Malaiarasan then develops various short- and long-term policy measures to address the identified lacunae.

To the Readers

The essays in this book have been written in as non-technical a manner as is possible by a set of academic authors. These can be read by all types of readers, particularly those who are not put off by the business press. We sincerely hope that apart from policymakers, academic audiences—of undergraduate and graduate economics students and faculty—too would have something for them. Given the feedback from people from different walks of life, we are bringing out a Tamil version of this book soon.

As this book has been written during the pandemic, we have not had the luxury of time either to wait for the pandemic to play out or to carry out new field or data-based research in the midst of it, given the additional constraints of lockdown. However, as pointed out in the preface, the challenges wrought by the pandemic call for academics to immediately reflect and act, based on available data and their own past research. This is one such attempt. We are in no position to foresee what the world would be in a year's time or for that matter, even six months from now. We are in the midst of a change and churn that is truly fundamental and far reaching, and also one that is likely to leave scars deeper than that of the Great Depression of the 1930s in all our souls as well as the economy. Hence, I ring this specific warning. Every crisis, though, opens a window to an opportunity, such as a new market; let us hope that the Covid-19 crisis would not be an exception to this age-old wisdom.

Notes and References

1. The data in this section come from the *World Economic Outlook* reports published by the International Monetary Fund (from October 2016) and the Pre Baseline Survey report prepared by the Tamil Nadu Household Panel Survey, which is an ongoing joint project between the Madras Institute of Development Studies, Department of Economics and Statistics of the Government of Tamil Nadu, and the Survey Research Center of the University of Michigan's Institute for Social Research.
2. See UNCTAD (United Nations Conference on Trade and Development), *World Investment Report 2020: International Production beyond the Pandemic*, New York, UN Publications, 2020.
3. Available at https://www.worldbank.org/en/news/speech/2016/10/03/speech-by-world-bank-president-jim-yong-kim-the-world-bank-groups-mission-to-end-extreme-poverty (accessed February 2022).

Section I

Macroeconomic Scenario

2

Pre– and Post–Covid-19 Macroeconomic Scenarios for India

Shesadri Banerjee

The outbreak of Covid-19 has triggered a public health emergency across the globe. Originating in December 2019 from China, it has spread like wildfire to almost all countries of the world, become a pandemic and has turned out to be the biggest health crisis of the century.

Although epidemics or pandemics have not been unusual in the history of human civilisation, the increasing frequency of pandemics is a grave concern (Fischer, 2020). Since the Spanish flu pandemic in 1918, the upsurge of coronavirus has become the greatest threat to public health (Ferguson et al., 2020). It is the fifth pandemic in the last 20 years and the ninth one in the past century (World Economic Forum, 2020). Covid-19 has two deadly characteristics. First, it is 3 to 30 times more fatal than seasonal influenza, and second, it is at least 10 times more contagious than Severe Acute Respiratory Syndrome (SARS)(World Bank, 2020).

Given the enormous potential of Covid-19 to wreak havoc on public health, the governments of both advanced and developing countries are toiling to contain the spread of the disease with policy actions such as social distancing, countrywide lockdown, and identification of containment zones. These policies, nevertheless, have come with inordinate socio-economic costs. In particular, the advent of the pandemic has posed a challenge for policymakers in terms of the need to have a trade-off between lives and livelihoods. These trade-offs are even more daunting for developing and low-income countries compared to those in advanced countries, primarily due to a lack of health infrastructure, the presence of a narrow fiscal space, labour market arrangements, poor governance, and uncertainties in policy implementation and coordination. This chapter intends to trace the probable impacts of the pandemic for India, an emerging market economy (EME), from national and subnational perspectives. Presenting an account of the pre–Covid-19 era, the economic developments of the post-corona episode have been illustrated narratively due to the paucity of systematic official data.

Indian Economy before Covid-19

The economic condition in India was not very promising in the pre-pandemic period. All the key macroeconomic and financial indicators reveal a clear downswing on both the demand side as well as the supply side. The staggering movements of the real side macroeconomic variables deteriorated further due to a logjam in the financial sector primarily on account of slow credit expansion by commercial banks and a decline in the lending potential of non-bank financial companies. Driven by falling demand, the headline consumer price index (CPI) inflation had been trailing below the target level for a consecutive 13 months until 2019–2020: Q2. However, it showed an uptick in the third quarter of 2019–2020, due to the food component in the CPI basket.

The aggregate demand and its key components show the downturn in the economy.[1] Demand for consumption had moderated sequentially, gross fixed capital formation had shown negative growth, and demand for exportable and importable had also comedown (Figure 2.1 and Table 2.1).

Rural demand could not pick up due to falling real wage of agricultural labour as the terms of trade moved in favour of the non-agricultural sector (Figure 2.2). Over the past couple of years, the excess supply of agricultural commodities and the accumulation of stocks had depressed agricultural prices. The Mahatma Gandhi National Rural Employment Guarantee Act (MGNREGA) did not support rural income much due to lower wages, delayed payments, and scanty budgetary allocations. Also, the slowdown of the construction sector had contributed to subduing rural wages.

Figure 2.1: Comparing Growth Rates of Components of Aggregate Demand

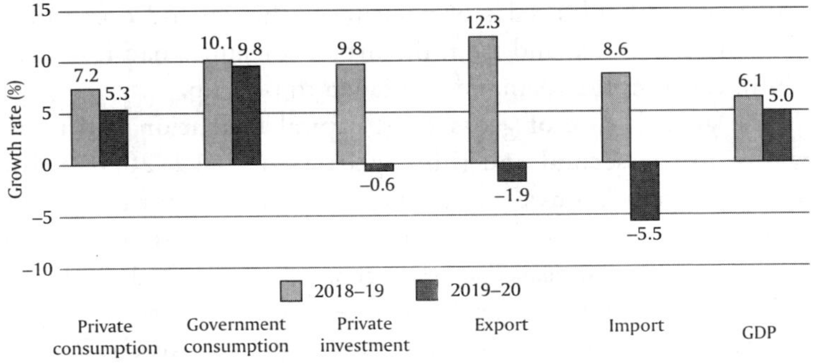

Source: Based on data from National Statistical Office, cited in RBI (2020), p. 30.

Table 2.1: Key Components of Aggregate Demand: Growth Rate over 2018–2019 and 2019–2020

Component of Aggregate Demand	*Q1*		*Q2*		*Q3*		*Q4*	
	2018–2019	*2019–2020*	*2018–2019*	*2019–2020*	*2018–2019*	*2019–2020*	*2018–2019*	*2019–2020*
Private consumption	6.7	5	8.8	5.6	7	5.9	6.2	4.9
Government consumption	8.5	8.8	10.8	13.2	7	11.8	14.4	4.9
Private investment	12.9	4.3	11.5	−4.1	11.4	−5.2	4.4	2.5
Export	9.5	3.2	12.5	−2.1	15.8	−5.5	11.6	−2.8
Import	5.9	2.1	18.7	−9.3	10	−11.2	0.8	−3

Note: Quarter-to-quarter comparison.
Source: RBI (2020), p. 30.

Figure 2.2: Agricultural vis-à-vis Non-agricultural Real Wages (per cent)

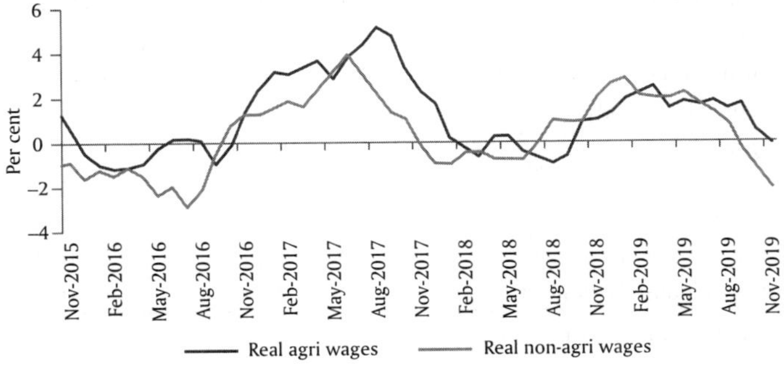

Source: Reproduced from RBI (2020), p. 35.

In parallel to this, several high-frequency indicators, such as sale of consumer durables, sales of passenger vehicles, and domestic air travel, show that demand from the urban consumer had lost steam. In sum, consumption demand had failed to pick up.

The growth rate of gross fixed capital formation had turned negative in the second and third quarters of 2019–2020. Private corporate organisations mobilise their funds mainly for the purpose of fixed asset formation and deleveraging. The total cost of sanctioned projects had also increased in the second half of 2019–2020 over 2018–2019. Moreover, financial channels were squeezed as the gross domestic saving rate had decreased to 30.1 per cent of GDP (Gross Domestic Product) in 2018–2019 from 32.4 per cent in 2017–2018.[2]

Following the depressed demand, both from consumption and investment, the aggregate supply of the economy had shrunk. Table 2.2 shows the growth rates of production across sectors. The index of industrial production and its constituents, in every sector, except mining, had recorded a negative growth rate in March 2020 as compared to March 2019. Specifically, capital goods, consumer durables, construction, and manufacturing sectors had undergone a remarkable slump. Reinforcing the observation, Figure 2.3 shows that capacity utilisation in the manufacturing sector had declined steeply during first to third quarters of 2019–2020.

Table 2.2: Sectoral Growth Rates of Production in India between 2018–2019 and 2019–2020 (Percentage)

Sector	*March 2019*	*March 2020*
Mining	0.8	0
Manufacturing	3.1	–20.6
Electricity	2.2	–6.8
Primary goods	2.6	–3.1
Intermediate goods	12.4	–18.5
Capital goods	–9.1	–35.6
Construction goods	5.1	–23.8
Consumer durables	–3.2	–33.1
Consumer non-durables	1.4	–16.2
Index of Industrial Production	2.7	–16.7

Source: tamilnadustat.com.

Figure 2.3: Capacity Utilisation in Manufacturing Sector in India (per cent)

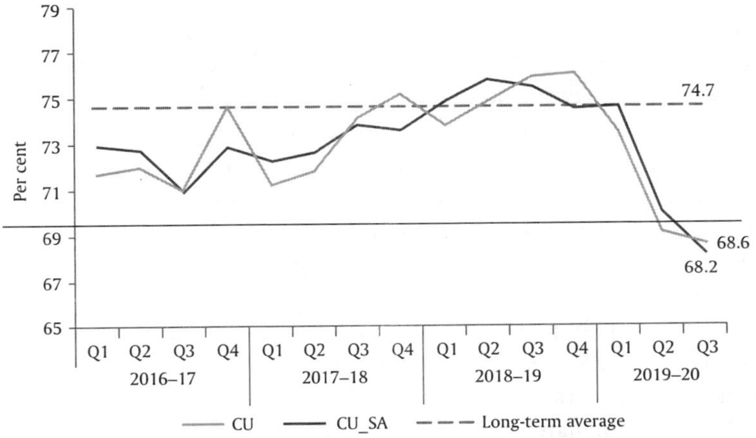

Notes: CU = capacity utilisation; CU_SA = seasonally adjusted series of capacity utilisation.
Source: Reproduced from RBI (2020), p. 36.

Domestic financial markets were overwhelmingly influenced by the twin balance sheet problems, one for the commercial banks and the other for the corporate sector. As a consequence of high levels of non-performing assets (NPAs) in the less capitalised position, banks had become increasingly risk-averse for extending loans, causing a sluggish growth of bank credit. From the borrowers' point of view, due to the high level of uncertainty in market demand and regulatory interventions, investors were reluctant to borrow and mobilise their funds.

Hence, the bank-based financial sector was unable to adequately fuel economic activities through the credit channel. Other market segments of the financial sector had witnessed heightened volatility beginning from February 2020, which had led to a sharp contraction in trading activity. Search for yield and flight to safety resulted in large-scale capital outflows which had pushed equity markets into a nosedive and had exerted a pressure of depreciation on the Indian Rupee.

Outbreak of Coronavirus: National and Subnational Scenarios

India recorded its first case of coronavirus on 30 January 2020. Given the scale and breadth of the crisis, and the highly contagious nature of the disease,[3] governments—both at the central and state-levels—have proposed ways of containing the spread, including policy actions such as the imposition of social distancing, self-isolation at home, closure of institutions and public facilities, restrictions on mobility and public gathering, and lockdowns and curfewsin the entire country or particular states. These policy measures are similar to those followed by many other countries.

Until now, India has gone through four phases of lockdown with periodic relaxation to allow for essential activities. At present, the most common strategy is to identify hotspots of Covid-19 outbreaks (which are designated containment zones) within the states, districts, and cities, and enforce strict lockdowns there till no further cases in that area remain active. Based on the number of active cases, the containment zones were classified red, orange or green and the restrictions on activity depended on the classification—red zones had the maximum restrictions and green zones had minimal curbs. The hotspots of infection are primarily located in the metropolitan areas of the affected states.[4]

The lockdown of the country has come with a substantial cost. According to a research conducted by the State Bank of India, the estimated growth rate of nominal GDP was 2.6 per cent at the beginning of the first lockdown, which had come down to a negative (–4.7 per cent) by the end of May 2020. The SBI report estimated that the rate of real gross value added and GDP growth could hit to –3.1 per cent and –6.8 per cent, respectively, in FY21. For the states, the loss of total GSDP amounts to ₹30.3 lakh crore, which is 13.5 per cent of total Gross State Domestic Product (GSDP) and 50 per cent more than the Covid-19 relief package (₹20 lakh crore) announced by the central government. The state-wise analysis further shows that the top five coronavirus affected states in 2020 account for 44 per cent of the total loss of GDP. For these states, the break-up of the share of loss and its disaggregation across the red, orange and green zones are depicted in Figures 2.4A and 2.4B.

Figure 2.4A: Break-up of Shares of Total Output Loss during the Lockdown Period of the Top Five Covid-Affected States in 2020

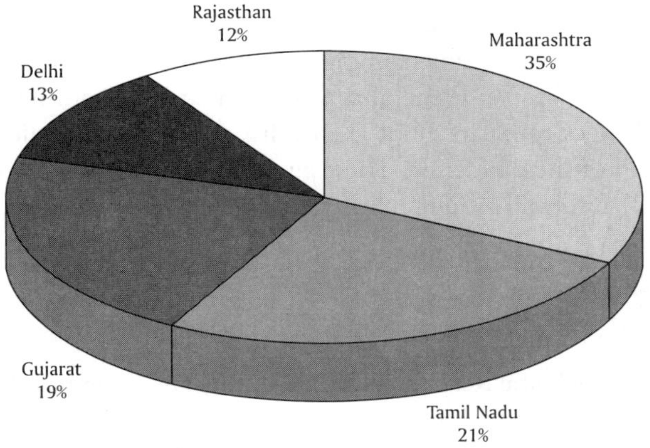

Source: State Bank of India (2020).

Figure 2.4B: Composition of Output Loss in Different Categories of Coronavirus-affected Zones (Percentage)

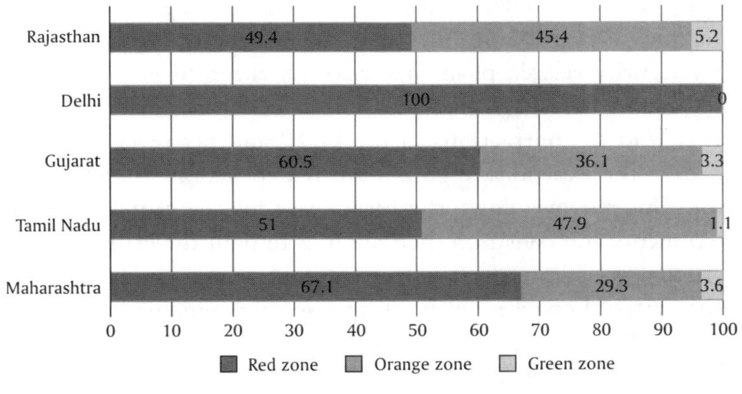

Source: State Bank of India (2020).

Areas of Concern During the Post-Pandemic Period

It is increasingly becoming evident that human lives will not be the same in the post–Covid-19 period. While the outbreak of the disease has caused a massive pressure on the government's exchequer to accommodate the requirements of the public healthcare system, the containment policies have also raised many concerns related to the economic well-being of individuals and the country as a whole. We address three issues which might be of significant concern in the aftermath of the pandemic and reflect on the policy interventions and challenges to balance out the health risk and economic risk for mitigation of the pandemic. These areas are as follows: (1) low fiscal space, (2) informal labour market, and (3) macroeconomic policies for recovery.

Low Fiscal Space

Given that the Fiscal Responsibility and Budget Management (FRBM) Act is in place and the target for gross fiscal deficit (3 per cent of the GDP) needs to be adhered to, the lack of fiscal space is one of the major concerns in efforts to handle the ongoing pandemic, both for central and state governments. The spread of the pandemic impacts the fiscal deficit in India in two major ways. First, the governments have to allocate a substantial portion of their budget to tackle the pandemic. This primarily includes expenditure on healthcare, and social security related payments. Second, enforced lockdowns and containment measures lead to a fall in economic activity, which further lead to contractions in the GDP and tax revenue. So not only does the expenditure go up, but tax collection will also comes down. This narrows down the fiscal space for the central and state governments and constrain their abilities to fight the crisis.

In the pre-Corona period, the combined revenue and fiscal deficits of the states showed a tendency to rise, but remained within the limit stipulated by the FRBM Act. Revenue deficit had risen from 0.1 per cent in 2018–2019 to 0.7 per cent (as per revised estimate) in FY 2019–2020. Gross fiscal deficit (as a percentage of GSDP) had been rising over the last couple of financial years successively—2.4 per cent in 2018–2019, 2.5 per cent as per budget estimate of 2019–2020, and 2.9 per cent as per revised estimate of 2019–2020 (RBI, 2020). It was argued that such levels of deficits at the sub-national level were on the higher side and could be unsustainable (Roy and Kotia 2018). These fiscal deficit numbers were expected to slip to

3.5 per cent in the FY 2020–2021 (Adhikari 2020). In anticipation, the states had started requesting the Centre to relax the provisions of the FRBM Act.

The states/UTs, which are facing the brunt of the spread of the pandemic, such as Delhi, Gujarat, Maharashtra, Rajasthan and Tamil Nadu, have undergone a diverse level of budgetary positions in their fiscal front. While the first three states had managed to remain within the specified limit of three per cent, the latter two overshot the three per cent limit during the period of 2011–12 to 2018–19. The situation is more problematic because of little budgetary allocation for public health and social security (see Table 2.3). Expenditures under the heads of medical infrastructure and social security, as a percentage of state domestic product were very low. In other states, barely two to four per cent of the total capital outlay was allotted for medical and public health expenditure during 2019–2020. At present, in terms of revenue expenditure in medical and public health, Kerala is spending the most (5.14 per cent of its total expenditure; ₹6,389 crore), followed by Tamil Nadu (4.15 per cent; ₹8,814 crore), Maharashtra (4.07 per cent; ₹13,636 crore) and Uttar Pradesh (3.63 per cent; ₹13,247 crore). Clearly, other states have to significantly reallocate their financial resources towards public health facilities and social payments to deal with the pandemic.

Table 2.3: Budgetary Position (as per cent of GSDP) of States facing High Impact of the Pandemic (Sample period: 2011–12 to 2018–19)

	Gross Fiscal Deficit	*Revenue Expenditure on Medical and Public Health*	*Revenue Expenditure on Social Security*
Delhi	0.3	0.7	0.4
Gujarat	2.2	0.5	0.1
Maharashtra	1.8	0.5	0.2
Rajasthan	4.6	0.9	0.7
Tamil Nadu	3.2	0.6	0.9

Source: EPWRF Database and Author's Calculation.

From the forecasts of various national and international agencies, it is projected that the Indian economy would contract by around 10 per cent in FY 2020–21. The same is also likely to happen for the GSDP. However, the size of contraction of state-level economic activities is critical to understand the how the fiscal deficit evolves in subsequent periods. Following the quantitative assessment of Balajee, Tomar and Udupa (2020), one can gauge the state-level fiscal space subject to output contraction for the pandemic. In a pessimistic scenario, if the GDP falls by 20 per cent, the fiscal deficit for the central government can ascend to 8.4 per cent of the GDP and 3.6 per cent of the GDP for (all) states. As per the Annual Report of the RBI (2019–20), the fiscal space for the states is likely to shrink so much that they may need to cut down even growth-yielding capital expenditure.

In a slowing economy, higher spending on medical expenditure and public health would either result in shifting of resources from their designated heads or dipping into borrowings from the market or the central government. As an alternative source of fund, the states may seek emergency funds or overdraft facility from the RBI through the central bank's ways-and-means window. The RBI has increased the limit from the existing level under this facility by 30 per cent for the states. With the finances of the Central Government already stretched, states have to find other sources of revenue generation in the coming days.[5]

While addressing the issue of fiscal space, it is imperative to pay special attention to the state finances of Tamil Nadu. The state has the second largest economy after Maharashtra and occupies a central position in the southern region of the country. During the period of 2005–06 to 2016–17, key parameters of government finance of Tamil Nadu, such as the revenue deficit, fiscal deficit and public debt relative to GSDP, had remained within the norms of the FRBM legislation. However, these indicators had deteriorated over the last few years, which have raised concerns regarding the fiscal capability of the state to handle the ongoing pandemic. In the pre-Corona period, on the inflow side of the budget, tax to GSDP ratio had declined from 8.94 per cent to 6.42 per cent due to various factors like the introduction of State VAT, the slowdown of the economy, abolition of vend fees and additional vend fees for liquor and spirits. On the outflow side, mounting pressure of the revenue expenditure on account of payment of salaries, wages and pensions, and servicing the interest on public debt had trimmed down the fiscal space. In addition, although the capital expenditure directed towards investments had increased substantially from 2.6 per cent to 3.5 per cent, adequate resources had not been allocated for the health sector. In fact, during the period of 2006–07 to 2018–19 (BE) the Government of Tamil Nadu spent less than 1 per cent of GSDP on public health, a level that was well below recommended international standards (Shanmugam 2018). In the post-Corona period, however, there has been a shift in priorities and subsequently, greater expenditures have been incurred on improving health infrastructure, setting up a corpus fund under a new health insurance scheme for the treatment of government employees and pensioners affected by Covid-19, providing social assistance to marginalised sections, and providing free ration and assistance to migrant labourers (RBI 2020). Such new accounts of expenditures and sudden reallocation of resources across these heads have undoubtedly taken a toll on the state government exchequer and posed a steep challenge in trying to maintain fiscal parameters at the stipulated level. In such a scenario, the fiscal authority may find some respite by tapping other sources of non-tax revenue, rationalising its expenditure (e.g. winding up non-productive public sector units, streamlining usage of manpower etc.), incentivising economic activities of Micro, Small & Medium Enterprises (MSMEs) and exploring the scope for state excise duties.

Informal Labour Market

Informality is one of the inherent features of the labour market in India. The containment policy in the form of lockdown has badly affected the informal labour of the unorganised sector, which occupies nearly 92 per cent of the labour market. There has also been a huge retrenchment of labours who are working in the service sector, manufacturing, transportation, travel and tourism industries, and construction sites, in different parts of the country, leading to a severe unemployment problem (24 per cent in May 2020, as per the estimate of Centre for Monitoring Indian Economy (CMIE)). All metro cities, which had undergone a sustained process of urbanisation over the past couple of decades, with a boom in infrastructure projects like housing and large commercial spaces, have witnessed a severe jolt for the large number of native workers and the small-to-moderate number of migrant workers due to the lockdown. The challenge for the central government as well as for state governments and local administrations has been to minimise the adverse effects of the ongoing situation. Although it may be argued that the containment policy is necessary toreduce the spread of the disease, it is imperative to find a cost-effective way to minimise the recessionary effect of the pandemic (Figure 2.5). Cost-effective containment policies need to be investigated in India (specifically in states like Tamil Nadu, which host a large percentage of migrant workers) keeping in mind the presence of a large informal labour market.[6]

Figure 2.5: Containment Measures and Severity of Recession

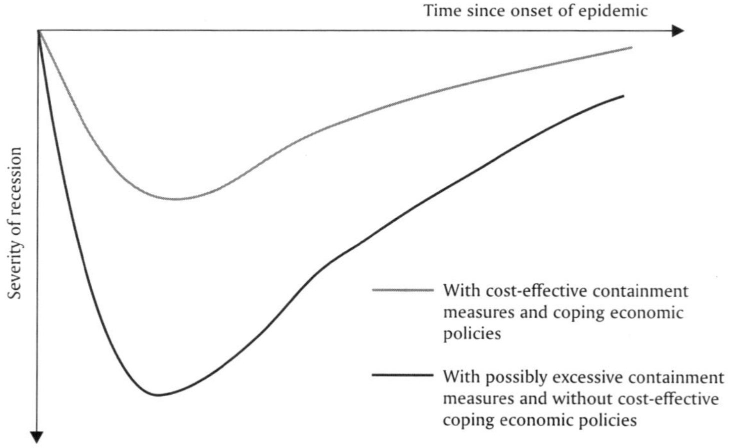

Source: Loayza and Pennings (2020), p. 3.

By now, the central and state governments have come up with some major policy measures that include the rehabilitation of the migrant labours in their own states, ensuring their social security, and the containment of the spread of the disease (ILO 2020).

At the central level, the Garib Kalyan Rojgar Abhiyaan (GKRA) has been launched to increase employment and livelihood opportunities for the migrant workers returning to villages (and similarly affected citizens in rural area) in the wake of coronavirus outbreak and the subsequent enforcement of the nationwide lockdown at the end of March 2020. The GKRA has set a target of generating employment for 6.7 million of the 10 million migrant labours. Moreover, the government intends to pursue 25 rural-centric employment generation schemes to provide work for 125 days in 25 areas for the migrant workers in 116 districts of six states. These states include Bihar, Uttar Pradesh, Rajasthan, Madhya Pradesh, Odisha, and Jharkhand.

Complementing the effort of the central government, various state governments have initiated the process of skill mapping so that the skills of workforce can be tracked and deployed to improve the economic activities in the non-containment zones. In addition, efforts have been made to ensure medical support, rapid testing facilities, and arrangements for food, clean drinking water and sanitation for the migrant workers at the relief camps and shelters in various parts of the states. However, the success of the policies for job creation, social security and insurance largely depends on the potential of labour absorption of different economic sectors, scope for skill development and fiscal support from the state.

Macroeconomic Policies for Recovery

The macroeconomic effects of Covid-19 can be analysed from various angles and subsequently the possible policy responses can be envisaged. Nevertheless, it is perceivable that the process of recovery from such adversities will require a strong and concerted effort from the monetary and fiscal authorities.

Considering that the outbreak of Covid-19 came as an uncertainty shock, Pellegrino, Castelnuovo and Caggiano (2020) have argued that it could result in a loss of output twice as big as that of the Great Recession. According to them, such a contraction of real activity can be mitigated partially by an aggressive monetary policy. In EMEs like India, however, the question remains as to how monetary authorities can exercise aggressive policy interventions to combat pandemic-driven economic recession. Empirical evidence suggests that the effectiveness of monetary transmission through interest-rate–based policy instruments is weak due to the presence of frictions in the financial markets (Banerjee et al. 2018). An alternative is to opt for quantitative measures of different scales which would have a more direct effect in reviving the aggregate demand (Banerjee et al., 2020). In this direction, some steps have already been taken. The RBI has come up with long-term repo operation (LTRO 2.0) of ₹50,000 crore to free up more capital for the banks for their lending purposes. Such an intervention can reduce the liquidity stress of shadow banks and microfinance institutions along with credit easing support from successive policy rate cuts.

Along with monetary policy, the role of expansionary fiscal policies using different policy instruments can be explored. With limited fiscal space and the traditionally small size of fiscal multipliers, the effectiveness of demand-oriented policy management needs to be reassessed. Several policy actions are in the process of being announced by the central and state governments. But, perhaps, the need of the hour is to provide direct cash transfer support to the lower tiers of the income groups in the economy. The purchasing power of the marginalised section of the population, whom we call 'hand-to-mouth' households, needs to be reinstated, so that the consumption demand can be geared up. To restore investment demand, investor-friendly climate with a strong expectation anchoring and policy support are required to rebuild the confidence of the entrepreneurs.

The economic slowdown in the pre-pandemic period was also attributed to policy uncertainty created by regulatory bodies (IANS 2019). Restoring the confidence of corporates is of paramount importance. In addition, these uncertainties, which have further snowballed in the aftermath of rapid changes in ground realities of the economy during the coronavirus pandemic need to be moderated through continued support to healthcare for the working population. Policy coordination at the international level among peer countries as well as at a subnational level across the states can be useful as it would provide opportunities to internalise the positive externalities from the multiple waves of infections and help in preventing the adverse effects of the pandemic.

Notes

1. A sentiment index based on the high-frequency data indicates a downturn in the aggregate output (RBI 2020).
2. The saving rate of the household sector, which is a net supplier of funds to the economy, declined from 23.6 per cent of GDP in 2011–2012 to 18.2 per cent in 2018–2019 (RBI 2020).
3. Transmissibility of a virus represents the average number of people to which a single infected person will transmit the virus. On 23 January 2020, WHO estimated the transmissibility of Covid-19 which lies in between 1.4 and 2.5. Other preliminary studies had estimated it to be between 1.5 and 3.5. (*Source*: Worldometer, available at https://www.worldometers.info/coronavirus/, accessed February 2022).
4. In Chennai, the northern part of the city has reported the majority of cases (65 per cent) owing to high population density and increased testing.
5. Recently, the Department of Expenditure, Ministry of Finance, has granted permission to Tamil Nadu to raise an additional amount of Rs. 9,627 crore through open market borrowings to meet the shortfall arising out of GST implementation. This may provide some respite in the fiscal space for the Government of Tamil Nadu (*Source*: CMIE: Indian Economy Today, 14 October 2020).
6. It can be noted that the containment policy does not allow the population to be immune to the virus as social interaction is restricted, and therefore, in case of subsequent waves of infection, population may be rendered vulnerable to those.

References

Adhikari, A., 'Coronavirus impact: Maharashtra, Kerala, Tamil Nadu, UP stare at big fiscal hole', *Business Today*, 3 April 2020, available at https://www.businesstoday.in/current/economy-politics/covid-19-impact-maharashtra-kerala-tamil-nadu-up-stare-at-big-fiscal-hole/story/400084.html, accessed on 23 September 2021.

Balajee, A., S. Tomar, and G. Udupa, 'Fiscal Situation of India in the Time of COVID-19', Indian School of Business,12 April 2020, available at https://ssrn.com/abstract=3571103 or http://dx.doi.org/10.2139/ssrn.3571103, accessed on 23 September 2021.

Banerjee, S., P. Basu, and C. Ghate, 'A monetary business cycle model for India', *Economic Inquiry*, 58(3), 2020, pp. 1362–1386.

Banerjee, S., H. Behera, S. Bordoloi, and R. Kumar, *Role of financial frictions in monetary policy transmission in India* (Study No. 44), Department of Economic and Policy Research, Reserve Bank of India, 2018.

Ferguson, N. M., D. Laydon, G. Nedjati-Gilani, et al., *Impact of non-pharmaceutical interventions (NPIs) to reduce COVID-19 mortality and healthcare demand*, Imperial College, London, 16 March 2020, available at https://www.imperial.ac.uk/media/imperial-college/medicine/sph/ide/gida-fellowships/Imperial-College-COVID19-NPI-modelling-16-03-2020.pdf, accessed on 23 September, 2021.

Fischer, R. S. B., 'What's the difference between pandemic, epidemic, and outbreak?', *The Conversation*, 9 March 2020, available at https://theconversation.com/whats-the-difference-between-pandemic-epidemic-and-outbreak-133048, accessed on 23 September 2021.

IANS., 'Regulatory uncertainty played role in India's slowdown: IMF', *Outlook*, 20 December 2019, available at https://www.outlookindia.com/newsscroll/regulatory-uncertainty-played-role-in-indias-slowdown-imf/1690379, accessed on 23 September 2021.

ILO, 'COVID-19 in India: Labour market measures taken by the central and State governments', 6 June 2020, live document available at https://www.ilo.org/newdelhi/whatwedo/publications/WCMS_741923/lang--en/index.htm, accessed on 23 September 2021.

Loayza, N. V., and S. Pennings, *Macroeconomic policy in the time of Covid-19: A primer for developing countries*, Research and Policy Brief No. 28, World Bank Malaysia Hub, 26 March 2020.

Pellegrino, G., E. Castelnuovo, and G. Caggiano, 'Uncertainty and Monetary Policy During Extreme Events', CAMA Working Paper 80/2020, Centre for Applied Macroeconomic Analysis, Crawford School of Public Policy, September 2020, available at https://crawford.anu.edu.au/sites/default/files/publication/cama_crawford_anu_edu_au/2020-09/80_2020_pellegrino_castelnuovo_caggiano1.pdf, accessed on 23 September 2021.

Reserve Bank of India (RBI), *Annual Report: 2019–20*, 25 August 2020, available at https://m.rbi.org.in/scripts/AnnualReportPublications.aspx?Id=1296, accessed on 23 September 2021.

———, *Monetary policy report: April 2020*, available at https://rbidocs.rbi.org.in/rdocs/Publications/PDFs/MPRAPRIL2020E3D4AD8245734F27B6C5688F22B4FA2F.PDF, accessed on 23 September 2021.

Reserve Bank of India, *State Finances: A Study of Budgets of 2020–21*, October 2020, available at https://rbidocs.rbi.org.in/rdocs/Publications/PDFs/0SF_271020FCF77451F1DF744B2B244875C785B8EF3.PDF, accessed on 23 September 2021.

Roy, R., and A. Kotia, 'Should states target a 3 per cent fiscal deficit?', *Economic & Political Weekly*, 53(9), March 2018, p. 49.

Shanmugam, K. R., 'Tamil Nadu State Government Finances', *Madras School of Economics*, November 2018, available at https://fincomindia.nic.in/writereaddata/html_en_files/fincom15/StudyReports/24.pdf, accessed on 23 September 2021.

State Bank of India, *Ecowrap*, Issue 14, FY21, 26 May 2020, available at https://bank.sbi/documents/13958/3312806/2605201152-Ecowrap_20200526.pdf, accessed on 23 September 2021.

World Bank, *World Bank East Asia and Pacific Economic Update, April 2020: East Asia and Pacific in the Time of COVID-19*, 2020, available at https://openknowledge.worldbank.org/handle/10986/33477, accessed on 23 September 2021.

World Economic Forum, *A Visual History of Pandemics*, 15 March 2020, available at https://www.weforum.org/agenda/2020/03/a-visual-history-of-pandemics/, accessed on 23 September 2021.

3

Employment and Covid-19

Trends and Issues in Tamil Nadu

P. G. Babu, Vikas Kumar and Poonam Singh

The Covid-19 pandemic has disrupted economies across the world and presented policy makers with the unenviable task of sustaining employment amidst lockdowns. This chapter explores the challenges facing Tamil Nadu, one of the highly industrialised and urbanised states of the country, and which was also one of the states worst hit by the pandemic.

Academic and political debates in India on unemployment, which is widely attributed to jobless growth amidst stagnation in the agricultural and manufacturing sectors, predate the pandemic. It will, therefore, be useful to contextualise the disruption caused by the pandemic on a larger canvas so as to enable a comparative assessment vis-à-vis other recent economic shocks, such as the demonetisation of high value currency notes on 9 November 2016 and the introduction of the Goods and Services Tax (GST) on 1 July 2017. A comparison with other states that have a large manufacturing sector and are net recipients of migrants will also be instructive.

Data

Attempts to assess the opportunity cost of arresting the spread of the pandemic through prolonged lockdowns and figuring out the road ahead are hampered by the lack of government data for this period.[1] We have had to rely on data from the Centre for Monitoring Indian Economy (CMIE), even though its employment data series is relatively new, because it is among the very few sources that provide data covering the period of lockdown.[2] We have used the *States of India* monthly database (CMIE 2020a) to understand the impact of the pandemic on employment. This database includes monthly observations on Labour Participation Rate (LPR) for the period of January 2016 to July 2020, covering major states, including Tamil Nadu. The CMIE database also provides information on employment at lower levels of aggregation, including region (urban–rural), gender (male–female), and educational qualification.

The reach of CMIE surveys was limited by the lockdown, and the sample size had to be reduced sharply.[3] A few points are worth noting in this regard. First, the data for the lockdown period may not be comparable with the preceding and succeeding periods due to the reduction in sample size and the change in the process of interviewing. Second, the actual labour participation rate could be lower if the areas more affected by the pandemic were also more likely to be left out of the survey. Third, the extent to which the changes in employment indicators between March and July are driven by changes in sample non-coverage is not clear. Fourth, the data cannot be used to understand the impact on narrower categories such as rural, college graduate women due to the smaller-than -usual sample size and unknown differences in non-coverage rate across categories.

Trends in Labour Participation Rate and Unemployment

Short Run

Tamil Nadu's unemployment rate[4] increased sharply during the strict lockdown in late March and April 2020 but registered a large turnaround in May when lockdown was eased to some extent. While unemployment rate fell further in June and July, the urban unemployment rate was much higher than the average for the year preceding lockdown. On the other hand, LPR continued to decline even though at a lesser rate in May and recovered in the next two months but remained below the average for the year preceding lockdown. The CMIE data seem to suggest that while the easing of lockdown allowed workers to return to work, they were initially either hesitant or unable to return due to transport and communications bottlenecks, lack of information, and fear of disease and that even after LPR began to rebound, work was not yet available for a large fraction of the workforce.

Unequal Impact

There is no clear trend vis-à-vis caste and religion. However, the decline in unemployment rate was faster in the case of urban areas, males, and those with higher education. The magnitude of increase, and subsequent decrease, in unemployment was largest in the case of those with no education.[5] Persons with intermediate levels of schooling were affected more than college graduates and the reduction in unemployment after relaxation of lockdown was also slower in their case even as their LPR continued to drop. If the level of education can be treated as a proxy for skill, the data seem to suggest that the lockdown affected semi-skilled workforce more than the skilled and unskilled workforce.

Long Run

The CMIE data suggest that at least since January 2016 there has been a steady decline in LPR[6] (Figure 3.1). However, there was no significant change in LPR after demonetisation in both rural and urban sectors, though the immediate effect of demonetisation on LPR was negative. In the case of GST, there was a significant decline in LPR only in the urban sector. The immediate effect of the Covid-19 lockdown was visible through a significant decline in LPR in both rural and urban sectors.[7]

Tamil Nadu and Other States

Tamil Nadu's LPR was lower compared to the median state, and unemployment rate was higher compared to the median state in both April and May (Table 3.1). Despite registering the largest decline in unemployment rate across major states, Tamil Nadu's unemployment rate was higher than the median state. In other words, employment indicators of Tamil Nadu have been worse than most other states. Two months later, Tamil Nadu's LPR continued to be low, even though unemployment rate had dropped below that of the median state.

Figure 3.1: Tamil Nadu: Labour Participation and Unemployment Rates (January 2016—May 2020)

Gender Divide

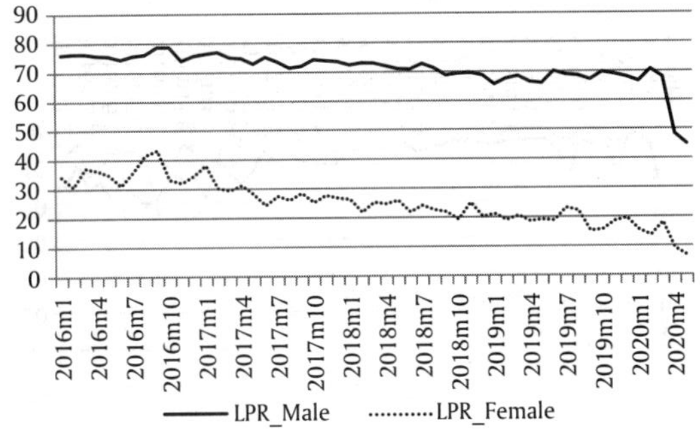

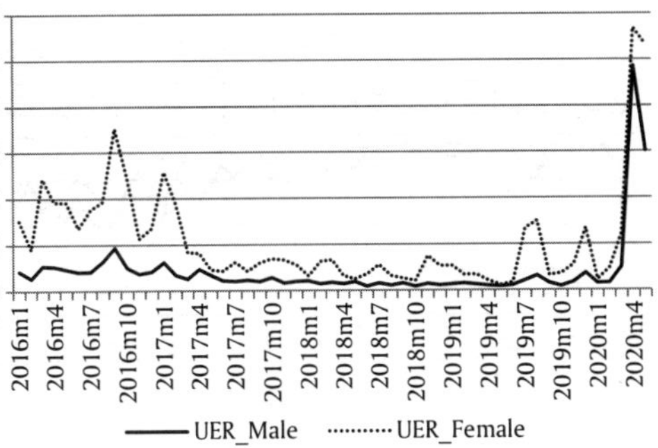

Rural–Urban Divide

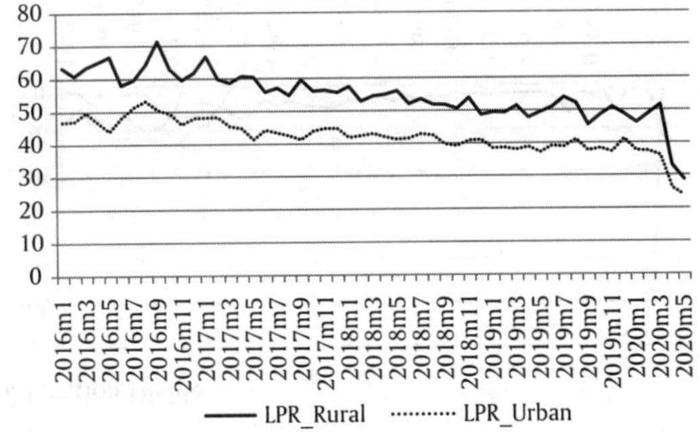

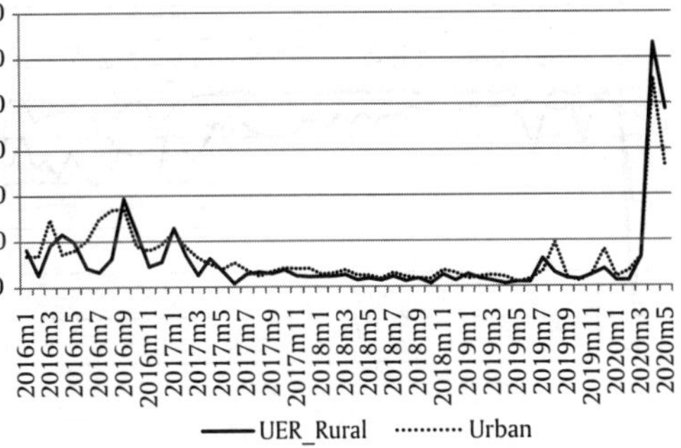

(Contd)

Figure 3.1 (Contd)

Education Divide

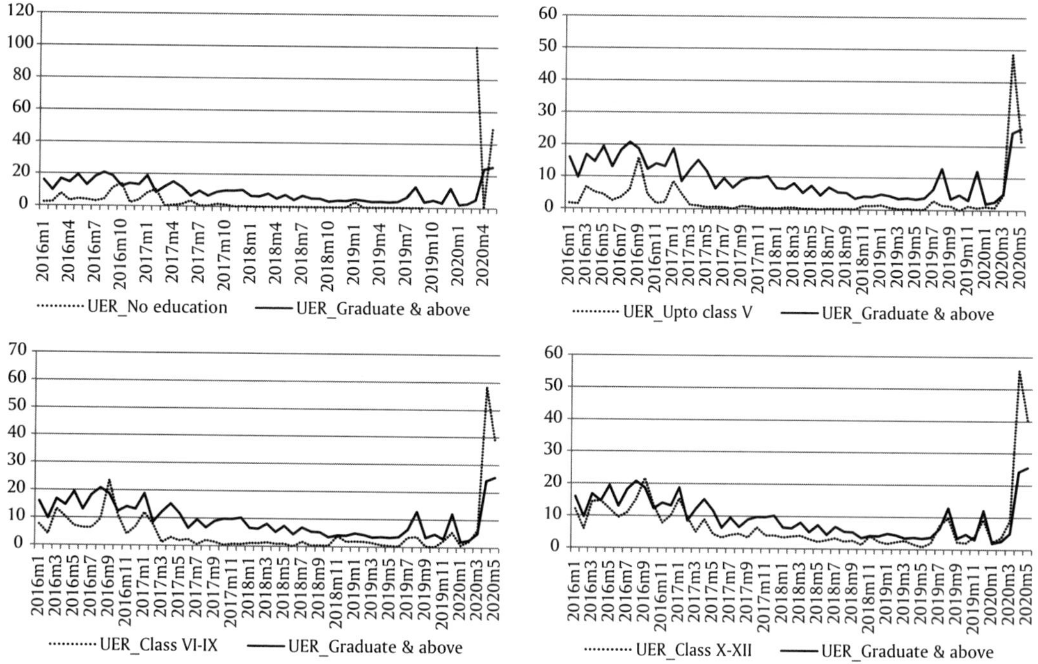

Notes: LPR and UER, respectively, stand for labour participation rate and unemployment rate.
Source: Prepared using CMIE (2020a).

Table 3.1: Tamil Nadu's Labour Participation Rate and Unemployment Rate vis-à-vis Other States (2020)

LPR		*May* Low	*May* High
April	Low	Kerala, NCT of Delhi, Odisha, **Tamil Nadu**, Andhra Pradesh, Uttarakhand, Maharashtra[#]	Himachal Pradesh, Punjab, Assam, Rajasthan
April	High	Madhya Pradesh,[##] Gujarat, Chhattisgarh, Jharkhand	Bihar, Uttar Pradesh, West Bengal, Telangana, Karnataka, Haryana
UER		*May* Low	*May* High
April	Low	Chhattisgarh, Uttarakhand, Assam, West Bengal, Rajasthan[#]	Himachal Pradesh, Punjab, Telangana, Madhya Pradesh, NCT of Delhi, Kerala
April	High	Gujarat, Andhra Pradesh, Maharashtra, Uttar Pradesh,[##] Odisha, Karnataka	Haryana, Bihar, Jharkhand, **Tamil Nadu**

LPR		*July* Low	*July* High
April	Low	NCT of Delhi, Kerala, Odisha, Uttarakhand, **Tamil Nadu**, Andhra Pradesh, Rajasthan[###]	Himachal Pradesh, Punjab, Assam, Maharashtra[#]
April	High	Jharkhand, Bihar, UP, Haryana	Madhya Pradesh, Gujarat, Chhattisgarh, Telangana, West Bengal, Karnataka
UER		*July* Low	*July* High
April	Low	Telangana, Assam, Madhya Pradesh, Kerala[###], West Bengal	Himachal Pradesh, Punjab, Chhattisgarh, Uttarakhand, NCT of Delhi, Rajasthan[#]
April	High	Gujarat, Maharashtra, Uttar Pradesh, Odisha, Karnataka, **Tamil Nadu**	Andhra Pradesh, Haryana, Bihar, Jharkhand

Notes: (i) The table covers 21 major states/union territories; (ii) [#] indicates the median state in April, whereas [##] and [###] indicate the median state in May and July respectively; (iii) Low (high) indicates that the state falls below (above) the median state. In each case, the median state has been included in the category 'Low.'

Source: Prepared using CMIE (2020a).

Tamil Nadu differs from other South Indian and other industrialised states with respect to the trend of LPR (Figure 3.2). Urban Tamil Nadu was initially comparable to urban areas of Gujarat and Maharashtra insofar as its labour participation rate continued to fall in May. Like Gujarat and Maharashtra, Tamil Nadu boasts of a large manufacturing sector, and these states were among the major Covid-19–affected states. While unemployment rate began to drop sharply in May in urban Tamil Nadu, it was rising in Gujarat and Maharashtra.[8] However, the recovery in urban areas has been faster in Gujarat and Maharashtra compared to Tamil Nadu, where LPR remains low even though its unemployment rate has dropped vis-à-vis the median state (Table 3.1, Figure 3.2). Interestingly, software and new economy hubs, such as Karnataka, and Telangana did not witness a very sharp decline in LPR; the former in fact, witnessed an increase. Both states, however, reported a decline in LPR in a more recent period (June–July) for which data is available. In most states, rural labour participation picked Covid-19 in rural areas and reverse migration from urban areas. However, rural Tamil Nadu suffered a decline in labour participation in both April and May. Interestingly, both rural and urban Tamil Nadu reported a rising LPR even as the figure had tapered off or declined in most other states in the following months.

Challenges Facing Industries in Tamil Nadu

The longer term decline in LPR in Tamil Nadu from 2016 reported by the CMIE could be attributed to general economic shocks, such as demonetisation and the introduction of GST, on the one hand, and a combination of industry-specific issues, such as changing tastes, tightening regulatory environment and growing international competition, on the other.

Demonetisation and the introduction of GST adversely affected industries such as the firecracker industry in Sivakasi and the textile industry in Tiruppur, both comprising a large number of small and medium units. It was reported that nearly 50,000 Micro, Small, and Medium Enterprises (MSMEs) were shut down in 2017–2018, due to demonetisation and GST, coupled with power problems and a

Figure 3.2: Rural and Urban Labour Participation Rates and Unemployment Rates Across States

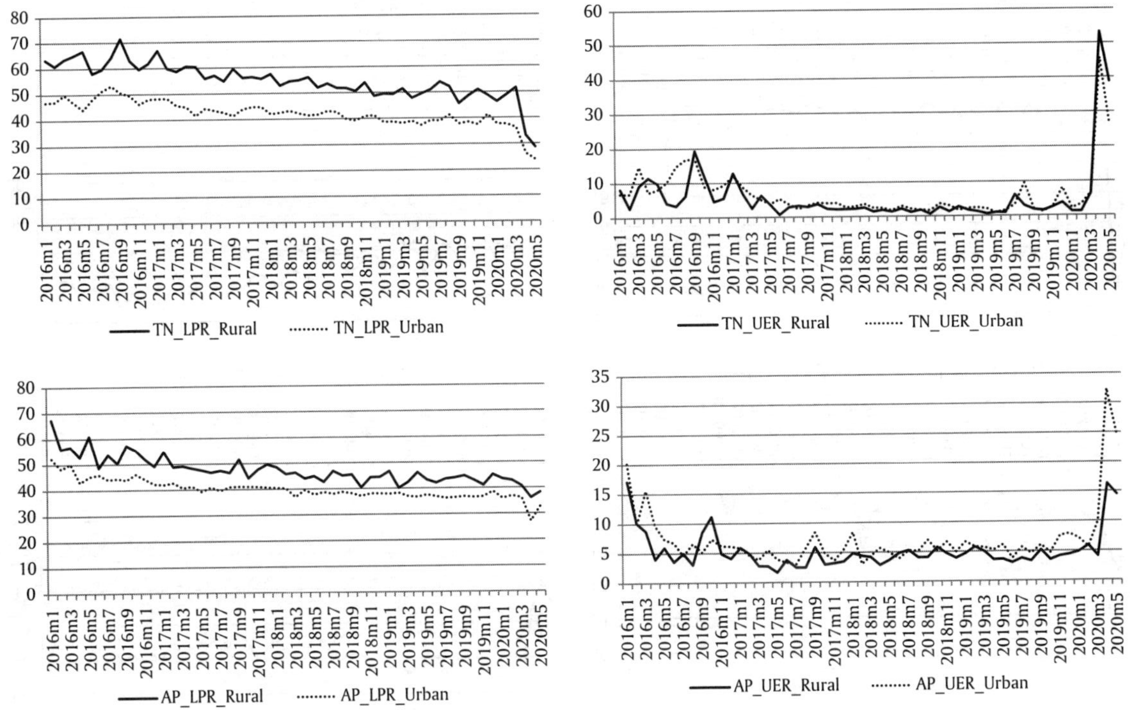

(Contd)

Figure 3.2 (Contd)

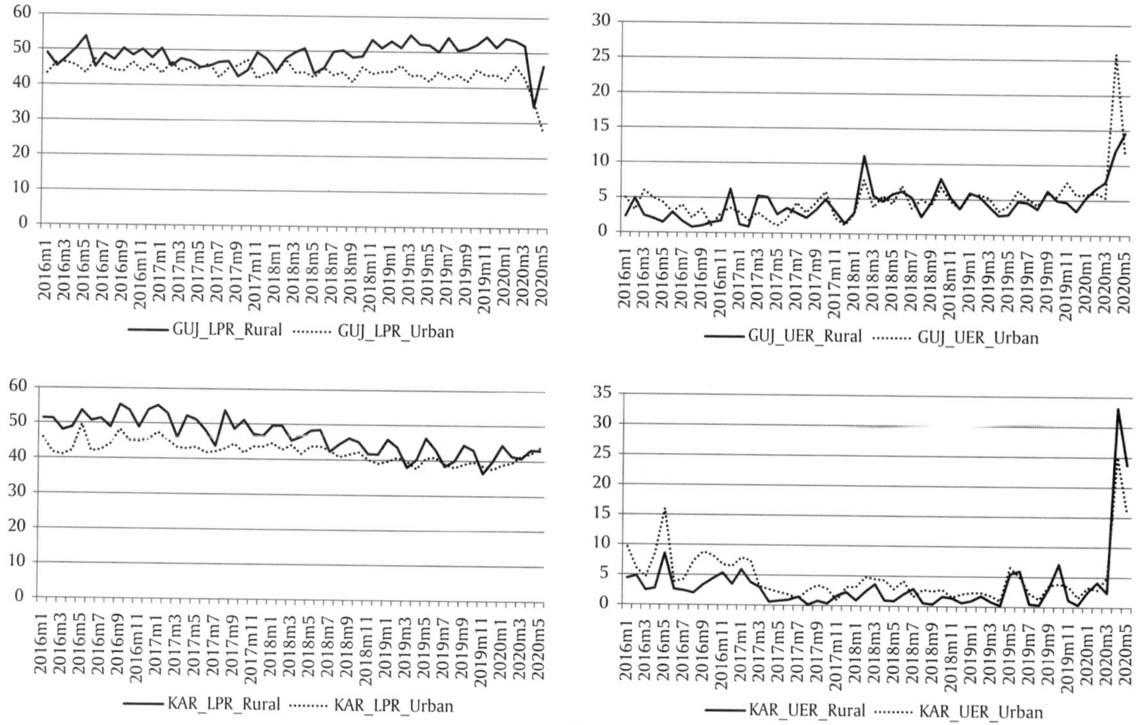

(Contd)

Figure 3.2 (Contd)

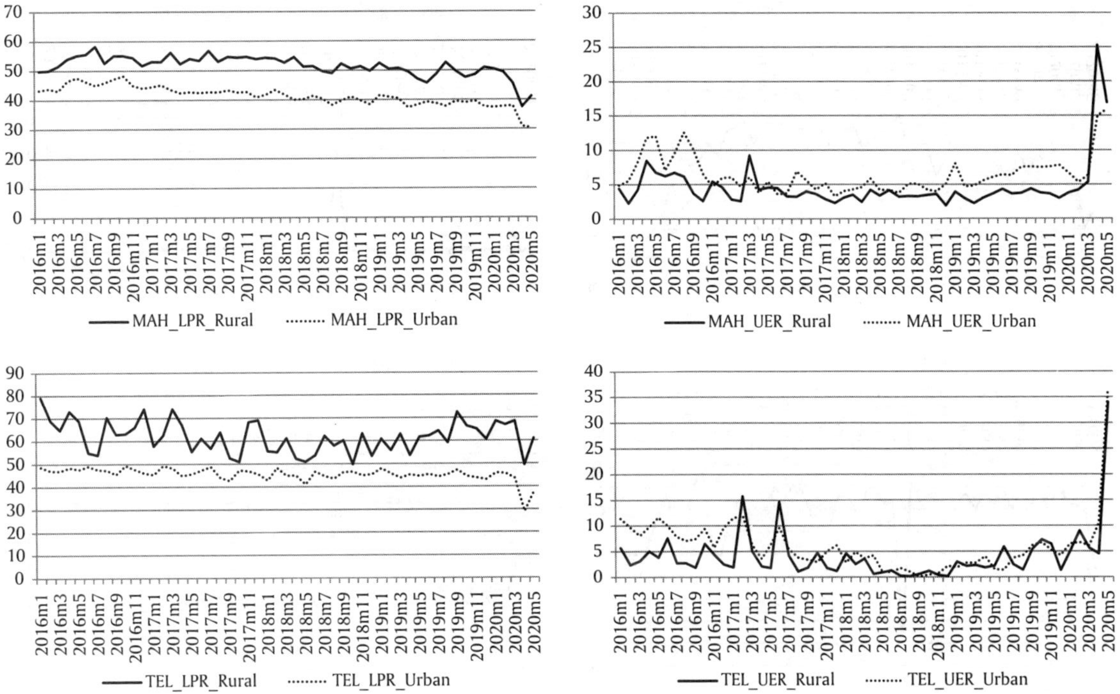

(Contd)

Figure 3.2 (Contd)

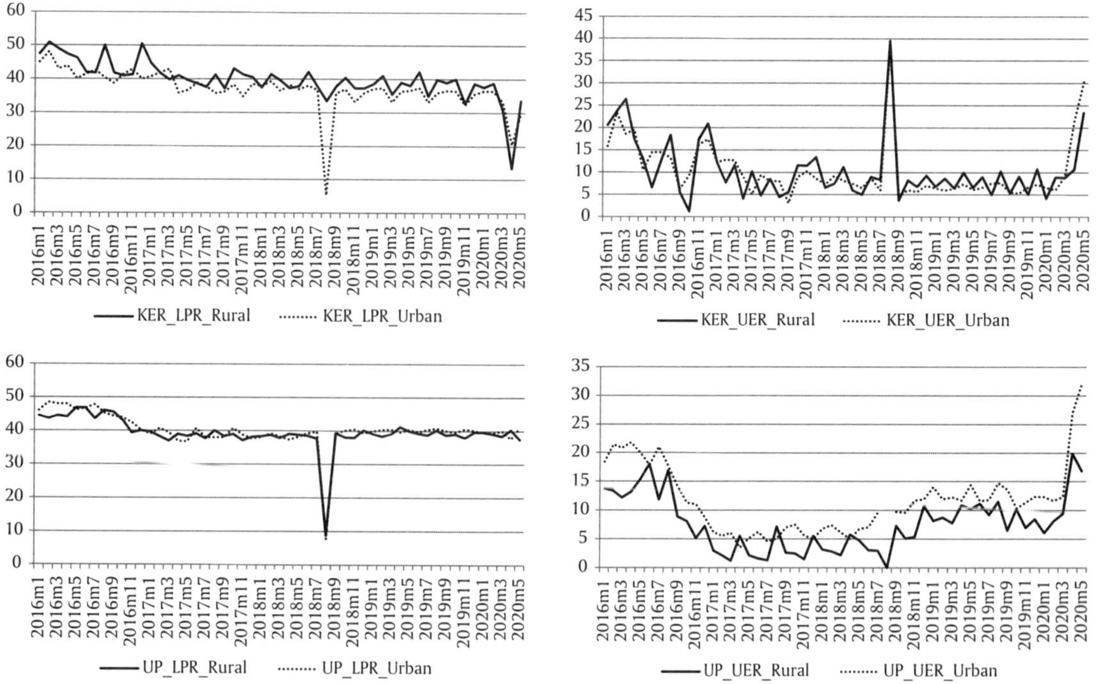

Notes: LPR and UER, respectively, stand for labour participation rate and unemployment rate.
Source: Prepared using CMIE (2020a).

delay in disbursement of subsidy by the central government to states (L. Rajagopal 2018).

The firecracker industry exemplifies the multidimensional character of challenges, which transcend sporadic shocks. Sivakasi accounts for 90 per cent of the firework production in the country and is one of the 'biggest local job creator, directly or indirectly, employing hundreds of thousands of people, many of them uneducated women' (Agence France-Presse 2019). The industry faces at least three challenges. First, it has been hit by campaigns calling for the boycott of polluting industries. Second, it faces major challenges due to a change in the regulatory environment. An October 2018 ruling of the Supreme Court permits only the use of green and improved firecrackers and also bans barium sulphate in the manufacture of firecrackers (K. Rajagopal 2018). Third, the industry also faces competition from illegal import of cheaper fireworks from China. So, the industry has had to cope with changing tastes, changes in regulations and growing international competition. The matchstick industry of Sivakasi is similarly facing multidimensional challenges due to a scarcity of raw material domestically and growing international competition (Krishnakumar 2015). This holds good for other industrial clusters in the Tiruppur, Erode, and Karur belt as well as in the Ranipet and Vellore belt.

Other industries in Tamil Nadu have also faced environmental challenges that are independent of the pandemic and the preceding economic shocks that include demonetisation. The Sterlite copper plant in Tuticorin failed to secure necessary approvals from the pollution control board due to fears of serious environmental damage (Vaitheesvaran and Mazumdar 2018). In 2018, following violent protests from people in the surrounding areas, the Tamil Nadu government had to close the factory. Likewise, leather tanning units in Vellore and textile units in Tiruppur, Karur, and Erode are facing increasing costs of pollution control. Tiruppur is referred to as an environmental 'dark spot' due to the large usage of water and emission of effluents by the textile industry (Deshpande 2020). Industrial pollution has not only adversely affected 'the production possibility in agriculture and allied activities but also brought a significant reduction in the economic opportunities in the industrial sector' (Venkatachalam 2019, p. 173).

Way Forward

A proper study of the economic impact of the Covid-19 pandemic will require combining models of epidemiology, migration, and economic activity. This chapter has tried to highlight some of the early trends. The CMIE data suggest that the experience of Tamil Nadu initially was comparable to that of urban Maharashtra and Gujarat, where labour participation declined in two consecutive months following the first lockdown. It is noteworthy that these three are among the states most affected by Covid-19 and at one point of time accounted for nearly half of the cases in the whole of the country.

Tamil Nadu, with a greater dependence on manufacturing, witnessed a delay in return to pre–Covid-19 levels of economic activities due to the inability of employees to work from home and the requirements of social distancing at the workplace. Additionally, Tamil Nadu's industries, as well as agricultural sector, depend a lot on migrant labourers, since most of the native workers are educated and unwilling to take unskilled jobs. For instance, studies of Tiruppur and the National Capital Region clusters show that 70–100 per cent workers are interstate migrants from Bihar, Uttar Pradesh and other poor states (Deshingkar 2020). This poses a dual challenge during the pandemic: on the one hand, Tamil Nadu faces a shortage of unskilled workers due to the reverse migration of labourers to their home state, and on the other hand, there is a supply of skilled workers seeking employment. In the short run, at least, the state, therefore, faces a skill mismatch. The state needs to create an environment conducive to attracting unskilled migrant labourers, to restart the industries, without which the local semi-skilled and skilled workers cannot be re-employed. In fact, after repeated disruption due to lockdowns, the Tiruppur garment industry appealed to the government to address the housing problem of the migrant labour (Saravanan, 2021).

The government also needs to be sensitive to social differences. After the relaxation of lockdown in May, unemployment dropped faster in the cases of males and those based in urban areas. Further, unemployment was lowest in the case of those with higher education. The government should pay special attention to bringing women and those without college education back into the labour force.

It, however, bears emphasising that Tamil Nadu's industrial woes predate the pandemic and will outlive it. The whole range of MSMEs in Tamil Nadu are faced with the challenge of coping with changing tastes, a tightening regulatory environment, and growing international competition. The answer to environmental challenges is not a complete shutdown of MSMEs. Either the industrial clusters should invest in research and development in order to find ways of circumventing the problems, or the government should step in with investment in public research and development to help the industry tide over environmental or technological crises, while keeping overall social welfare in mind.

Total bans on economic activities are often counterproductive in a welfare state. For example, the government cannot be oblivious to the fact that a complete ban on child labour in countries like ours can potentially push children from poor families into far worse forms of labour, such as bonded labour, or work with much lower wages, or extreme types of work such as child prostitution (Basu 1999). In other words, governments and courts ought to keep in mind unpleasant but unavoidable trade-offs and interlinkages. The closure of tanneries in Dindigul is a case in point. The effect of the ban on the local economy in order to safeguard the environment is illustrative of the impact of one-sided solutions—a double whammy of lost employment and unresolved environmental damages. It could have been possible to explore simultaneous mitigation strategies (Mondal and Singh 2011), much before the point of no return, in order to save both.

While the overall economic scenario is bleak, the present crisis perhaps has a silver lining. The pandemic has exposed India's unsustainable dependence on other countries, particularly China, for a variety of goods and has nudged the government to promote supply chains less dependent on foreign countries. In a parallel development, the unfortunate border clash in Ladakh had hardened a popular resolve to boycott Chinese goods. These developments may just as well offer a much-needed breathing space to domestic industries that have been battered by a series of economic shocks. States that are alert to the rapidly evolving economic environment will recover faster. State governments will have to look beyond traditional policy approaches and adopt innovative solutions to cope with the emerging challenges. This will require adapting quickly to shifting economic currents. State governments should commission focused need-based surveys that yield precise, even if less accurate, results that feed regularly into policymaking rather than wait for large-scale national surveys with long time lags in the release of reports.

Notes

1. Policymakers in India have hitherto depended upon the following for information on employment (last year for which data are available is indicated within parentheses): decennial population census (2011), quinquennial employment–unemployment surveys conducted by the National Sample Survey Office (2011–2012), annual employment–unemployment surveys of the Labour Bureau (2015), and Labour Bureau quarterly employment surveys (2017). None of these sources provide information for the recent years. The Periodic Labour Force Survey (PLFS) conducted by the National Sample Survey Office in 2017 is, therefore, the only government source of information on employment for the period after demonetisation. However, the PLFS provides only one observation, and even that is not comparable with the 68th Round of the National Sample Survey (National Statistical Office, 2019, pp. 1–5).
2. The CMIE has published monthly information on employment since 2016 and is perhaps one of the very few sources for the most recent period in which the economy has suffered multiple shocks. Since the CMIE sampling frame and methodology has not changed after September 2017 (CMIE 2020b, p. 194), we can possibly use their data to infer the direction of change notwithstanding concerns, if any, about the accuracy of its estimates of the level of, say, LPR.
3. Bertrand et al. (2020) note that 'CPHS has continued to run through the lockdown with roughly 45 per cent of its usual sample.' (CPHS stands for Consumer Pyramids Household Survey). While the latest

CMIE reports provides further information in this regard, it is not enough to infer the impact of non-coverage on estimates (CMIE 2020c). Vyas (2020: 15) notes that 'the larger states, Maharashtra and Tamil Nadu saw their share in total responses decline during the lockdown period compared to the responses accepted during the pre-lockdown period. Maharashtra saw its share fall from 11.7 per cent to 10.7 and Tamil Nadu from 5.7 to 4.8 per cent. Interestingly, both are largely urban and industrial states'. The urban-rural distribution of the sample in Tamil Nadu also varied sharply due to lockdown (ibid: 17). So, the Tamil Nadu sample was severely affected, but we do not have sufficient information about the geography and socio-economic distribution of non-coverage to be able to understand the impact of lockdown on the survey. The contribution of reverse migration to the patterns and trends observed in CMIE data is not clear either. See also Dreze and Somanchi (2021) and Pronab Sen quoted in Nahata (2021) for concerns about the quality of the CMIE data. Other data collection exercises have also been affected by the pandemic (Press Trust of India 2020).

4. The unemployment rate is computed as the number of persons who are 'unemployed who are willing to work and are actively looking for a job, expressed as a percent of the labour force' (CMIE 2020b, p. 191).
5. This seems to be an artefact of the idiosyncrasies of samples as there is no data in February and the data for later months swing wildly from 100 per cent to zero unemployment.
6. The labour force used as the base to calculate employment indicators includes persons aged 15 years and above, who fall into either of the two categories (a) persons employed and (b) persons unemployed, who are willing to work and actively looking for a job (CMIE 2020b, p. 190).
7. We regressed Tamil Nadu's rural and urban LPR on demonetisation, GST, and Covid-19 lockdown dummies after controlling for year- and month-specific effects. We ran two separate regressions, one covering the period up to July 2020 and the other restricted to the period 2016–2019. The results suggest demonetisation did not significantly impact either rural or urban LPR. GST, on the other hand, had a significant negative effect on urban LPR. The immediate impact of the Covid-19 lockdowns on both rural and urban LPRs are negative and significant.
8. States with low unemployment rates are not necessarily better off if their labour participation rates have dropped sharply.

References

Agence France-Presse, '$800 million firecracker industry in Tamil Nadu's Sivakasi hit by anti-pollution drive', *NDTV*, 25 October 2019, available at https://www.ndtv.com/india-news/800-million-firecracker-industry-in-tami-nadus-sivakasi-hit-by-anti-pollution-drive-2122542, accessed on 24 September 2021.

Basu, K., 'Child labor: Cause, consequence and cure, with remarks on international labor standards', *Journal of Economic Literature*, 37(3), September 1999, pp. 1083–1119, available at https://doi.org/10.1257/jel.37.3.1083, accessed on 24 September 2021.

Bertrand, M., K. Krishnan, and H. Schofield, 'How are Indian households coping under the Covid-19 lockdown? 8 key findings', *Rustandy Center for Social Sector Innovation*. The University of Chicago, 11 May 2020, available at https://www.chicagobooth.edu/research/rustandy/blog/2020/how-are-indian-households-coping-under-the-covid19-lockdown, accessed on 24 September 2021.

Centre for Monitoring Indian Economy (CMIE). *States of India* [Data set], 2020a, available at https://statesofindia.cmie.com/, accessed on 7 August 2021.

———. *Unemployment in India: A statistical profile, January–April 2020*, 2020b.

———. *Unemployment in India: A statistical profile, May–August 2020*, 2020c.

Deshingkar, P., 'Faceless and dispossessed: India's circular migrants in the times of COVID-19', *Down To Earth*, 16 June 2020, available at https://www.downtoearth.org.in/blog/economy/faceless-and-dispossessed-india-s-circular-migrants-in-the-times-of-covid-19-71782, accessed on 24 September 2021.

Deshpande, N., 'India's textile city of Tiruppur is an environmental dark spot', *The Wire*, 12 February 2020, available at https://thewire.in/environment/australian-open-tiruppur-dyeing-bleaching-groundwater-contamination-agriculture-noyyal-river, accessed on 24 September 2021.

Dreze, Jean and Anmol Somanchi. '"Bias it is": CMIE chief's defence of CPHS survey elicits fresh critical response from Jean Drèze, Anmol Somanchi', *The Economic Times*, 06 July 2021, available at https://economictimes.indiatimes.com/opinion/et-commentary/bias-it-is-cmie-chiefs-defence-of-cphs-survey-elicits-fresh-critical-response-from-jean-drze-anmol-somanchi/articleshow/83889707.cms, accessed on 21 July 2021.

Krishnakumar, P. K., 'Future of matchbox industry worth Rs. 1,500 crore fading away with time', *Economic Times*, 11 July 2015, available at https://retail.economictimes.indiatimes.com/news/food-entertainment/personal-care-pet-supplies-liquor/future-of-matchbox-industry-worth-rs-1500-crore-fading-away-with-time/48030617, accessed on 24 September 2021.

Mondal, N. C., and V. P. Singh, 'Hydrochemical analysis of salinization for a tannery belt in Southern India', *Journal of Hydrology*, 405(3–4), 5 August 2011, pp. 235–247, available at https://doi.org/10.1016/j.jhydrol.2011.05.058, accessed on 24 September 2021.

Nahata, Pallavi. 'CMIE Survey Limitations May Bias Unemployment Data, Says Pronab Sen', *Bloomberg Quint*, 29 June 2021, available at https://www.bloombergquint.com/economy-finance/cmie-survey-limitations-may-bias-unemployment-data-says-pronab-sen, accessed on 21 July 2021.

National Statistical Office, *Annual report, periodic labour force survey (July 2017—June 2018)*, Ministry of Statistics and Programme Implementation, Government of India, May 2019, available at http://mospi.nic.in/publication/annual-report-plfs-2017-18, accessed on 24 September 2021.

Press Trust of India, 'Govt holds back full IIP data for April', *Outlook*, 12 June 2020, available at https://www.outlookindia.com/newsscroll/govt-holds-back-full-iip-data-for-april/1864266, accessed on 24 September 2021.

Rajagopal, K., 'Supreme Court refuses blanket ban on firecrackers', *The Hindu*, 23 October 2018, available at https://www.thehindu.com/news/national/supreme-court-refuses-blanket-ban-on-firecrackers/article25294444.ece, accessed on 24 September 2021.

Rajagopal, L., 'Centre, Tamil Nadu blamed for 50,000 industries shutting down', *The New Indian Express*, 9 June 2018, available at https://www.newindianexpress.com/states/tamil-nadu/2018/jun/09/centre-tamil-nadu-blamed-for-50000-industries-shutting-down-1825739.html, accessed on 24 September 2021.

Saravanan, M. P., 'Garment makers of Tirupur seek solution to housing woes', *The New Indian Express*, 07 March 2021, available at https://www.newindianexpress.com/states/tamil-nadu/2021/mar/07/garment-makers-of-tirupur-seek-solution-to-housing-woes-2273289.html, accessed on 21 December 2021.

Vaitheesvaran, B., and R. Mazumdar, 'Tuticorin protest: Tamil Nadu government orders permanent closure of Sterlite plant', *The Economic Times*, 29 May 2018, available at https://economictimes.indiatimes.com/news/politics-and-nation/tamil-nadu-government-orders-permanent-closure-of-sterlite-plant-in-tuticorin/articleshow/64355730.cms, accessed on 24 September 2021.

Venkatachalam, L., 'Environmental implications of the manufacturing sector: A case study of textile manufacturing in Tiruppur, Tamil Nadu, India', *Review of Development and Change*, XX (2), 19 June 2019, pp. 165–175, available at https://doi.org/10.1177/0972266120150208, accessed on 24 September 2021.

Vyas, Mahesh, 'CPHS execution during the lockdown of 2020', Working Paper, Centre for Monitoring Indian Economy, 2020.

Section II

Agricultural Policy Reforms

4

Reforms in the Agriculture Sector in the Post–Covid-19 Era

L. Venkatachalam

Though the Covid-19 pandemic has devastated our economy, it can also be treated as an opportunity to revamp it. In this chapter we highlight some of the short- and long-term measures that can be undertaken in the agriculture sector in order to bring about a 'new normal' in that sector in the post–Covid-19 scenario.

During the Covid-19 pandemic, agricultural and allied activities have been the worst hit. As a result, there has been a disruption in the food supply in the economy. Due to the lack of transportation and marketing facilities during the lockdowns, many farmers could not sell their produce. The farmers had to either allow the unharvested produce to rot in the field itself or to harvest them and destroy them on the roadside.

There was a lack of demand as well for agricultural products. With the reduced purchasing power caused by income and job loss during the lockdown period, people had a tendency to purchase less agricultural products, a result of which was that a large number of poorer people were vulnerable to hunger. Using lockdown as an opportunity, some traders hoarded essential items, causing an artificial scarcity to make windfall profits. Increased quasi-rent for some of these items forced people to spend more on them, leading to a constant erosion in their purchasing power. Since disruptions in the supply of agricultural commodities caused forward and backward effects in the industry sector, these industrial activities were also paralysed, causing hardship to people dependent on it. For example, activities in the transportation industry carrying agricultural commodities and food processing industry had been severely hit, and a large number of small traders and labourers dealing with goods and services from agricultural and allied activities had lost their livelihood during the lockdown. In order to address these problems, we are proposing certain short- and long-term measures to be undertaken in agriculture and allied activities in Tamil Nadu.

Short-Term Measures (Up To 1 Year)

The supply chain had been adversely affected in the agriculture and allied sectors, despite efforts made by the state government to seamlessly sustain these activities. The following are some of the short-term measures that can be undertaken:

Faster Procurement

Interactions with farmers reveal that, at present, harvested products brought to the government market committees have not been adequately procured by government agencies. Farmers expect the government to procure these products at the minimum support price (MSP), but there is a huge delay in procurement. As a result, the farmers are forced to dispose of their products to private agents at a much cheaper rate. During the lockdown, for farmers already suffering from a lack of income, the non-procurement of their products caused an additional burden. Long delays in government procurement also increase their transaction cost. For example, the farmers have to employ a labourer to stay in the market yard to prevent the commodities from being stolen until they are procured and a delay in procurement increases the cost of policing significantly. Farmers reported that a delay of 5 days costs them an additional Rs. 1,500 for policing. Similarly, such delays increase loss to the farmers due to delays in repayment of their loan, delays in purchasing agricultural inputs for the next crop, and so on. So, timely procuring the agricultural commodities brought to the market committees should be undertaken on a war-footing to ease the burden of the farmers.

Direct Procurement

Many farmers feel that during the lockdown period, vegetables and other perishable commodities should be procured by government agencies directly from wherever they are produced. Since private agents are not willing to procure them (because of problems such as unavailability of transportation and a lack of demand) or are willing to pay only non-remunerative prices, government agencies procuring them will help farmers minimise losses.

Hassle-Free Transportation

Transportation of agricultural inputs and outputs should be made hassle-free both within and across the state.

Storage Facilities in Rural Areas

Farmers prefer the government to create adequate storage facilities in the rural areas itself so that they can store their unsold products in their own villages. This is due to the fact that when they take their commodities to the neighbouring towns, they are either not allowed by the police to cross the border of the town or do not find adequate demand for their products. In both cases, they have to bring the products back to their village, which involves paying additional transportation costs. Some farmers, who find this option to be costlier, are forced to dump their produce in open places.

Reduced Prices and Smooth Supply of Inputs

All government and private outlets selling inputs such as seeds, fertilisers, weedicides and pesticides should be made to function smoothly and sell these inputs to farmers at prices fixed by the government. Farmers feel that some of these inputs can be supplied at reduced rates, at least until the Covid-19 crisis is over.

Timely and Affordable Farm Machinery

Farmers complain that farm machinery are not readily available for use and that local officials indulge in malpractices in allocating these machines. Therefore, the government should ensure that such machines are made available on time through both government as well as private agencies at affordable rates and that small and marginal farmers be given preference in the allocation of these machinery.

Flexible Crop Loans

Crop loans should be made available to farmers with greater flexibility in norms. Farmers argue that agricultural loans against gold, availed at a 4 per cent interest rate in the past, have now become costlier, with an 8 per cent interest rate. They feel that in view of the current crisis, the rate of interest should be reduced to 3 per cent. They also would prefer that sanctioning of loans from public sector banks should be made faster.

Decentralised Agricultural Markets[1]

More decentralised agricultural markets should be opened up, especially in urban areas, so that agricultural products can directly be sold to consumers. For instance, rather than selling agricultural produce in a single wholesale market, such as the newly created Thirumazhisai market in the Chennai Metropolitan Area (CMA), decentralised markets can be created in each of the 15 zones in the CMA, and vehicles carrying the agricultural products can be diverted to these markets so that retailers and consumers can buy them within their neighbourhood. This will not only reduce the transaction costs to these agents but, due to better social distancing, also reduce the spread of Covid-19. Since Covid-19 is not likely to go away anytime soon, agricultural markets in urban areas should be designed to be operated in a completely decentralised manner so that the social costs involved in operating a single wholesale market can be minimised significantly. In these newly created markets, adequate storage facilities should be created.

How to bring farmers and consumers together—so that the exploitation of both producer and consumer surplus by the intermediaries can be minimised—has been an issue for a very long time. The reality has been that in the absence of proper marketing facilities, the elimination of intermediaries will indeed increase the transaction costs to farmers. For example, coconut farmers in Puducherry region reported that the procurement price paid to them by the intermediaries is three times lower (Rs. 10 per unit) than the retail price (Rs. 30 per unit) prevailing in places like Chennai. The farmers, however, cannot sell the coconuts in the retail markets due to difficulties such as non-availability of market yards and cartels among intermediaries and retailers (which creates problems for outsiders). A better strategy to deal with this issue is to increase competition among intermediaries so that farmers can have more bargaining power.

During the lockdown period, we have observed that state-established institutions, such as farmer producer organisations, have played a crucial role in making agricultural products directly available to consumers at reasonable rates. So, making full use of existing institutions and establishing similar new institutions is important, so that the negative impact of private intermediaries in the agriculture sector is minimised significantly not only at the present time, but also in the future.

Contract Farming[2] and Certification

The central government has now announced various measures for reviving the agriculture sector, such as allowing farmers to sell their produce directly to buyers, rather than through APMC (Agricultural Produce Market Committee) markets, and permitting electronic trading of farm produce. The state government should ensure that these measures are adequately implemented so that their benefits actually reach the farmers. For example, measures to establish institutions for contract farming need to be initiated in the state immediately. Right now, contract farming in Tamil Nadu operates in a very limited space and that too only in the private domain. The government should play a major role in establishing proper institutions to promote contract farming. For example, formal contracts are required in the cultivation and marketing of organic products. There is considerable demand for organic products in the state, but the asymmetric information problem plays a constraining role in the spread of organic farming in the state. Farmers do not have adequate information, such as the size of the demand for organic products, where the demand comes from, and what the maximum price the consumers are willing to pay for these products. The consumers, on the other hand, have asymmetric information on the quality and actual price of the products. Institutional intervention in the form of certification for organic products can bring about a desirable change in this area.

Linking of MGNREGA with Agriculture[3]

In recent years, a large number of migrant labourers from north India have been engaged in agricultural activities in different parts of Tamil Nadu. During the lockdown, most of the migrant labourers went back to their respective states and there has been no indication that they would ever return. With this being the case, we can expect labour scarcity in the agriculture sector—acute in some places like the Cauvery delta region—in the short run. In order to ease the situation, the Mahatma Gandhi National Rural Employment Guarantee Act (MGNREGA) activities can be linked to agricultural activities. MGNREGA workers can be effectively utilised for carrying out agricultural activities in private land and marginal and small farmers may be given priority in the allocation of these workers.

Long-Term Measures (1–5 Years)

Demand-Based Agriculture

The prices of many important agricultural commodities are observed to be unstable. This is because the supply of, and the demand for, these commodities are not balanced. In a classic example, when price of onion goes up, a large number of farmers start cultivating onion. Four months down the line, when the crop is harvested, the price crashes due to oversupply. As a consequence, a large number of loss-making onion-producing farmers withdraw from cultivating onion. A further four months down the line, there is a short supply, and the price goes up once again, which influences the farmers to cultivate onion once again. This vicious circle between supply and demand has become a regular phenomenon.

One of the major reasons for this is the herd behaviour of farmers. Such behaviour results in benefiting neither the farmers nor the consumers. How do we bring about a balance between supply and demand so that the prices can be stabilised in the long run? The solution lies in demand-based agriculture. All that we need to do is estimate the demand, both domestic and foreign, for all major agricultural commodities and ensure that these commodities are produced according to the size of the demand. Based on historical data, crops produced in excess of demand and crops produced in short supply can be identified. Two or three months before every cropping season, farmers can be asked two simple questions: (1) what crops are you planning to cultivate in the coming season? and (2) how much land area are you going to utilise for each crop? This information can be collected by the agricultural extension centres and village administrative officers at the micro level. Based on this information, the government can predict the expected supply of each crop. In case the output of a crop is going to be in excess supply, the extension officials can ask the farmers to switch over from that crop to another crop which is going to be in short supply. The farmers can be nudged to adopt a suitable cropping pattern, depending on their respective agro-climatic zones. The government machinery and the farmer producer organisations can be effectively utilised for bringing about a required behavioural changes among farmers in order to make supply–demand equal over a period. Though there may be some degree of error in predicting supply and demand in the short run, such errors can be rectified in the long run, providing a win-win outcome for both farmers as well as consumers.

Payment for Ecosystem Services Scheme

In the agriculture sector, supply–demand imbalance is caused by lack of diversification as well. One of the reasons for this is MSP. Of the

22 crops governed by MSP, most of the farmers prefer to cultivate paddy and sugarcane, leading to an excess supply of these products and a glut in the market. Since these crops are highly water intensive, their cultivation leads to serious environmental issues such as the over-exploitation of groundwater. Excess supply and environmental constraints increase not only the private cost to the farmers but also the social costs borne by society. A solution to this problem is a Payment for Ecosystem Services (PES) scheme. When farmers are nudged to change their cropping pattern in certain agro-climatic zones, they can be encouraged to cultivate specific environment-friendly crops. When farmers switch over to such crops, their agricultural practices generate social benefits in the form of increased ecosystem services (e.g., water saved for other uses). The social benefits are measured in monetary terms by using standard macroeconomic valuation techniques (such as Benefit Transfer Method) and additional payments are made to the farmers according to the size of the social benefits in terms of ecosystem services that they generate. An ecological indicator, consisting of different types of best practices (such as the use of micro-irrigation technology to save groundwater) conducive for each agro-climatic zone, can be established. Then the farmers using current practices would be encouraged to adopt best practices, for which they would be provided financial incentives.

Based on the number of best practices adopted, the farmers can be classified into three different categories and incremental payments can be made to them accordingly. Suppose there are three best practices, then the high adopters are those who undertake all three practices; medium adopters are those who adopt two practices, and low adopters are the ones adopting only one practice. Based on the value of ecosystem benefits, the amount of PES payment would be determined and used for compensating the farmers. An estimation of different levels of payment for the Indian farmers for their best practices is provided in Table 4.1.

A similar exercise can be done for each agro-climatic zone in Tamil Nadu, and the PES scheme can be implemented to make agricultural practices more efficient, equitable, and sustainable. The PES has great potential in the Tamil Nadu context. For example, implementing the carbon credit scheme to encourage Tamil Nadu farmers to cultivate tree crops (that sequester carbon responsible for global warming) on a vast area of uncultivable land in the state could be a viable option, which can be considered in the immediate future. The institutional arrangement for implementing the PES scheme can involve government agencies, the corporate sector, nongovernmental organisations, and farmers' organisations.

Table 4.1: PES-Based Income to Different Categories of Farmers

Farm size	*Size of land (ha)*	*Current annual income from all agricultural sources (2017 prices; Rs.)*	*High adoption (Rs.)*	*Medium adoption (Rs.)*	*Low adoption (Rs.)*
Marginal	<0.01	25,064	41,438	38,018	30,795
	0.01–0.40	26,712	43,086	39,666	32,443
	0.40–1.00	48,919	65,293	61,873	54,650
Small	1.01–2.00	84,958	144,576	132,589	105,824
Semi–medium	2.01–4.00	137,132	250,950	228,038	176,994
Medium	4.00–10.00	266,135	507,967	458,959	350,776
Large	10.00+	605,845	1,335,538	1,187,742	861,238
All size classes		62,850	114,132	104,480	82,749

Source: Kumar et al. (2009).[4]

Value-Added Products

Though agricultural production and productivity are relatively high in Tamil Nadu, the value-added in the agriculture sector has not yet been realised to its fullest potential. More focus is needed in that area so that more employment and income can be generated, especially at the regional level. In Tamil Nadu, for various reasons, an increasing number of farmers are gradually switching over from cultivating food-grains towards tree crops, such as coconut, mango, banana, jackfruit, areca nut, and palmyra. However, the greater part of their yield is being used only for direct consumption within the state. Much of the food produced is also wasted at different stages. There is greater potential for developing agro-based industrial units, such as food processing. For example, tender coconut water, if processed scientifically, can be exported to other states and countries. The coir and coconut-husk-based industry can be developed in the coconut belts in Tamil Nadu, which has greater export potential since there is considerable demand for coir and coconut husk, especially from Gulf countries. Palmyra products, such as *nungu* (ice-apple) also can be processed and exported, as has been done in the case of countries like Thailand. Gur extracted from the palmyra tree also has medicinal values, and the demand for it is also increasing. Similarly, mango- and jackfruit-processing industrial units can be established in Tamil Nadu. Further developing agro-based industry in Tamil Nadu will not only benefit farmers in helping them gain more income but also create employment and income for non-agricultural households.

Liquor Policy and Agricultural Benefits

Since coconut and palmyra trees are abundantly available in Tamil Nadu, their untapped benefits should be properly utilised. Toddy tapping from coconut and palmyra trees can be allowed in the state. Toddy tapping can bring the following benefits: (1) there will be direct employment and income generation for the households involved in toddy tapping; (2) the farmers of coconut trees will get additional income from renting the trees for toddy tapping, apart from regular income from selling ripe coconut, tender coconut, and other coconut-based products; (3) if coconut trees are used for toddy tapping, the coconut yield is expected to increase (this is because, during toddy tapping, the tree is regularly cleaned, and insects and diseases attacking the trees are contained); (4) on top of everything, as toddy is considered to be a close substitute for Indian-made foreign liquor (IMFL), alcohol consumers can consume toddy at a much cheaper rate and save a significant amount of their income spent on IMFL. Since toddy is not as harmful to health, consumers can minimise their health cost as well. So, allowing toddy tapping will lead to multiple uses of these crops, leading to increased income and employment, and reduced health impacts in the economy. Since a large number of farmers in the state are switching over from conventional crops to tree crops, a liberal liquor policy can benefit farmers substantially.

Alternate Medicines and Agriculture

In addition to modern medicines, traditional medicines also played a major role in containing the impact of Covid-19 on the people of

Tamil Nadu. In the state, people commonly use alternate medicines (Siddha, Ayurveda, etc.) in order to strengthen their immune system. The same phenomenon was also seen during recent dengue fever outbreaks. Given that there is a huge market for immunity-producing medicines, such as zinc and vitamin tablets, traditional Tamil Nadu herbal medicines can be converted into tablet or capsule form and marketed. This means that the Tamil Nadu government should promote the use of these medicines, ensure that these medicinal plants are cultivated and that such medicines are produced on a large scale and exported to other states and countries in the coming years. Since Covid-19 is expected to stay with us for the foreseeable future, this is a good opportunity to promote effective alternate medicines. This will encourage the industry to establish units to produce these medicines as well as encourage farmers to cultivate the herbs used as inputs in these units. This will increase employment and income in the industry and in the agriculture sectors, apart from bringing substantial export earnings to the country.

Notes and References

1. For a detailed discussion on agricultural market reforms, please see Chapter 6 of this book.
2. Please see Chapter 6 of this book for a detailed discussion on contract farming.
3. See also, Chapter 6, this book.
4. Kumar, L., M. Manjula, R. Bhatta, L. Venkatachalam, D. S. Kumar, P. I. Devi, and P. Mukhopadhyay, 'Doubling India's farm incomes: Paying farmers for ecosystem services, not just crops!' *Economic and Political Weekly*, 54(23), 2019, pp 43–49.

5

Irrigation in Tamil Nadu Pre– and Post–Covid-19 Eras

K. Sivasubramaniyan

This chapter discusses the inputs, some of which already exist in the current policy domain, which can profitably be implemented for the development of agriculture in Tamil Nadu.

Trends in Agriculture Sector Before Covid-19

In Tamil Nadu, the share of contribution of agriculture to Gross State Domestic Product (GSDP) has been steadily declining over the past 50years. It declined from 35 per cent in 1970 to 17 per cent in 2000, 14.5 per cent in 2011, and further to 11.5 per cent in 2016 (Department of Evaluation and Applied Research 2011, 2012, 2013; Sivasubramaniyan 2016). Hence, the revival of agriculture will require a big push, for a minimum period of at least five years.

One of the main factors that determine the prosperity in agriculture is the extent of irrigation sources available for enabling better cropping pattern. In Tamil Nadu, it is important to ensure that canal and tank irrigation systems are revived in order to increase the irrigated area from a little more than a million hectares at present to their potential limit of about two million hectares.

What is the present status of different sources of irrigation in Tamil Nadu?

Canal Irrigation

The registered command area of canals is about a million hectares. But irrigating this much area has never been achieved even in a year of normal rainfall, or in a year of supply of water through canals (Table 5.1). A good option is to increase canal-irrigated area in river basins with an 'alternate irrigation system', dividing the entire command area into two halves or zones, and providing irrigation for each zone every alternate year. For instance, although the Cauvery canal irrigation serves more than two-thirds of the total canal-irrigated area in 8 districts of Tamil Nadu, this area has been decreasing gradually. To compensate for this and to increase this assured Cauvery canal area, its command area needs to be doubled by dividing the Cauvery ayacut into two zones so that each zone can be irrigated every 'alternate' year. The prime reason is that in 4 of these 8 Cauvery districts, 53 per cent of net sown area (NSA) remains unirrigated. This task can be done as already practised in the Parambikulam Aliyar Project command and the Lower Bhavani Project command.

Presently, the efficiency and productivity of water use in the prime Cauvery delta districts are well below the state and national averages, which indicates that the efficiency of water use in the basin is very low. If alternate irrigation is carried out successfully towards exploiting the existing potential, this can be replicated in other river basins like that of the Tamirabarani. This can enhance canal-irrigated area substantially, thereby increasing agricultural production and employment opportunities.

Tank Irrigation

The importance of tank irrigation is multifaceted. As per the state government data, Tamil Nadu has 41,127 tanks serving small (<40 ha; 33,142) and large (>40 ha; 7,985) ayacuts. The registered ayacut of all tanks is a little more than one million hectares (Department of Economics and Statistics 2018: 581; Vaidyanathan and Sivasubramaniyan 2001).

A majority of tanks have their own catchment area, and a limited number of large tanks have wider catchment supplies through canals linked to rivers and dams. Usually, tank irrigation does not involve interstate disputes. To develop tank irrigation, all Tamil Nadu has to do is to construct many check dam–based small anicuts across a river to link them to the tanks.

Table 5.1: Net Irrigated Area (NIA) by Sources in India and Tamil Nadu from 1950–1951 to 2014–2015 (in lakh hectares)

Source	*1950–1951 to 1959–1960*		*1960–1961 to 1969–1970*		*1970–1971 to 1979–1980*		*1980–1981 to 1989–1990*		*1990–1991 to 1999–2000*		*2000–2001 to 2009–2010*		*2010–2011 to 2014–2015*	
	Area	*Per cent of NIA*	*Area*	*Per cent of NIA*	*Area*	*Per cent of NIA*	*Area*	*Per cent of NIA*	*Area*	*Per cent of NIA*	*Area*	*Per cent of NIA*	*Area*	*Per cent of NIA*
India														
Canals	91.9	41.2	111.9	41.9	137.7	40.1	163.1	38.3	173.4	32.7	156.9	26.4	159.6	24.0
Tanks	41.5	18.6	44.5	16.6	38.1	11.1	29.9	7.0	31.1	5.9	19.8	3.3	18.4	2.8
Wells + tube wells	66.3	29.8	87.1	32.6	144.1	41.9	207.8	48.7	292.5	55.2	364.1	61.2	412.8	62.1
Other sources*	23.2	10.4	23.9	8.9	23.8	6.9	25.4	6.0	33.1	6.2	53.9	9.1	73.5	11.1
Total NIA	222.9	100.0	267.3	100.0	343.6	100.0	426.3	100.0	530.1	100.0	594.7	100.0	664.3	100.0
Tamil Nadu														
Canals	8.0 (8.7)	37.6	8.8 (7.9)	35.6	8.9 (6.5)	33.2	8.2 (5.0)	33.0	8.3 (4.8)	29.3	7.3 (4.7)	26.8	6.8 (4.3)	24.4
Tanks	7.8 (18.7)	36.8	9.1 (20.5)	36.8	8.5 (22.3)	31.5	6.2 (20.6)	24.7	6.3 (20.4)	22.4	5.1 (25.6)	18.6	4.2 (22.8)	14.9
Wells + tube wells	5.0 (7.5)	23.5	6.5 (7.4)	26.0	9.2 (6.4)	34.1	10.4 (5.0)	41.6	13.5 (4.6)	47.7	14.8 (4.1)	54.2	16.9 (4.1)	60.5
Other sources*	0.5 (2.0)	2.2	0.4 (1.6)	1.6	0.4 (1.5)	1.3	0.2 (0.7)	0.8	0.2 (0.5)	0.6	0.1 (0.2)	0.4	0.07 (0.1)	0.2

(Contd)

Table 5.1 (Contd)

Source	*1950–1951 to 1959–1960*		*1960–1961 to 1969–1970*		*1970–1971 to 1979–1980*		*1980–1981 to 1989–1990*		*1990–1991 to 1999–2000*		*2000–2001 to 2009–2010*		*2010–2011 to 2014–2015*	
	Area	*Per cent of NIA*	*Area*	*Per cent of NIA*	*Area*	*Per cent of NIA*	*Area*	*Per cent of NIA*	*Area*	*Per cent of NIA*	*Area*	*Per cent of NIA*	*Area*	*Per cent of NIA*
Total NIA	21.2 (9.5)	100.0	24.8 (9.3)	100.0	27.0 (7.8)	100.0	25.0 (5.9)	100.0	28.4 (5.4)	100.0	27.3 (4.6)	100.0	28.0 (4.2)	100.0
Total NSA	55.45		60.26		61.35		56.22		56.33		50.22		48.04	

Notes: Figures in parentheses indicate source-wise percentage compared to India. NIA = Net Irrigated Area. NSA = Net Sown Area.
*indicates anicuts, *bhandaras*, springs, *kuttai*, *thangal*, small diversion networks, and so on.

Sources: Centre for Monitoring Indian Economy (various years); Directorate of Economics and Statistics (2000); Directorate of Economics and Statistics (1993); Department of Evaluation and Applied Research (various years); Department of Economics and Statistics (various years); Indiastat Agri (n.d.).

Up to the 1960s, tank irrigation was the prime source of irrigation in Tamil Nadu. During the 1960s, 9.1 lakh ha were irrigated via tanks. But now, tank irrigation has lost its glory. The area served by tanks has steadily declined and dropped to 2,58,207 ha in 2016–2017. This is roughly 25 per cent of the area registered (more than a million hectares) under tanks. The several factors responsible for such decline can be broadly classified into physical, institutional, and technical. All these prevailing factors merit attention if there has to be a revival of the tank irrigation system.

The current status shows the potential for construction of small anicuts for prudently linking with the tanks to ensure effective use of water. This possibility helps in generating short- and medium-term employment in addition to developing the long-neglected sources of tank irrigation. Also, once revived, tank irrigation will enable income generation to marginal and small farmers through agriculture for a long period of time.

In its latest state focus paper for Tamil Nadu, the National Bank for Agriculture and Rural Development (NABARD) has noted, 'Water availability is a key as also a limiting factor influencing the production and productivity in agriculture sector. It is essential to provide timely irrigation for effective utilisation of agricultural land, and hence irrigation availability for all cultivable land within the next 10 years has been identified as a key objective under *Tamil Nadu Vision 2023* prepared by GoTN.' (NABARD 2020: pp. x–xi).

The Impact of Covid-19 in the Surface Irrigation Sector

There are three dimensions to the impact of Covid-19 in the minor irrigation sector.

The first relates to the period of the pandemic in Tamil Nadu. The period started from the last week of March 2020. Usually the summer (April–May) is important for agriculture, because during this period farmers collectively undertake preparatory farm works, such as summer ploughing, maintenance, and improvement of minor irrigation structures through *kudimaramathu* for the *kuruvai* (short-term) crop. This work is essential for sowing and continues till the southwest monsoon arrives in June. Kudimaramathu is required in pre- and post- southwest monsoon periods, for canal maintenance and tank infrastructure–related maintenance, respectively, since tanks in Tamil Nadu get copious inflows mainly from northeast monsoon. If this basic work is not undertaken on time, there are severe problems, in terms of delays in sowing, more wastage of water, and flooding due to weak tank- or river-bund and other infrastructure, which adversely affect the cultivation of crops. In 2020, due to Covid-19, planned cultivation could not be carried out prudently with effective use of all farm inputs to enhance productivity.

The second dimension relates to availability of farm labourers during the Covid-19 period. Agricultural labourers carrying out routine farm work and activities related to minor irrigation, such as kudimaramathu, abstained from work and stayed home due to the implementation of lockdown measures. This adversely affected the routine maintenance of minor irrigation and related agricultural activities. Further, the phenomenon of inter-district and intra-district displacement of agricultural labourers due to lockdown aggravated labour scarcity in agriculture, despite some relaxation to the farm sector for carrying out essential operations. It is necessary that in thepost–Covid-19 period, time should be fruitfully utilised for the maintenance of both canal and tank infrastructure to reap good outcome from irrigation facilities and to ensure more income to farmers.

The third dimension relates to the healthcare of people in the farm sector in rural areas. Lack of awareness and lack of seriousness in adherence to mandatory preventive norms—namely, physical distancing, face masks, and washing of hands—resulted in large-scale violation of such norms. The intensity of the spread of Covid-19 in rural areas was also impacted by the 'Koyambedu factor'[1] at the community level. These developments aggressively affect the ecosystem by paralysing the supply and demand value chains in agricultural sector, more particularly in horticultural sector.

In addition to these Covid-19 related issues, severe storms and heavy rain in summer also led to a loss of crops and a reduction in farm income.

Short-Term Policy Measures

1. The defunct Tamil Nadu Farmers' Management of Irrigation Systems Act, 2000 (TNFMIS Act) can be revived to empower farmers who utilise tanks for irrigation and to manage the tanks under the supervision of Public Works Department (PWD) authorities. More importantly, this Act was created not only to revive tanks but also to strengthen the management of canal irrigation. The Act safeguards Water Users' Associations (WUAs). Were this Act to be re-implemented, and not only in the Covid-19 period, the farmers would be vigilant in protecting and maintaining the tank and canal system to get adequate water supply and enable better cropping. Once this has been implemented, productivity will improve and farmers' income will rise. This has not been happening in the past few decades.
2. The income from tank fisheries, wherever possible, can be shared on a 50:50 basis between the WUAs and the Government of Tamil Nadu, as stipulated in the TNFMIS Act.
3. The farmers should be permitted to remove the silt deposited in the tanks, as and when it is necessary, free of cost. Although in the past, the government had given permission to remove silt, this is now politically oriented, and disputes are reported frequently. This can be solved through the implementation of the TNFMIS Act.
4. WUAs should be created for all tanks and canals, and non-functional tanks and canals should be made functional again. These associations should be empowered to take care of kudimaramathu in tanks, channel maintenance, and management of field-level water distribution. For this too, the basis is the recognition of the TNFMIS Act.
5. As per the TNFMIS Act, PWD officials have been tasked with duties such as the removal of encroachments in the canals, channels, and water bodies, and to sort out related issues as quickly as possible. This has not been done so far, and the situation needs to be rectified.
6. Since irrigation water has been released from Mettur dam, it is time for proper maintenance of canals and channels throughout

the Cauvery command area. For this purpose, the government should release an order indicating that proper canal maintenance should be undertaken by the farmers themselves in their village jurisdiction through the WUAs, and wherever this is not feasible the government should take steps to do the maintenance on time to ensure efficient water use in the channels. Although the state government has appointed a few special officers of the IAS cadre for this purpose, the main objective is to ensure that the tail end of the Cauvery command areas get adequate supply of irrigation water. Only when the tail end of the command area get the required water supply, can we say that the maintenance system is functioning well. This has not been possible for many decades.

7. Although irrigated agriculture produces relatively more yield than unirrigated land, the transport and marketing problems often lead to heavy losses for farmers in general. Under this circumstance, the supply chain issue needs to be thought of in agriculture and irrigation alone will not be enough. The supply chain during post-production period needs to be strengthened in every district, with the intensive promotion of collective marketing structure, like farmer producer organisations and farmer promotion committees. Village- and block-level marketing facilities are inadequate and lead to heavy loss of marketing of farm produce. Block-level *uzhavar sandhai* (farmers' markets) should be equipped with facilities, such as water, sanitiser, face masks, and physical-distance marking, to prevent the spread of corona virus.
8. In order to supplement the state budget, NABARD may consider focusing on funding of minor irrigation works under the Rural Infrastructure Development Fund (RIDF). More attention could be paid to construction of check dams and river-based anicuts, and direct supervision of the status of maintenance of existing minor irrigation works already financed could be carried out. Remedial action will need to be given attention on priority. Inlet channels of all minor irrigation tanks need to be revived fully.

9. To ensure that adequate healthy workforce is available for maintenance work on irrigation, an intensive awareness campaign on the significance of disease prevention norms needs to be arranged through various kinds of cultural programmes that are designed based on indigenous knowledge, like street theatre and drama, folk songs, village Koothu and puppetry (*Bommalattam*), and hoardings in places like shanties and temple premises. These activities need to be implemented and monitored by different departments (health, PWD, agriculture, fisheries, forestry) and involve the people under a participatory approach. Apart from Covid-19 prevention messages, a message about the importance and usefulness of the TNFMIS Act can also be propagated. For these purposes, social capital, such as self-help groups, WUAs, farmers' clubs, and joint liability groups along with village organisations need to be utilised.

Medium-Term Policy Measures (3–5 Years)

Wherever irrigated agriculture is practised, many indirect problems are faced by farmers. These problems are mainly in terms of non-availability of adequate storage (eg., for onion) and cooling (eg., for tomato) facilities, since crop outputs due to irrigated agriculture are high, but farmers lack storage facilities to house this increased yield. That leads to heavy damage of output due to the perishable nature of these commodities. Further, a large majority of farmers are small and marginal landholders and their economic position is very weak. If these farmers have good irrigation facilities, but no access to proper credit to buy other inputs on time, then they will not cultivate in general. Even if the farmers make an attempt at cultivation, the yield level will be very low, in the absence of adequate inputs. So, credit is another crucial factor even in irrigated agriculture. This credit is also the base for improving the farmers' soil quality and raising crop productivity, provided the farmers have a good irrigation facility. Increasing labour costs in irrigated agriculture is yet another major concern. Thus, considering these complicated issues in irrigated agriculture, one has to address these indirect issues, especially during the Covid-19 pandemic, to support agriculturists and encourage government intervention to help the farmers in multiple ways, so that they do not incur losses in their agricultural operations.

1. The current package announced by the state finance ministry is not adequate, and the problem in the irrigation sector is entirely different. The suggestion is to develop and upgrade infrastructure facilities of surface irrigation—canals and tanks—systems that, in the past, have been grossly neglected. A special five-year perspective Covid-19 plan (2020–2021 to 2024–2025) for provision of infrastructure is required for minor irrigation works under the Rural Infrastructure Development Fund (RIDF) by NABARD. In addition, farm output–based storage facilities (e.g., godowns) at village and block levels need to be developed.The present RIDF plan by NABARD needs to be revisited to identify the rural infrastructural works, related to farm sector, in all the districts of Tamil Nadu to be taken up on priority basis to overcome the hurdles in the supply chain caused by the pandemic. For example, private investment-based storage structures like godowns need to be encouraged with proper subsidy component for ensuring adequate storage and cooling facility for crop output, including horticulture products, in a majority of revenue villages. NABARD may study the potential demand-based special plan for storage and cooling centre at block level in every district and include this in their Potential Linked Credit Plan as this would supplement the state budget under RIDF allocation.
2. The four lead banks (State Bank of India, Indian Overseas Bank, Indian Bank, and Canara Bank) can prepare special three-year (2020–2021 to 2022–2023) perspective Covid-19 special credit plan in consultation with NABARD and the respective district consultative committees to identify the different activities in the farm sector and to bridge the credit gap caused by the pandemic. The State Level Bankers' Committee (SLBC) can take the initiative on planning this. Under the lead bank scheme (LBS) of the Reserve Bank of India (RBI), this potential credit plan includes cooperative banking and micro financing (through non-banking financial companies,

microfinance institutions, and nongovernmental organisations). Insurance players also come within the purview of LBS. So, a comprehensive Covid-19 special three-year plan for covering both potential credit plan linked with insurance on farm sector (including animal husbandry and fisheries) under LBS may be considered. SLBC, NABARD, and RBI need to prepare the guidelines for this Covid-19 special comprehensive plan for Tamil Nadu, as has been suggested.

3. Based on soil quality map, crop, and water productivity, suitable measures need to be taken by farmers to increase the maximum yield of a particular crop. For this, adequate and timely outreach to farmers may be extended by agricultural universities as well as by the agriculture-related departments.
4. Wherever water deficiency is noticed, water intensive crop cultivation must be stopped and only dry irrigated seasonal crops should be grown. In those areas, advance farming methods using modern technology, including drip-, sprinkler-, or water gun-based irrigation need to be adopted. For this, intensive groundwater recharge programmes and river extension programmes need to be undertaken. River water should be made available to all basin areas (including new extension areas) at least for one season in a year. Scepticism regarding availability of water leads to non-adoption of technology in most areas. As long as wells are available, usage of this modern technology would not be a problem. The problem is the availability of water.
5. In agriculture, the cost of cultivation has been steadily increasing due to increases in input costs to the point that farmers are unable to bear the burden. Labour cost is the highest component of input costs. In many places, despite high labour cost, labourers are not readily available for agriculture works. To avoid such a situation and help farmers, the Mahatma Gandhi National Rural Employment Guarantee Act (MGNREGA) labourers can be utilised by the farmers when they need to get work done on their farm. Farmers can meet 50 per cent of the labour cost, and the remaining 50 per cent can be borne by the government through the allotted MGNREGA funds.

6. In many government-aided programmes, the involvement of the beneficiaries has been grossly neglected. Consequently, without their participation, the accountability and success of the programme becomes questionable. A good example is the recently completed first phase of the Irrigated Agriculture Modernisation and Water-Bodies Restoration and Management (IAMWARM) project aided by the World Bank. The basic objective of the programme—more income per drop of water—and the involvement of eight line departments (agriculture, agricultural engineering, animal husbandry, agricultural marketing, horticulture, fisheries, TNAU [Tamil Nadu Agricultural University], and PWD) to achieve the objective have been wonderful as per the guidelines given by the funding agency. However, the desired outcomes of the project, in terms of assured water supply to crops and envisaged cropped area, have not been achieved, mainly due to total exclusion of beneficiary farmers in the development activities. As seen in Table 5.1, despite this phase of the project being implemented between 2007 and 2014), the area irrigated by tanks steadily decreased in the 2010s (only 4.2 lakh ha against the registered ayacut of a little more than a million hectares in Tamil Nadu). The government should take appropriate steps to fulfil these targets, at least in the ongoing second phase of the project, to raise the tank ayacut area for cultivation adequately in Tamil Nadu.

Since farmers' income through agriculture is not always appreciable, and the irrigation sector is performing poorly, the pandemic and post-pandemic periods should be utilised to develop this vulnerable sector.

Linkages with Interrelated Sectors and Issues

Other Steps for the Betterment of Agriculture in Tamil Nadu

1. Since the MGNREGA programme is active, this labour force should be used prudently to help the farmers to carry outtheir agricultural activities, through an expansion of the irrigation

sector. For this, half the cost of the wages should be shared by the government through MGNREGA funds and the other half by the beneficiary farmers.

2. To solve the credit problems of the farmers, strict instructions should be given to all banks to give liberal credit, based on the farmer's landholdings. The interest levied could be 4 per cent per annum. This demand for credit for farm sector needs to be included in the Covid-19special three-year credit plan by lead banks, as discussed under medium-term policy.
3. In Tamil Nadu, 42.3 per cent of net sown area is still rain-fed (average of 2010–2011 to 2016–2017). To solve water scarcity problems, especially in agriculture, the central and state governments should give priority, in the planning process, to link the southern peninsular rivers. These rivers should then be interconnected to bigger tanks. Currently, the available rainwater and river water are not stored or utilised properly due to the lack of or poor maintenance of tanks, inlet channels, and other storage reservoirs. So, during good rains, water could be stored properly to irrigate additional areas which are always affected by water scarcity. Consequently, in these water-scarce areas, the farmers may be able to cultivate their crops at least during the monsoon season and raise their income level. This is where WUAs need to be created and strengthened (TN–IAMWARM 2014).
4. A village development plan is prepared by the village panchayat in every village in Tamil Nadu, and committees are constituted—such as village works committee, planning committee, and group for supervising MGNREGA scheme—with people in the village as members, for planning and implementing village-level development programmes. Due to the imperative need for adoption of preventive norms (namely, physical distancing, facemask, and handwashing), to safeguard the human being in the last mile, a 'Covid-19 Healthcare Committee' may be constituted and entrusted with raising awareness at individual and community levels in the village and for supervision of these measures, under the participatory approach to healthcare at the village level.

Note

1. Spread over 65 acres, the Koyambedu market is one of Asia's largest wholesale vegetable markets. The market was shut down in May 2020 after the government declared it a Covid hotspot after hundreds of coronavirus cases were found linked to this market. The decision left the traders in distress. Due to this decision, around 215 wholesale traders and over 2,500 retailers were affected. Consequently, agriculture-related market chain was disturbed and farmers around 150 kms distance from this market were affected heavily in the short run. Available at https://www.bbc.com/news/world-asia-india-52674639, https://www.livemint.com/news/india/covid-19-chennai-s-super-spreader-koyambedu-market-closed-traders-miffed-11588682956956.html, accessed February 2022.

References

Centre for Monitoring Indian Economy, *Agriculture,* (Various years).

Department of Economics and Research. *Quick study on Farmers' Clubs Programme in Tamil Nadu for redesigning the policy guidelines on Farmers' Club Programme,* Unpublished manuscript, December 2017.

Department of Economics and Statistics, *Statistical handbook of Tamil Nadu.* Government of Tamil Nadu, 2018 and various years.

_______. *Season and crop report.* Government of Tamil Nadu, various years.

Department of Evaluation and Applied Research, *Tamil Nadu: An economic appraisal,* Government of Tamil Nadu, 2011–2013 and various years.

Directorate of Economics and Statistics, *Indian agricultural statistics, 1985–86—1989–90,* Vol. I, Department of Agriculture & Cooperation, Ministry of Agriculture, Government of India, 1993.

_______. *Indian agriculture in brief,* Department of Agriculture & Cooperation, Ministry of Agriculture, Government of India, January 2000.

Indiastatagri (n.d.), available at https://www.indiastatagri.com/, accessed on 27 September 2021.

National Bank for Agriculture and Rural Development (NABARD), *State Focus Paper 2020–21: Tamil Nadu,* Tamil Nadu Regional Office, 2020, available at https://www.nabard.org/auth/writereaddata/tender/1802201021Tamil%20Nadu-SFP.pdf, accessed on 26 September 2021.

_______. *Impact evaluation study on agriculture (irrigation) and connectivity (roads & bridges) sector projects supported under RIDF in Tamil Nadu,* unpublished, October 2016.

Sivasubramaniyan, K., *Performance of irrigation in Tamil Nadu: A macro perspective* (Working Paper No. 224). Madras Institute of Development Studies, December 2016, available at http://www.mids.ac.in/assets/doc/WP_224.pdf, accessed on 27 September 2021.

Tamil Nadu—Irrigated Agriculture Modernisation and Water-Bodies Restoration and Management (TN–IAMWARM), *Final impact evaluation report*, Submitted to Multi-Disciplinary Project Unit, Water Resources Organisation, Public Works Department, Government of Tamil Nadu, June 2014.

Vaidyanathan, A., and K. Sivasubramaniyan, 'Tank irrigation in south India: An overview', in A. Vaidyanathan (ed.) *Tanks of south India*, Centre for Science and Environment, 2001, pp. 5–30.

6

Reforms in the Farm Acts

Agriculture Markets[1]

P. G. Babu, A. Ganesh-Kumar and Chandan Kumar

Three acts[2] have recently been passed by the Government of India, which have now been withdrawn, to spearhead agricultural market reforms to increase productivity through better price realisation and to encourage farmers to adopt contract farming for a stable income. It was a long-awaited reform in agricultural marketing, moving from oligopsony to free market, which allowed the farmers to sell their produce to anyone, anywhere. The concept of 'One Nation, One Market' is opening new opportunities to the states but throwing up new challenges as well. These opportunities, if capitalised at the right time, will not only help Tamil Nadu to overcome the recessionary state of the economy, but will also benefit it, in the long run, to rise as a leader in the agricultural market and as an export hub for agro-products. However, that aspiration needs to be balanced against deep-rooted organisational and regulatory challenges.

Opportunities: Oligopsony to a Competitive Market

Turning an oligopsony (many sellers and few buyers) market to a competitive (many sellers and many buyers) market will allow many players and investors to enter the market, who have, so far, been restricted due to limited permits and licences and several restrictions of a regulatory nature. This will not only help farmers to realise better prices for their produce but can also take the agro-industry to the next level if implemented with the right set of policies, regulation, and institutional support. We can, therefore, expect changes in the current market mechanism or market strategies driven by innovative ideas that can lead the market towards greater efficiency. The origins of these changes would stem from the multilayers of competition.

Multilayers of Competition

Traditional Mandis *versus Open Markets and New Players*

The first layer of competition will be between traditional *mandis*—i.e., Agricultural Produce Market Committees (APMCs)—and new players or open mandis. The traditional mandis will be forced to become more efficient to survive in the business by sharing the deserved benefits with farmers. This competition can help farmers to realise better prices for their produce.

Competition among Businesses and Investors

The next level of competition would be among businesses (such as large aggregators, processors, and organised retailers), investors (including local and foreign players) and others, to either enter into this market or increase their market share. This competition, with proper regulation, can help the agro-industry, food processing industry, and other allied sectors to flourish. It can also help to develop the requisite infrastructure like cold storage, storehouses, and logistics. Players can choose their field or subsector as per their expertise or business plans. It can also strengthen the interlinkages between the agricultural markets and other sectors. E-platforms or innovative information technology (IT) solutions can further speed up the process of integrating or unifying the markets and sectors.

Competition among States

To harness these two levels of competition in the 'One Nation, One Market' scenario, the next level of competition will be among states to extract the maximum benefits for their farmers and to the state economy at large. It will be up to the states to enact policies that attract new regional and national market players, especially from the formal sector that can improve the linkage between farmers and consumers. States will have the responsibility of enacting policies that create a level playing field for all players, including existing and potential entrants. Another important responsibility of the states would be to provide the requisite infrastructure in terms of better connectivity to farms through quality roads and land. Ease of doing business through less documentation and fewer permissions and approvals can smoothen and speed up the entry of new players. States would need to pay special attention to competition policies to promote healthy competition and to avoid any market capture or dominance.

First-Mover Advantage

Considering the nation as a single market,[3] the first-moving states can reap extra benefits by gaining a larger market share. The competition will be to attract more players to invest in the state. Therefore, to gain first-mover advantage, states would need to be proactive in setting up policies and regulatory frameworks to open up and allow the market to function with market principles and the right set of regulatory policies to safeguard all stakeholders. The best part of this competition would be the limited state fiscal commitments. It is likely to turn the competition into one of showcasing political willpower and capabilities of states rather than their fiscal strengths.

Challenges

If the past is any guide, one should draw lessons from history. The success of the Green Revolution in India hinged on its integrated and comprehensive support from various walks of public policy, such as focused research and technology development, irrigation expansion,[4] proper information dissemination, and requisite rural infrastructure development. Similarly, harnessing this opportunity and taking the first-mover advantage will hinge on a state's multidimensional actions. A state is likely to face three major challenges while designing plans and the policy framework—the right incentives, appropriate regulations, and a robust support system.

Comprehensive Plan to Targeted Incentives

To attract investors, states would need to design incentive schemes. The challenge is to design targeted incentives that match with its objectives or plans for the sector. For instance, if the objective is to fetch maximum investment into a particular sector or region, then a progressive incentive scheme would be appropriate, where larger the investment, greater the incentive. But if the objective is to bring investment into a specific subsector or region, then the incentives can be targeted towards that subsector or region to fulfil the objective. It is, therefore, necessary to draw up a long-term plan and strategy to develop the market, and accordingly design incentives aligned with the comprehensive plan.

Regulatory Framework for Markets, Information, Contract Farming, Environment, and Food Safety

Formulating an appropriate regulatory framework is a challenging task, where a lot of careful deliberations over conflicting ambitions are needed to articulate suitable and transparent regulations for society.

Markets

The key to market regulation is to encourage competition, creating a level playing field for both new and existing players, including state agricultural agencies and marketing boards that currently are instruments of state intervention in agricultural markets for specific commodities. As part of bringing in a level playing field, it is critical to stop, or at least limit, the preferential treatment that state agencies and marketing boards receive, such as easy access to cheaper credit and the right to procure at government-announced prices (in contrast to market determined prices). Bringing in reforms in this would be challenging due to, among others, political economy considerations—the organised and unionised workforce in the state agencies would resist these changes that erode their privileged position.

Regulation should not only promote competition but also allow enterprises to achieve economies of scale to scale up the operations in order to compete in the national market as well as sustain their exports to the world market. Competition without appropriate regulation, however, can take a distorted form, which may not be ideal for society. Another serious challenge for a regulatory framework would be to avoid, or at least limit, the corporatisation of agriculture, where a few large corporations can influence the market in their favour, at the cost of farmers.

A plausible perspective that might fit the Covid-19 scenario can be gleaned from Edmund Phelps' work on 'mass flourishing' (Phelps 2013). Among the many ideas that he puts forth, two stand out starkly—corporatism and flourishing. He argues that 'modern corporatism' is founded on the idea that national governments ought to provide benefits in the form of tax exemptions or grants or merely free service to groups that are better able to organise themselves, such as corporations, unions, or select consumer groups (Phelps 2016). This further aggravates the initial lack of inclusion of the less advantaged who have limited access to jobs that provide them 'self-respect' in terms of the nature and dignity of work and pay.

Flourishing too has a philosophical origin in the notion of 'good life' which, according to Phelps, is an experience that deeply involves employing one's imagination and creativity in finding new ways to produce or new things to produce. In short, it is 'the experience of using one's mind' irrespective of social class. The Green Revolution in India is, perhaps, an example of mass flourishing that created 'a "good-enough" economy' with 'high-enough wages, low-enough unemployment and wide-enough access to engaging work' (Phelps 2016, p. 6), which the proposed agricultural reforms could aspire to.

Information

The smooth functioning of a market relies on seamless availability of information, that is, symmetric information. Any constraints to information sharing or availability can result in market failures that, in turn, can lead to market abuse by the players who possess the information; that is a case of asymmetric information. The success of the Green Revolution in India can partially be credited to the comprehensive strategy of information dissemination (through various communication channels, such as television, radio, and local media) among the stakeholders, particularly the farmers (Varshney

1995). On the other hand, failures in information diffusion of the expected benefits and potential pitfalls of Bt cotton variety became problematic in Maharashtra and Andhra Pradesh (including parts of current Telangana) (Sahai 2002), where several farmers, under pressure of huge credit burdens and heavy losses due to ill-informed decisions about the Bt cotton crop, were left with no choice but to end their lives (Gruère and Sengupta 2011; Stone 2011). The proponents of Bt cotton, however, argued that spurious seeds sold in the black market (that has grown rapidly due to initial high prices of Bt cotton seeds) were responsible for crop failure; insufficient information about the increasing number of seed varieties further confused the farmers (Gruère and Sengupta 2011; Herring 2007). The Bt cotton saga highlights the crucial role of information in successful policy implementation.

Moreover, any market transaction involves information search, which is a part of transaction costs; hence, ease of information accessibility is key to reducing transaction costs. If farmers can access information at the least possible cost, it will help them to reap more benefits by minimising their transaction cost. Therefore, the state governments need to put extra efforts to create regulatory institutions to make information available easily and cost-effectively. With the penetration of mobile telephony increasing among farmers, e-platforms, e-markets, and other innovative IT solutions could be instrumental in filling this gap in the digital era. Information through digital platforms, if unchecked, however, can also result in mushrooming of information providers that, in turn, will bring about the problem of plenty. Therefore, a regulation or supervision by the state would be necessary to maintain the balance between information providers and seekers and to have a set of credible sources of information.

Contract Farming

The current reforms through the third act legalise and stress on contract farming. The regulation of contract farming through a state-level authority would be the state government's responsibility. The contracting agencies are usually organised and large entities, whereas the farmers are engaged in individual capacity with limited knowledge, human resources, and contracting experience; hence, it is difficult for the farmers—both individually and collectively—to match the bargaining power of the larger contracting agencies. Moreover, if unchecked, there is a possibility of cartelisation of formal or bigger players, which can distort and skew the distribution of benefits against the contracting farmers. Therefore, the government needs to put extra effort into contract farming regulation to encourage a balance on both sides.

Studies on contract farming in India highlight the success in terms of risk-free farming and stable income for farmers, where the contracting company (for instance, Pepsico, which procures potatoes through contract farming) buys the final produce at predetermined prices and procures at the farm gate, along with providing additional services, such as farm and crop inputs, technology and knowledge transfer, credit facility, and insurance for the crop (Dutta et al. 2016). The literature, however, also cautions about considering only these positive outcomes based on overlooked or missing aspects of contract farming. Evidence suggests that contract farming has, so far, mostly remained restricted to medium and large farms in India and the majority of the farming community—small and marginal farmers—have not been able to take advantage of contract farming (Singh 2002). It also highlights the complex nature of power equations within rural society, which exacerbates the inequality within the farming community, through the unequal distribution of the benefits of contract farming (Vicol 2017). These issues need to be addressed through a thoughtful regulatory framework in order to have a larger economic and social impact.

A diverse support system would need to be devised covering various aspects related to contract farming. Contract farming may be a new concept for many farmers and hence they may be reluctant to adopt it even if it has the potential to be more remunerative and provide them a more stable income. A state helpline or authority could help to prepare farmers to understand contract farming and their obligations to honour the contracts as well as comply with routine procedures of inspection, completion formalities, and so on. Also, such neutral agencies should help farmers to learn how to choose the right partner among the many options available. The states may need to initiate a campaign for wider dissemination of information and enhance awareness about the benefits and pitfalls of contract farming among farmers and even traders.

Once contract farming is in practice, the next challenge would be to ensure efficient and effective contract enforcement. The role of a third party in contract enforcement is widely acknowledged in contract theory literature. A government organisation or authority can play the role of third party to verify or standardise quality parameters for easy authentication, or verification of quality and other parameters of farm produce in order to reduce the likelihood of disputes. For instance, invoking the clause of force majeure due to untimely rain or pest attack would need verification or certification from the third party. Therefore, a well-trained, resourceful, and adequately powerful, independent third-party institution would be needed.

Even with the well-engineered contract enforcement system, disputes arising out of contracts are difficult to avoid. It leads to the challenge of creating a robust dispute resolution system that can resolve disputes within a stipulated period and with cost-economising effort. The proximity of such a redressal system to the farmers and other stakeholders can create long-term benefits.

Environmental Safeguards

While increased competition can bring several advantages to farmers and consumers, unbridled and unregulated competition can play havoc on natural resources if traders, private processors, and farmers aggressively pursue short-run profits at the cost of long-run resource sustainable farm practices. The experience of aquaculture cultivation in parts of Tamil Nadu and Andhra Pradesh is a pointer to the pitfalls of unregulated competition (Kagoo and Rajalakshmi 2002). Indeed, government policies of subsidising inputs, such as chemical fertilisers, water, and electricity, can also have similar adverse effects on the natural resource base required for agriculture, as has been seen in many of the north-western states of the country (International Food Policy Research Institute 2007). An appropriate regulatory framework for natural resource management, based on local conditions, including state input subsidy policies, should be devised by the state governments to strike a balance between short-term necessities of livelihood and the long-run sustainability of agriculture.

Food Safety Standards and Sanitary and Phytosanitary Measures

The discovery of the Covid-19 virus in largely unregulated food markets in the Wuhan province of China as well as Tamil Nadu's experience of the Koyambedu agricultural market becoming a hotspot for the spread of the virus, bring out the importance of food safety standards and Sanitary and Phytosanitary (SPS) measures. These standards and measures cover not only the products themselves and the inputs used in their production, but also the entire food supply chain in terms of handling, storage, processing, and transporting the product from the farm to the final consumer. India, in general, like many developing countries in South Asia and elsewhere in the world, does not have a strong regulatory framework on food safety and associated SPS measures. It is time that the country pays attention to this, as failures in this can have large economic costs, as the pandemic and the consequent lockdown measures have shown. Tamil Nadu, which experienced this issue in one of its large agricultural markets, can take a lead and integrate food safety and SPS regulations into its framework for encouraging private sector investments in agriculture. Implementing such regulations would involve some fiscal costs, including in investments on appropriately-trained human resources, laboratories for testing, and certification of products. Such investments, however, will yield large benefits for the society at large—better health status of its citizens and products that are in demand because they are certified to be safe in terms of the inputs used and of handling, storage, processing, and transportation. These benefits would easily outweigh the fiscal costs involved in implementing the food safety standards and SPS measures.

The Way Ahead

With the new set of reforms, the oligopsony market is targeted to be turned into a free competitive market. The destination of these reforms is clear (a free competitive market), but the path is unknown. However, the reforms initiated so far go only halfway towards this destination. A major deterrent for greater investments and participation by private sector in agriculture in the country is the policy of public procurement at administratively announced minimum support prices (MSP), aided and implemented through an elaborate set of institutions and government agencies, both at the union and state levels. Public procurement of specific commodities (rice, wheat, etc.) at administratively-set MSP distorts the risk-return profile of various agricultural products, which in turn affects farmers' production decisions. This can raise the risks faced by potential entrants, which would curtail investments and hence not serve the purpose of ushering in greater competition in agricultural markets. It, therefore, is critical to reform the system of public procurement and MSP as has been pointed out by several studies (see for instance, Ganesh-Kumar et al. 2009).

Several states—Andhra Pradesh (Rythu Bazaar), Karnataka, Maharashtra, and Tamil Nadu (Uzhavar Sandhai)—allow direct marketing by farmers of farm products, especially horticultural products, in urban centres, bypassing the APMC. These experiments have had mixed outcomes in different products and in different states. One shortcoming of these farmer markets is that they are subject to several municipality regulations that are not necessarily farmer friendly. They often lack investments, especially in preserving the shelf life of products, thereby resulting in greater wastage, a loss which has to be borne by the farmers. In many instances, these farmer markets also suffer from poor food safety practices. State governments can strengthen these markets by institutionalising them in all urban centres, facilitating easy access to credit, and organising programmes that bring greater awareness about food safety standards in these farmer markets.

The evolving nature of the market always responds well to innovation and openness to adopting new ideas. It also gives freedom to experiment. Hence, states should not hesitate to experiment and implement any idea or policy that has the potential to take the market to its destination—free competitive market. One possible option is to set up private markets, in the form of special economic zones (SEZs), closer to farms.

These SEZs can play multiple roles—as an open market, as aggregator of players related to agro-industry, and as a key point in the supply chain logistic. These SEZs will be an alternative to traditional markets (APMCs) and hence promote competition in the market. These SEZs can also house other market players involved in the agro-industry, such as supply-chain logistic players of cold storage, warehousing, packaging, and gamma irradiation. It will be like a one-stop solution for the agro-industry. It can help to reduce logistic efforts and costs.

Promoting these SEZs can provide deeper and wider infrastructure for the agro-industry and will further strengthen the linkages of agro-industry to other sectors. Therefore, developing a smaller SEZ in each taluk, and a bigger SEZ at the district level may achieve maximum outreach to farmers as well as economies of scale for businesses. Apart from providing basic infrastructure for SEZs, like good quality roads and land, the state will have limited fiscal commitment. The development of these SEZs can mostly be through private financing, with some initial incentives from the government. State governments may also modify their policies to attract foreign direct investment and foreign players into this market.

A New Journey for States: Opportunities and a New Conundrum

As the recent laws open up the agricultural market and create opportunities for farmers (to sell to anyone and anywhere), businesses (to enter the market as per their choice and expertise), and the states (to go beyond their geographical boundaries for a larger market share), they unleash multilayer competition in the agricultural sector. A state can take the first-mover advantage through proactive measures to benefit its farmers and the state at large. The best part of this competition would be the limited state fiscal commitments. It is likely to turn the competition into one of showcasing the political willpower and capabilities of states rather than their fiscal strength.

States, however, will have a new conundrum of having to create a policy framework that has multiple challenges. The first challenge is to create a level playing field for all, including existing players and potential entrants. Another important responsibility of the state would be to provide the requisite infrastructure in terms of better connectivity to farms through quality roads and land. The next challenge—the most critical too—is to ensure the balance between buyers and sellers (i.e., businesses and farmers). The policy framework should boost competition, minimise collusion (and the influence of powerful 'within state' entrenched interest groups and cartels), safeguard the vulnerable (farmers), and minimise the chances of market abuse or market capture.

States would need to put special efforts in formulating plans and choosing the right incentives and the regulation of markets, information, contract farming, environment, and food safety. Designing incentive structures that match the comprehensive development plan for the sector would be crucial for sectoral development. Ease of information accessibility to the farmers is the key to pass on the benefits to the farmers and to reduce their transaction costs. The presence of e-platforms, e-markets, and other innovative IT solutions could be instrumental in the digital era in filling this gap. However, mushrooming of information providers can bring the problem of plenty. Similarly, contract farming has the potential to provide stable and higher incomes to farmers, but asymmetric power relations between the contracting agency and farmers need to be balanced through proper regulation and a robust support system. Private open markets in the form of SEZs could be a good starting point in the direction of competitive markets. Construction of SEZ infrastructure can generate employment and augment demand in the state economy.

Notes

1. For other reforms in the agriculture sector in Tamil Nadu, please see Chapter 3 in this book.
2. Essential Commodities (Amendment) Act, 2020, the Farmers (Empowerment and Protection) Agreement of Price Assurance and Farm Services Act, 2020, and the Farmers' Produce Trade and Commerce (Promotion and Facilitation) Act, 2020.
3. We can consider the export market too for competition among states.
4. A detailed discussion on irrigation reforms is available in Chapter 4 in this book.

References

Dutta, A., A. Dutta, and S. Sengupta, 'A Case Study of Pepsico Contract Farming For Potatoes', *IOSR Journal of Business and Management*, 2016, pp. 75–85, available at http://www.iosrjournals.org/iosr-jbm/papers/ICSE%20Conference/14.75-85.pdf, accessed on 28 September 2021.

Ganesh-Kumar, A., A. Gulati, and Jr. R. Cummings, 'Reforming foodgrains management: Achieving food security with cost-effectiveness', in Surjit Singh and V. Ratna Reddy (eds), *Changing contours of Asian agriculture: Essays in honour of Prof. V.S. Vyas*, Academic Foundation, 2016, pp. 475–478.

Gruère, G., and D. Sengupta, 'Bt cotton and farmer suicides in India: An evidence-based assessment', *The Journal of Development Studies*, 47(2), 27 January 2011, pp. 316–337, available at https://doi.org/10.1080/00220388.2010.492863, accessed on 28 September 2021.

Herring, R. J., 'Stealth seeds: Bioproperty, biosafety, biopolitics', *The Journal of Development Studies*, 43(1), 31 Jan 2007, pp. 130–157, available at https://doi.org/10.1080/00220380601055601, accessed on 28 September 2021.

International Food Policy Research Institute. *Withering Punjab agriculture: Can it regain its leadership?* March 2007, available at https://pdf.usaid.gov/pdf_docs/Pnadk223.pdf, accessed in July 2020.

Kagoo, I. E., and N. Rajalakshmi, 'Environmental and Social Conflicts of Aquaculture in Tamilnadu and Andhra Pradesh', *Journal of Social and Economic Development*, 4(1), 14 February 2002, pp. 13–26, available at http://www.isec.ac.in/JSED/JSED_V4_I1_13-26.pdf, accessed on 28 September 2021.

Phelps, E. S., *Mass flourishing: How grassroots innovation created jobs, challenge, and change*. Princeton University Press, 2013, available at https://doi.org/10.2307/j.ctt32bbrz, accessed on 28 September 2021.

———, 'What is wrong with the West's economies?', *Homo Oeconomicus*, 33(1–2), 29 June 2016, pp. 3–10, available at https://doi.org/10.1007/s41412-016-0006-3, accessed on 28 September 2021.

Sahai, S., 'Bt cotton: Confusion prevails', *Economic and Political Weekly*, 37(21), 25 May 2002, pp. 1973–1974, available at https://www.epw.in/journal/2002/21/commentary/bt-cotton-confusion-prevails.html, accessed on 28 September 2021.

Singh, S., 'Contracting out solutions: Political economy of contract farming in the Indian Punjab', *World Development*, 30(9), September

2002, pp. 1621–1638, available at https://doi.org/10.1016/S0305-750X(02)00059-1, accessed on 28 September 2021.

Stone, G. D., 'Field versus farm in Warangal: Bt cotton, higher yields, and larger questions', *World Development*, 39(3), March 2011, pp. 387–398, available at https:/doi.org/10.1016/j.worlddev.2010.09.008, accessed on 28 September 2021.

Varshney, A., *Democracy, development, and the countryside: Urban–rural struggles in India*, Cambridge University Press, 1995, available at https://doi.org/10.1017/CBO9780511609367, accessed on 28 September 2021.

Vicol, M., 'Is contract farming an inclusive alternative to land grabbing? The case of potato contract farming in Maharashtra, India', *Geoforum*, 85, October 2017, pp. 157–166, available at https://doi.org/10.1016/j.geoforum.2017.07.012, accessed on 28 September 2021.

Section III

Environmental Markets and Policy

7

Environmental Reforms in Tamil Nadu after Covid-19

P. Durairasu and L. Venkatachalam

The Covid-19 pandemic and subsequent lockdown has brought about certain positive impacts on India's environment (Goswami 2020), including an improvement in the air quality in major cities, an improvement in water quality in most river systems, and a reduction in solid waste generated in urban areas. Though temporary in nature, some of the environmental impacts are remarkable. For example, the lockdown achieved a milestone in terms of making water in the Ganges potable, which could not be achieved despite the governments' massive efforts and expenditure (Rs. 4,800 crore) from 1986 till 2017 to clean the Ganges (Press Trust of India 2017).

Before the arrival of the pandemic, India's environmental status was poor, with the country ranked low (168th out of 180 countries) on the global 'environmental performance index' (Wendling et al. 2020). India accounted for 23.7 lakh pollution-related mortality in 2017 (Fuller et al. 2019). The country's estimated economic cost of environmental damages stood at Rs. 3.75 trillion, which was equivalent to 5.7 per cent of its gross domestic product (GDP) in 2009 (Mani 2013). Unestimated pecuniary (e.g., cost of morbidity) and non-pecuniary (e.g., aesthetic value) costs imposed by various environmental problems are manifold. The secondary effects of environmental damage (e.g., rural-to-urban migration) cause various hardships to people dependent on the environment for their livelihoods. Rural-to-urban migration is attributed largely to the failure of agriculture in generating adequate employment and income in rural areas. Environmental refugees constitute a significant portion of these migrants (Warrier 2020) since failure of agriculture is caused primarily by chronic environmental tragedies, such as over-exploitation of groundwater and shrinking of village commons. By this, we understand that environmental degradation is the root cause of India's painful reverse migration that took place during the pandemic. Most of the reverse migrants are likely to stay back in their original places during the post–Covid-19 period, putting pressure on scarce environmental resources. Since a self-reliant economy is likely to be the 'new normal' in the Covid-19 era, strengthening the environment is a necessary condition to make the new normal economy stronger and sustainable.

It should be noted that, in general, usually there is a trade-off between economy and environment, and as a result, the improvements in environmental quality during the lockdown were achieved at the cost of the economy. When the lockdown is fully relaxed, India's environmental status will once again become poorer due to the revival of consumption and production activities—probably, with a greater intensity. A poor quality of environment has a harmful effect on people's health, making them more vulnerable to Covid-19 infections, and therefore, measures to improve environmental quality would not only help to fight Covid-19 infections at present but also reduce the risk of future epidemics (World Health Organization 2020). Strengthening the environment in rural areas will help in arresting future rural-to-urban migration, in addition to enhancing health benefits, livelihood options, and overall well-being.

Tamil Nadu is both an environmentally rich state as well as a state facing serious environmental negative externalities, such as pollution from the industry and from urban waste, solid waste, groundwater over-exploitation, land degradation, coastal erosion, seawater intrusion, and loss of biodiversity (Centre of Excellence in Environmental Economics 2016). Results from micro-level studies suggest that the damage cost imposed by industrial pollution in certain environmental hotspots of the state has made regional economies unsustainable (see Venkatachalam 2005). The economy-wide aggregate environmental damage cost imposed by all major negative externalities has not yet been quantified, and as a result, the direction and magnitude of the environmental impact of development policies being pursued in the state are not known, especially to policymakers. Many development and infrastructural projects in the state—for example, leather tanning industry in Ambur, Vaniyambadi, and Dindigul, knitwear industry in Tiruppur, Erode, and Karur, fireworks industry in Sivakasi, the Sterlite factory in Tuticorin, the eight-lane expressway between Chennai and Salem, hydrocarbon projects in the Cauvery delta region, the Neutrino Observatory Project in Theni, and the Enayam port in Kanyakumari—face environmental challenges, and therefore, the future growth of Tamil Nadu's economy depends mainly on how effectively the government addresses the environmental issues through appropriate institutional reforms in its development and environment sectors. Hence, the state government will have to make use of the Covid-19 crisis as an opportunity to carry out environmental reforms which would not only benefit the people of the state but also the society at large. In this context, we propose some important measures that can be undertaken by the state government to strengthen the environment and make the economy more sustainable in the years to come.

Short-Term Measures

The closure of tourism activities due to Covid-19 crisis, especially in the 'recorded forest areas' consisting of reserved forests and protected areas (e.g., national parks and sanctuaries) in Tamil Nadu, should be extended at least for a year after the end of the lockdowns so that the natural rejuvenation of forests and biodiversity can continue to prevail for some more time. The Government of Tamil Nadu should notify the priority wetlands in all districts before the end of this year so that focused attention can be given to protect the precious wetlands in the state. Increasing the tree cover in urban areas helps to minimise air and noise pollution, and therefore, steps to greening the corporations and municipalities will have to be initiated. To enable this, 'tree officers' may be appointed to ensure adequate green cover as well as to closely monitor greening activities in urban areas.

Long-Term Measures

Green GDP

The GDP is considered an indicator of 'economic welfare'. The way the State GDP (SGDP) is currently measured, it cannot be treated as a proper indicator of economic welfare as the GDP measurement does not make necessary adjustments for changes in the value of the environment. Human–environment interaction takes place at three levels:

a. Economic agents utilise innumerable non-market ecosystem services[1] in their various production and consumption activities.
b. Negative externalities cause a reduction in the quantity and quality of the ecosystem services, which is reflected in terms of environmental damage costs borne by the economic agents.
c. Economic agents take up preventive and remedial measures by incurring a substantial amount of expenditure—called 'environmental defensive expenditure' (EDE)—to defend themselves from the harmful effects of environmental externalities.

On the one hand, the economic value of non-market ecosystem services is not included in the estimation of SGDP, making it an underestimate; on the other hand, any increase in the environmental damage cost and EDE wrongly expands the size of the SGDP, making it an overestimate. For example, the total turnover of knitwear industry in Tiruppur was Rs. 50,000 crore in 2018–2019 (Ravichandran 2019), which is included as 'income' in SGDP estimation. However, the un-quantified environmental damage costs inflicted by the industrial activities on society (i.e., in terms of health cost, cost on agriculture and allied activities, and cost of biodiversity loss) as well as the EDE (in terms of, for example, cost of hospitalisation or additional fertilisers to improve soil quality) will amount to several thousand crores which are not quantified and netted out from the SGDP. Therefore, the current SGDP does not indicate if the economy is moving on an environmentally sustainable path or reflect true economic welfare of the society. The government, therefore, should take the initiative to periodically estimate the economic value of non-market ecosystem services, environmental damage costs, and EDE, and make necessary adjustments in the SGDP so that appropriate environmental policy can be initiated in the relevant sector and the SGDP becomes an indicator of both sustainable income as well as true economic welfare of the society.

Environmental Accounting System

In general, Environmental Accounting System (EAS) is a prerequisite for overall environmental management, and for computing green GDP to monitor if the state income is sustainable in particular. Environmental accounting needs to be developed for all major environmental resources—water, forests, and biodiversity—so as to monitor the interaction between the economy and the environment. EAS should periodically measure the change in the 'stock' of the environmental resource and 'flow' of ecosystem benefits emanating from it.

EAS has two components: physical accounting and monetary accounting. Physical accounting measures the stock and flow of resources in terms of physical units. For example, to take a physical accounting of water stock, one needs to consider the total stock of water (both surface and subsurface) available at the beginning of the accounting period, the changes in the stock in terms of 'additions' (rainfall, return flow, contribution from tributaries, and import from other basins) and 'subtractions' (withdrawal for various uses, run-offs, export to other basins, evaporation, and evapotranspiration) throughout the entire accounting period. The total stock at the end of the accounting period is measured systematically in terms of physical units (usually, in million cubic feet). Based on the total stocks at the beginning and at the end of the accounting period, the net 'surplus' or 'deficit' can be calculated (i.e., net surplus or deficit equals the stock at the end minus the stock at the beginning).

An alternative way of measuring the net surplus or deficit is to deduct 'subtractions' from 'additions'. Flow accounting measures the flow of physically measurable ecosystem benefits, such as quantity of water used in agriculture sector, how much is used for different crops, and how much water is used in allied (e.g., livestock) and non-agricultural (e.g., household and industry) activities. Flow accounting informs decision-makers whether water is used efficiently in a particular activity, how much water can be transferred from one crop to another crop (or from one place to another place), how much water can be transferred from agriculture to industry without affecting agricultural productivity, and so on.

Physical accounting, though essential for effective decision-making, poses some problems. For example, ecosystem benefits are measured in different units (e.g., water used in industry is measured in kilo litres, but recreational benefits in the number of tourists visited), which creates an 'aggregation' problem. Similarly, many ecosystem services are qualitative (e.g., cultural benefits), which cannot be quantified in physical units.

Monetary accounting overcomes these problems by estimating the economic values in terms of monetary value (e.g., in rupees). In most cases, deterioration in the quality of environment may reduce the benefits of ecosystem services even if the stock of the resource is increasing in size. For example, a river basin may be full of water, but if it carries pollution, then the ecosystem services become unfit for any use. So, physical accounting should be modified to incorporate quality issues, by taking into account problems like pollution and biodiversity loss. EAS is a prerequisite for designing appropriate institutions and policies in the environmental domain, and therefore, the state government should take up this task on a priority basis.

Accounting for Biodiversity

By establishing an accounting framework for specific environmental resources, one can analyse the critical relationship between changes in environmental quality (e.g., water quality) and changes in biodiversity. A recent study by the Salim Ali Centre for Ornithology and Natural History (SACON 2019) has provided baseline data for developing an accounting framework for capturing the interaction between changes in the quality of wetlands and their impact on biodiversity. SACON developed a Wetland Heath Status Score based on:

a. change of land-use patterns;
b. threats to wetlands (e.g., pollution); and

c. biodiversity value measured in terms of total flora and fauna of 141 prioritised wetlands in Tamil Nadu.

The combined value of these three aspects gives the health status of a wetland (Table 7.1), and policymakers can take an informed decision to improve the quality of the wetland and to protect biodiversity. Such an exercise should be carried out periodically to monitor the dynamic relationship between environmental change and its impact on biodiversity.

Table 7.1: Health Status of 141 Prioritised Wetlands in Tamil Nadu

Sl No.	*Wetland Health Status Score group*	*Number of Wetlands*	*Status*	*Action Needed*
1.	–0.75 to 0.00	04	Critical and serious concern	Most urgent and immediate
2.	0.001 to 0.500	19	Critical and serious concern	Urgent and immediate
3.	0.501 to 1.00	21	Serious concern	Immediate
4.	1.001 to 1.500	40	Advance concerns	Threats need to be addressed on a priority
5.	1.501 to 2.00	25	Threats are in initial stages	Conservation measures need to be initiated
6.	Above 2.000	32	Stable conditions	Conservation plan should be implemented

Source: Salim Ali Centre for Ornithology and Natural History (SACON 2019).

Economic Valuation of Ecosystem Services

Most ecosystem services originating from environmental systems are not traded in markets, and as a result, their economic importance is either not known or not readily available to decision-makers. This being the case, policy decisions undermine the importance of environmental protection, leading to a loss of social welfare. To protect the environment and increase the social benefits, an informed decision will require information about the economic value of the ecosystem services enhanced due to certain policy interventions (e.g., how much additional health benefits can come from pollution control measures to improve air quality). So, estimating ecosystem benefits in terms of monetary values serves multiple purposes, which include computing green GDP and assessing social benefits and costs of different policy interventions. But how can we estimate the economic values of non-market ecosystem benefits (and costs) in monetary units? Based on information from existing data sources, we estimated the monetary values of ecosystem benefits of 141 prioritised wetlands in Tamil Nadu.

The average per hectare economic value (called global value) of different types of wetlands (e.g., coastal and inland wetlands) has been estimated (de Groot et al. 2012). We utilised the global values to estimate the total economic value of 141 prioritised wetlands in Tamil Nadu (Table 7.2). The potential economic value is the monetary value of total ecosystem services generated when the wetland is maintained at its best quality level. In that sense, the potential economic value of all the 141 prioritised wetlands is Rs. 11,283.09 per year. In reality, however, the wetlands are not maintained at their best quality level. They experience depletion (e.g., due to siltation) and degradation (e.g., due to pollution), and as a result, most ecosystem services either shrink or vanish. This reduces the actual value of ecosystem services to much less than the potential value.

Table 7.2: Economic Value of Ecosystem Services of 141 Prioritised Wetlands in Tamil Nadu

Wetland type (Nos.)	*Method*	*Total value of ecosystem services (in Rs. crore)*
Coastal wetland (5)	66,017 ha × Rs. 16,15,922.94 per ha	10,336.89
Inland wetland (135)	45,294.14 ha × Rs. 2,14,089.26 per ha	944.00
Reservoir (1)	633 ha × Rs. 34,617.62 per ha	2.20
All (141)		11,283.09

Source: Authors' study.

The SACON study documented the currently available ecosystem services of 141 wetlands in the state, and based on the information, we estimated the actual value of the wetlands to be Rs. 1,343.32 crore per year (SACON 2019). Subtracting the actual value from the potential value, we get the net economic loss—Rs. 9,940 crore per year. The policy implication is that if the wetlands are maintained at their best-quality level, society will be able to gain a gross economic benefit of

Rs. 9,940 crore per annum. If 141 wetlands alone can generate this much of benefit, maintaining over 41,000 water bodies across the state can generate a much higher level of social benefits. If we add ecosystem benefits from other forms of environmental resources—forests, land, and biodiversity—it will increase the size of the SGDP by several trillion crore rupees. This implies that income growth can significantly be enhanced not only by promoting industry and service sectors but also by strengthening the environmental sector in the state. Therefore, economic valuation of ecosystem services of environmental resources in Tamil Nadu should be taken up on a priority basis to make informed decisions regarding protection and management of the environment.

Payment for Water Ecosystem Services

As far as the water bodies are concerned, the traditional *kudimaramathu* system, which had prevailed for centuries in the state, had fully empowered the communities to manage water bodies—especially, the irrigation tanks—on an efficient, equitable, and sustainable basis. This system gradually disappeared from the state due to several reasons such as the government agencies taking over the control of water bodies, and farmers switching over from tank irrigation to modern tube-well irrigation. In recent years, the Government of Tamil Nadu has been trying to revive the kudimarmathu system in the state. The issue is that the government agencies themselves are carrying out most of the activities under the kudimaramathu system, without adequate community participation. Lack of community participation does not increase social welfare; it indirectly increases the government's transaction costs of water management, which in turn increases the tax burden on the public. Community participation can be made more effective by way of designing an appropriate incentive mechanism. This is where a scheme like 'payment for water ecosystem services' (PWES) can play a profound role.

Under a PWES scheme, user rights over ecosystem services can be assigned to communities so that they can manage the water bodies and share the ecosystem benefits with other users through mutual negotiations. For example, Chennai Metropolitan Water Supply and Sewerage Board (CMWSSB) draws around 150 million litres of water per day from Veeranam lake to serve consumers in Chennai. When water becomes scarce in the lake, water transfer produces an economic trade-off wherein the consumers in Chennai are made better off by making the farmers in the Veeranam command areas worse off. How do we address this trade-off? If the stakeholder villages are assigned with the right to manage Veeranam lake, CMWSSB can buy raw water from the villagers through mutual negotiations. Studies found that water users in Chennai spent around Rs. 1,250 crore in 2017 on purchasing water from private vendors (Schneider 2017). If good quality water is supplied by the CMWSSB, users will be willing to pay an amount equivalent to what they already pay in the private water market at present. A significant share of that money can be transferred to the villages managing Veeranam lake. Through proper institutional arrangements (such as bringing representatives from all stakeholder villages to form a group) and involving other institutions (e.g., government, market, corporate firms, and non-governmental organisations), a PWES scheme can bring about a win-win outcome for all stakeholders (Venkatachalam and Balooni 2017). The Government of Tamil Nadu may think of implementing such a scheme for managing not only water bodies but also other forms of environmental resources, namely, forests and biodiversity. For example, farmers may be provided additional incentives for cultivating perennial tree crops for enhancing ecosystem benefits in the long run; similarly, incentives may be given to farmers to cultivate organic products to protect soil quality, reduce groundwater pollution, and enhance agro-ecosystems.

Tradable Water Rights

How can we allocate surface water amidst scarcity or conflicts among water users? Tradable water rights (TWRs) are a promising instrument in resolving this issue. In the Bhavani river basin, for example, the present pattern of water allocation on the basis of 'senior appropriation rights' between the old canal system (consisting of Arakkankottai, Thadapalli, and Kalingarayan canals) and the new canal system (the Lower Bhavani Project) has resulted in a conflict between farmers across these canal systems (Rajagopal and Jayakumar 2006). A pilot study found that introducing TWRs would not only resolve the present conflict but would also lead to efficient utilisation of scarce water through 'water trading' arrangements. The study found that the farmers in the new canal system were willing to pay for obtaining additional irrigation water, and farmers in the old canal system were willing to accept compensation for saving their irrigation water and subsequently transferring it to the needy farmers in the new canal system. Around 63 per cent of the farmers would participate in trading irrigation water voluntarily, which would make more water available to the new canal system farmers without reducing production and productivity in the old canal system (Venkatachalam and Narayanamoorthy 2012). If TWRs are implemented in Tamil Nadu, the authorities can initially allocate TWRs to all farmers on the basis of their current irrigation entitlements. For example, if a farmer is entitled to 90 irrigations during a particular cropping season, then 90 units of TWRs can be assigned to that farmer. In case the farmer utilises only 80 irrigations through efficient irrigation practices and saves 10 irrigations, then the farmer can transfer 10 units of TWRs to a needy farmer who is willing to purchase them. During the next cropping season, fresh TWRs can be distributed to all farmers again based on their original entitlements. TWRs provide incentives for farmers to utilise water efficiently, thereby achieving a win-win outcome for buyers and sellers as well as increasing social benefits. TWRs can be coordinated by the water users' associations in different river basins in Tamil Nadu. Not only within the agriculture sector, TWRs can also facilitate efficient water allocation between agricultural and non-agricultural sectors. For example, industry can buy water rights from willing farmers so that irrigation water can be transferred for industrial use. Since the percentage of water used in non-agricultural sectors is comparatively small (19 per cent) and 15 per cent of irrigation water used at present can be transferred to non-agricultural sectors without any reduction in agricultural output just by increasing efficiency of water utilization, TWRs can play a major role in efficiently facilitating inter-sectoral water allocation. The state government can think of introducing similar innovative economic instruments to make policy decisions more effective in inter-sectoral and intra-sectoral allocation of water.

River-Basin Boards

The Integrated Water Resources Management approach suggests that treating the river basin as a unit of analysis is a prerequisite for better water governance. Institutional reforms for water governance include creating river-basin boards (RBBs) which can coordinate all water allocation and management activities. Water accounting, economic valuation of water ecosystem services, exchange of water entitlements, and other institutional arrangements for overall water governance at the basin level will have to be coordinated by the RBBs. The RBBs should consist of elected representatives from all stakeholders so that decisions regarding water management and allocation are mutually agreeable to all parties. Since water-related issues are site-specific, creating RBBs for all 17 major river basins in Tamil Nadu will significantly improve the social benefits from water use.

Revamping Pollution-Control Policies

Industrial pollution and urban sewage are the major culprits in degrading the environment in Tamil Nadu. Despite several measures, industrial pollution continues to be a serious issue in the state, threatening not only agriculture and the environment sectors but also the industry sector. The present pollution control policy, based on command-and-control (CAC) approach, is responsible for the current situation. The CAC approach does not provide adequate incentive for polluters to mitigate pollution. This is because the current approach forces both high-cost and low-cost polluters to reduce pollution, irrespective of the size of the abatement cost, which varies across polluters. Similarly, when pollution is controlled through common-effluent treatment plants and polluters have to pay the average abatement cost, it results in a situation where the high-cost polluters end up paying less than their actual abatement cost, and the low-cost polluters paying more. Such an arrangement punishes the efficient polluter and rewards the inefficient polluter.

Therefore, there is a need to move away from the CAC approach towards a more incentive-oriented and market-based approaches. Rather than the CAC approach, tradable pollution permits provide incentive for the low-cost polluters to mitigate a greater quantity of pollution and the high-cost polluters to outsource their pollution control activities to the low-cost polluters so that the level of pollution is reduced to the prescribed level at the least cost. Market-based instruments, such as tradable pollution permits, have proved to be efficient in reducing pollution in Gujarat (Gopal 2019). These instruments can be introduced in controlling air and water pollution as well as sewage pollution in the state.

Creating an Environmental Database

In Tamil Nadu, many government agencies like the Tamil Nadu Pollution Control Board (TNPCB), the Environment Department, the Forest Department, the Regional Environment Cells of Water Resources Organisation, the Institute of Water Studies (IWS), Tamil Nadu Water Supply and Drainage Board (TWAD Board) are engaged in collecting various types of data on the environment. The same type of data are collected by more than one agency—for example, water quality data is being collected by the TNPCB, the regional environment cells, and the TWAD Board. However, these data are not of much use for some specific purposes, such as computing environmental accounting, ecosystem valuation, environmental impact assessment, and social benefit–cost analysis. In future, collection and maintenance of environment-related data will have to be channelised, and data will have to be collected based on specific policy requirements. All the environment-related data collected should be maintained by a single agency.

Capacity Building

As we have seen in the past, many development and infrastructural projects face resistance from people on environmental grounds. Resistance of this nature will hamper economic growth, thereby shrinking income- and employment-generating opportunities in the state. At the same time, uncontrolled economic growth hampers the environment, thereby affecting the employment and livelihood opportunities of many. The prevailing 'economy versus environment' approach is harmful, but an 'economy and environment' approach is desirable. Projects become environmentally controversial due to social preferences not being adequately incorporated in environmental impact assessments. Environmental resistance, in many cases, takes place due to inadequate information or wrong information available to the stakeholders. To overcome environmental controversies, capacity will have to be built in the state in the areas of environmental policy, environmental impact assessment, economic valuation of ecosystem benefits and damages, social benefit-cost analysis, and environmental education among all stakeholders—staff in government departments dealing with environmental matters, environmental lawyers, judges, non-governmental organisations, environmental activists, farmers' organisations, corporate firms, consumer groups, teachers, and panchayat leaders. These measures would help in formulating better economic policies that provide due attention to the environment, thereby making future economic growth more sustainable.

Note

1. Ecosystem services are benefits derived from environmental capital and utilised for the benefit of human well-being. The ecosystem services of, say forests, are classified as: (*a*) provisioning services (e.g. minor forest products); (*b*) regulating services (e.g., groundwater regulation); (*c*) cultural services (e.g., religious benefits); and (*d*) supporting services (e.g., maintenance of biodiversity) (The Economics of Ecosystems and Biodiversity, 2010).

References

Centre of Excellence in Environmental Economics, *State of environment report for Tamil Nadu*, Madras School of Economics, January 2016, available at http://www.tnenvis.nic.in/WriteReadData/LatestNewsData/SoERTN_MSE_Final_Jan_27_2016%20(1).pdf, accessed on 30 September 2021.

de Groot, R., L. Brander, S. van der Ploeg, et al., 'Global estimates of the value of ecosystems and their services in monetary units', *Ecosystem Services*, 1(1), July 2012, pp. 50–61, available at https://doi.org/10.1016/j.ecoser.2012.07.005, accessed on 30 September 2021.

Fuller, R., K. Sandilya, and D. Hanrahan, *Pollution and health metrics: Global, region, and country analysis*, Global Alliance on Health and Pollution, December 2019, available at http://www.indiaenvironmentportal.org.in/files/file/PollutionandHealthMetrics.pdf, accessed on 30 September 2021.

Gopal, S., 'Gujarat pilots emissions trading programme to tackle air pollution', *Mongabay*, 4 September 2019, available at https://india.mongabay.com/2019/09/gujarat-pilots-emissions-trading-programme-to-tackle-air-pollution/, accessed on 30 September 2021.

Goswami, K., 'Covid-19: 4 unbelievable environmental changes seen in India since lockdown', *India Today*, 2 May 2020, available at https://www.indiatoday.in/education-today/gk-current-affairs/story/covid-19-4-vital-environmental-changes-evidenced-in-india-since-lockdown-1673726-2020-05-02, accessed on 30 September 2021.

Mani, M. S. (ed.), *Greening India's growth: Costs, valuation and trade-offs*, Earthscan, 2013, available at https://openknowledge.worldbank.org/bitstream/handle/10986/22048/Greening0India0tions0and0trade0offs.pdf?sequence=1&isAllowed=y, accessed on 30 September 2021.

Press Trust of India, 'Ganga action plan: Over Rs. 4800 crore spent since 1986, says Ministry of Environment and Forests', *NDTV*, 11 July 2017, available at https://swachhindia.ndtv.com/ganga-action-plan-over-rs-4800-crore-spent-since-1986-says-ministry-of-environment-and-forests-9829/, accessed on 30 September 2021.

Rajagopal, A., and N. Jayakumar, 'Equity, Access and Allocation: Conflict in the Bhavani', *Economic and Political Weekly*, 41(7), 18 February 2006, pp. 581–582, available at https://www.epw.in/journal/2006/07/water-conflicts-india-special-issues-specials/equity-access-allocation-conflict, accessed on 30 September 2021.

Ravichandran, R., 'Tirupur garment exports grow 8% in FY19 to Rs. 26k crore', *Financial Express*, 18 April 2019, available at https://www.financialexpress.com/industry/tirupur-garment-exports-grow-8-in-fy19-to-rs-26k-crore/1551567/, accessed on 30 September 2021.

Salim Ali Centre for Ornithology and Natural History (SACON), *Criteria for prioritisation and framework for wetland monitoring in the state of Tamil Nadu* (Report). Submitted to State Planning Commission,

Government of Tamil Nadu, 2019, available at https://drive.google.com/file/d/1XxsDu8bwj-P910LlZFC9qjMIMy8q7U3Y/view?usp=sharing, accessed February 2022.

Schneider, K., 'The story behind the $180-million industry fuelled by Chennai water crisis", *Citizen Matters*, 17 May 2017, available at https://chennai.citizenmatters.in/chennai-water-crisis-180-million-dollar-bottled-water-industry-2058, accessed on 30 September 2021.

The Economics of Ecosystems and Biodiversity (TEEB), *Mainstreaming the economics of nature: A synthesis of the approach, conclusions and recommendations of TEEB* (Report), 2010, available at http://www.teebweb.org/wp-content/uploads/Study%20and%20Reports/Reports/Synthesis%20report/TEEB%20Synthesis%20Report%202010.pdf, accessed on 30 September 2021.

Venkatachalam, L., 'Damage assessment and compensation to farmers: Lessons from verdict of loss of ecology authority in Tamil Nadu', *Economic and Political Weekly*, 40(15), 9 April 2005, pp. 1556–1560, available at https://www.epw.in/journal/2005/15/special-articles/damage-assessment-and-compensation-farmers.html, accessed on 30 September 2021.

Venkatachalam, L., and K. Balooni, 'Water transfer from irrigation tanks for urban use: Can payment for ecosystem services produce efficient outcomes?', *International Journal of Water Resources Development*, 34(1), 3 July 2017, pp. 51–65, available at https://doi.org/10.1080/07900627.2017.1342610, accessed on 30 September 2021.

Venkatachalam, L., and A. Narayanamoorthy, 'Estimating economic value of irrigation water through contingent valuation method: Results from Bhavani river basin, Tamil Nadu', *Indian Journal of Agricultural Economics*, 67(3), July-September 2012, pp. 308–315, available at https://ageconsearch.umn.edu/record/204814/files/03-Venkat-%20Narayanamoorthy-Final.pdf, accessed on 30 September 2021.

Warrier, S. G., 'India's Covid-19 relief package has environmental consequences', *Quartz India*, 28 May 2020, available at https://qz.com/india/1861793/indias-covid-19-relief-package-has-environmental-consequences/, accessed on 30 September 2021.

Wendling, Z. A., J. W. Emerson, A. de Sherbinin, D. C. Esty, et al., *2020 environmental performance index: India*, Yale Center for Environmental Law & Policy, 2020, available at https://epi.yale.edu/epi-results/2020/country/ind, accessed on 30 September 2021.

World Health Organization, *Protecting nature protects health – lessons for the future from COVID-19*, 5 June 2020, available at https://www.euro.who.int/en/health-topics/environment-and-health/pages/news/news/2020/6/protecting-nature-protects-health-lessons-for-the-future-from-covid-19, accessed on 30 September 2021.

8

Covid-19 and Tamil Nadu's Marine Fisheries Sector

Ajit Menon and Maarten Bavinck

The Covid-19 pandemic and its subsequent lockdowns have adversely impacted the marine fisheries sector in Tamil Nadu. This chapter discusses the cumulative and differential impacts of both state and local institutional restrictions on different actors within the fisheries sector, considers the type of relief available, and suggests remedial and rehabilitation measures to cope at present and deal with similar emergencies in the future. In addition, considering the wider vulnerabilities of the sector, it suggests some longer-term policy options.

Status of Tamil Nadu Fisheries Sector

The Tamil Nadu marine fisheries sector became number one in the country in 2019 in terms of annual fish production. There were 10.48 lakh marine fishers[1] in the state in 2019–2020 (Animal Husbandry, Dairying and Fisheries Department 2020a) and likely a similar number of people engaged in the post-harvest sector, though those numbers are hard to determine accurately.[2] Women comprise more than 50 per cent of those involved in post-harvest activities and are particularly prominent in jobs such as fish handling, sorting, grading, drying, and retail marketing (Sudhakara et al. 2003).

Tamil Nadu's fisheries sector comprises both mechanised and small-scale[3] (motorised and non-motorised) crafts. The mechanised sector, which comprises 5,893 crafts, accounts for 83.3 per cent of the 7.75 lakh tonnes landed in 2019, whereas the motorised and non-motorised small-scale sectors, which together comprise 38,779 crafts, account for 16.3 per cent and 0.4 per cent, respectively (Sivadas et al. 2019, p. 10). However, small-scale fishers account for a large proportion of sea-going fishers in the state as is evidenced by the large number of small-scale crafts. Though according to official statistics, approximately 90 per cent of the fisher population is below the poverty line and dependent on fishing (Department of Fisheries 2019), inward migration of labour into fishing continues because of relatively better incomes in comparison with many other rural livelihoods (Bavinck 2014).

The fisheries sector in Tamil Nadu depends highly on resources in the territorial sea (the sea up to 12 nautical miles from the coast), which are becoming depleted (Department of Animal Husbandry, Dairying and Fisheries 2017). In addition, the sector is frequently crippled by conflict between fisher groups. Governance structures and processes are generally considered to be weak and in need of reinforcement (see 'Challenges and Way Forward' section).

The Tamil Nadu fisheries sector has often been affected by disasters, including frequent cyclones and floods, and a tsunami in 2004. The Covid-19 crisis is a new type of unfolding disaster, for which short-term relief measures and longer-term adaptation and rehabilitation are required.

Covid-19 Impacts on the Fisheries Sector

The Tamil Nadu government, like most state governments, imposed a total ban on fisheries when India went into lockdown from 24 March 2020 to 14 April 2020. Fisheries, unlike agriculture, was not considered an essential service. After fishers raised their voice, the Government of India relaxed restrictions and instead issued model Standard Operating Procedures (SOP) on 10 April 2020, to include marine fisheries and aquaculture, movement of fish and movement of workers along the fishery value chain, and subsequently inland fisheries from 15 April 2020. The SOP contained instructions for all four phases of fishing operations: before departure, during fishing, at the time of arrival, and post-harvest and transportation. The SOP was aimed at the safety and better hygiene of fishers (Department of Fisheries, 2020). Fishing was resumed under the guidance of crisis management committees that comprised members of fisher associations and fisheries vessel owner associations. Local institutions (*ur* panchayats and fisher organisations)[4] imposed their own sets of restrictions.

Despite these measures, the fisheries economy was impacted in multiple ways:

a. The loss to fisheries production in India as a whole was estimated to be around Rs. 6,700 crore per month (based on April 2020 data) as the fisheries sector functioned at less than one third of its capacity (Kurien 2020).[5]
b. The livelihood of all fishers, both mechanised and small-scale, was adversely impacted due to the lockdowns and because of transportation hurdles and safety concerns when fishing was eventually permitted (Vohra 2020). Trawl fishing did not resume till June 2020 because of the two-month (15 April–14 June) fishing ban.[6]
c. Fishers on mechanised vessels had no employment till June 2020 because by the time fishing resumed, the two months' fishing ban had started.
d. Migrant fishers, who work on vessels[7] in other parts of India during the lean fishing season on the East Coast, and in Gulf countries, were left stranded upon vessels with no wages.
e. The post-harvest sector was equally affected. Exporters, traders, auctioneers, and small-scale fish vendors lost out due to dwindling markets and transport facilities.
f. Women fish vendors were particularly affected because of a scarcity of fish, high local prices, and restrictions on movement imposed upon them by local village institutions.
g. Other allied workers, like those who transported fish, worked in ice factories, and repaired boats, had almost no employment.
h. Fish workers in many other parts of the world were similarly impacted (Bennett et al. 2020).

Immediate Relief Measures in the Covid-19 Context

The impact of the lockdown and local restrictions were, to some extent, cushioned by government relief measures and measures taken by village institutions, fisher organisations, and individual vessel owners. These included the following:

a. Fisher families, like all families with ration cards, were entitled to the Rs. 1,000 relief amount given by the Government of Tamil Nadu. Fishers registered with the Tamil Nadu Fishermen Welfare Board were given additional two payments of Rs. 1,000 (i.e., Rs. 2,000) during the lockdowns. All fishers received Rs. 5,000 during the two-month-ban period.
b. Local institutions (ur panchayats and fisher organisations) provided rations in some villages and neighbourhoods, whereas in others they urged fishers to prioritise supply of fish to local households first.
c. Vessel owners provided rations to fishers engaged on board their vessels, often by taking loans themselves.

According to fishers, these measures, however, were inadequate. The government's relief package was much less than the average earnings of fishers and fish workers. Moreover, the support provided by the Tamil Nadu Fishermen Welfare Board excluded most vulnerable groups, such as women fish vendors.

Suggestions for Improving Short-Term and Medium-Term Responses

What can we learn from the first months of the Covid-19 pandemic? How can relief measures in Tamil Nadu be improved in future? What measures can be taken so that the fisheries economy is better able to deal with pandemics of this sort that have a strong impact on both public health and livelihood? The following actions will, to some degree, address these concerns:

a. While adequate safety precautions must be taken, fishing—especially non-intensive fishing operations—should generally be permitted during such crises. Safety measures must also be ensured at fish markets, with proper hygiene measures and physical distancing.
b. Relief measures should depend on the duration of the crisis. The government can give fisher families Rs. 250 per day, the same

amount it gives to fisher families whose kin, while fishing, are apprehended by neighbouring countries. Further discussions must take place on whether all transfers should be only in the form of cash or whether it also can be in the form of social insurance.

c. A systematic updating of the list of those entitled to benefits must be done, and should not be limited to active fishers alone. Many women fish vendors, for example, were excluded from relief from the Board. Migrant workers involved in the fish value chain—from fishers, to loaders and unloaders, and workers in ice and allied factories—were also excluded.
d. Prioritising women fish vendors and implementing targeted policies that improve transportation facilities for them may help them to sell their fish in neighbouring areas. The government can consider a scheme similar to the Amma Two-Wheeler Scheme for working women.
e. The government should ensure that internal migrant fishers and fish workers are registered so that they are entitled to government benefits that other informal sector workers get, including access to relief during disasters and crises, and welfare benefits.
f. The government should provide access to safe and reasonably priced housing near major harbours in the country to migrant fish workers, to give them more security.
g. Close to 10 per cent of highly skilled fishers, especially from the southern districts of Tamil Nadu, migrate to the Gulf countries for fishing. The government should make Pravasi Bharatiya Bima Yojana insurance compulsory for all migrant fish workers irrespective of their status (Emigration Clearance Required or Emigration Clearance Not Required) and create awareness about the renewal and claims processes of this policy. This policy provides benefits in the event of accidental death or permanent disability, covers repatriation of migrants if medically unfit or made redundant, and allows for family hospitalisation insurance cover and maternity benefits.
h. All measures regarding migrant workers will require better data on the status of migrant fish workers to facilitate informed

policy decisions. Existing data sets do not cover migration or labour mobility outside fishing—one can only assume this from the declining numbers of full-time fishers. The 64th round of the National Sample Survey in 2007–2008 involved a migration survey (National Sample Survey Office 2010). However, it is difficult to match this with the fishing villages and habitations, given the definition of zone in the national sample survey. In 2011, for the first time, the Census collected data on migration (D-series). Unit-level data is not yet available, making it difficult to distinguish between fishing hamlets and the larger revenue village.

i. The government should ensure better implementation of the kisan credit card scheme for fishers, and banks should provide them credit against their entitlement as and when they require. Fishers, at present, are largely dependent on moneylenders, who charge high rates of interest.

j. The government should go ahead and implement a centralised insurance scheme for owners of small-scale crafts, as specified in the latest Government of Tamil Nadu's *Fisheries: Policy Note 2020–2021* (Animal Husbandry, Dairying and Fisheries Department 2020b). Tamil Nadu State Apex Fisheries Cooperative Federation Limited can help fishers get insured and help them liaise with insurance companies.

Policy Measures to Improve the Resilience of the Fisheries Sector

In addition to addressing the immediate consequences of socio-ecological crises, the policies of the state government must also aim to strengthen the fisheries economy in the medium term so that it becomes more robust and is able to deal with such crises in the future. The following measures could go some way in strengthening resilience:[8]

a. The Fisheries Department should set a minimum floor price for all species for the small-scale fisheries, based on market data, similar to the minimum support price for major crops, to ensure fishers get a fair price. The government should communicate these base prices widely through television, radio, and newspapers.

b. The government can provide support, if needed, to a range of collective organisations including cooperatives, ur panchayats, or other local institutions, in control of local village and market infrastructure, including cold storage. The state could encourage women microcredit groups to take the lead as a way to integrate women empowerment with infrastructure development. This will ensure that those who provide credit to fishers do not have first rights to their fish.

c. The small-scale fisheries sector must be enabled to use technology during fishing as well as for marketing. Small fishing craft need to be equipped with global positioning system and smartphones for tracking fish, weather information, price information, and so on. New forms of linkages between producers, distributors, and consumers can be built through digital platforms, such as online marketing, Whatsapp groups, and online transactions (Kurien 2020).

Challenges and the Way Forward: Strengthening Marine Fisheries in Tamil Nadu

The Covid-19 pandemic has given us an opportunity to look at the long-term status of the marine fisheries sector and marine fishing livelihood. Although, as noted, the marine fisheries sector has hitherto performed well in terms of production, it faces various long-term challenges. These emerge from both external as well as internal sources.

Challenges External to the Fisheries Sector

a. The industrialisation of the Indian coast that is taking place in the name of creating a Blue Economy, with projects such as Sagar Mala, has had an adverse impact on the coastal environment in terms of coastal erosion, deterioration of mangrove forests and coastal wetlands, and pollution of ocean waters, and thereby on the marine fisheries sector. Firm safeguards are, therefore, required for the continued access of marine fishers to coastal and marine space and resources. The recent draft Environmental Impact Assessment Notification, 2020, which further dilutes the environmental clearance process and the involvement of public participation, must be subjected to greater deliberation.

b. The promotion of aquaculture and mariculture in Tamil Nadu's coastal space, such as advocated by Tamil Nadu's *Fisheries: Policy Note 2019–2020* (Animal Husbandry, Dairying and Fisheries Department 2020a) and the National Policy on Marine Fisheries (Department of Animal Husbandry, Dairying and Fisheries 2017), potentially affects the fisheries sector. Not only do these activities occupy similar spaces as those required for marine fishing, they also introduce negative externalities that affect the fisheries indirectly, such as through pollution or the introduction of alien species.

c. To counter the negative effects, such as those mentioned in the previous two points, marine fishers in Tamil Nadu require a clear set of rights, such as those advocated by the Food and Agriculture Organization's (FAO) Code of Conduct for Responsible Fisheries (1995), which is recognised by the Government of India. These rights over fishing grounds and resources should be incorporated in coastal zone regulations. This will contribute to a confidence in the long-term sustainability of the sector and a continued willingness to invest therein.

d. Climate change is increasing the intensity of storms, resulting in sea-level rise and influencing the distribution of fishery resources. Ensuring the safety of fishers at sea and their households on land is increasingly important and requires preventive measures of various kinds. A study done by a team led by Ramachandran illustrates that the fisheries sectors of Thoothukudi, Thiruvallur, Chennai, Villupuram, Cuddalore, and Kanyakumari districts are highly vulnerable in the current climate scenario (Ramachandran et al. 2016). In 2008, the Government of India encouraged all states to come up with a State Action Plan for Climate Change. Tamil Nadu formulated such a plan in 2014 and has now released a draft of a new plan

(Department of Environment 2020). Chapter 5 of the draft plan deals with sectoral issues including coastal management. The report recognises problems of coastal erosion, coastal flooding, water pollution, saltwater intrusion, and sea-level rise, all of which impact fish workers in general, and small-scale fish workers in particular.

Challenges Internal to the Fisheries Sector

Tamil Nadu's *Fisheries: Policy Note 2019–2020* formulates a future perspective for the marine fisheries sector (Animal Husbandry, Dairying and Fisheries Department 2020a). The vision could be construed as further capitalisation of fisheries and the creation of additional infrastructure. While the Policy Note recognises the possible adverse impacts of excessive capitalisation, for example in the Palk Bay, the solutions it offers, such as deep sea fisheries, do not address the basic problem of over-capitalisation, but rather move the problem further out into the Bay of Bengal, with the government heavily subsidising these initiatives.[9] The rapid capitalisation of even the small-scale fisheries in Tamil Nadu over the past 40 years has significantly increased not only the costs of purchasing boats, but also the cost of operations relative to returns, resulting in many fisher families suffering from high levels of indebtedness (Salim et al. 2017). The National Fishworkers' Forum (NFF), for one, has criticised the draft National Fisheries Policy, 2020, with which the Tamil Nadu Policy Note is largely in line, for not being people-centric and equitable, and for not articulating any vision regarding the rights of fishing communities (Kumar 2020).

The Fisheries Management for Sustainable Livelihoods (FIMSUL) project, jointly carried out in 2010 and 2011 by the governments of Tamil Nadu and Puducherry together with the FAO, concluded that 'the fisheries management system as a whole [in Tamil Nadu] is "weak"' (FIMSUL 2011a, p. x). It therefore advocated a Fisheries Reform Programme that (1) strengthens policy and management requirements at a government level, (2) installs a fisheries co-management process, and (3) enables fisheries stakeholders (fishers and others) to develop the sector (FIMSUL 2011a, p. xv). One decade later, these recommendations continue to hold true.

The inshore and offshore marine resources of Tamil Nadu are recognised as being in decline (Bhathal and Pauly 2008), and this trend needs urgently to be reversed. One of the core recommendations of the FIMSUL report is to introduce capacity controls, particularly for the mechanised fleet, 'as it is the most over capitalised part of the sector and having a seriously negative impact on fishing habitat, fish resources, and on other fishermen' (FIMSUL 2011a, p. xii). This would serve to reduce environmental pressure and help alleviate the many conflicts that permeate the fisheries.

In addition, the report calls for a reorganisation of fisheries governance: 'Co-management is considered the most suitable approach to manage fisheries in Tamil Nadu and Puducherry, given that the fishing community has its own management traditions and institutions' (FIMSUL 2011a, p. xii). A better connection between government and the fisher organisations that play an important role is highly desirable. The installation of harbour management committees is a step in the right direction.

The suggestions made by the FIMSUL report are in tune with FAO's *Code of Conduct for Responsible Fisheries* (FAO 1995) and its *Voluntary Guidelines for Securing Sustainable Small-Scale Fisheries in the Context of Food Security and Poverty Eradication* (FAO 2015), both of which the Government of India has recognised. Recognising the contribution that small-scale fisheries make to employment, income and food security, the Code of Conduct urges governments to protect the rights of such fishers, who make up a large segment of the fishers in Tamil Nadu. The Sustainable Development Goals (SDGs), which were adopted by the United Nations in 2015, similarly seek governments and other stakeholders to 'provide access for small-scale fishers to marine resources and markets' (SDG 14.b, available at https://sdgs.un.org/goals, accessed February 2022).

While the fisheries sector in Tamil Nadu faces important challenges, we believe, if properly addressed, it also has a promising future. The fishing grounds are rich, and the fishing population is skilled and committed. The key to addressing these challenges is good governance. What remains to be done is the formulation of a long-term vision for the sustainability of the sector. This needs to be done in active collaboration with the fishing population. After all, fisheries and fish workers have constituted a vital part of the history of Tamil Nadu and should be part of its future too.

Conclusion

This chapter has discussed the effects of the Covid-19 pandemic on the fisheries sector of Tamil Nadu, pointing out some ways to improve short- and medium-term responses to disasters of this sort. It must be noted that this chapter was written before the conclusion of the pandemic and should be taken as no more than an interim assessment.

We have pointed out that the lockdown measures as well as the relief measures that were issued in response to their emerging side effects, have already had great impact on the marine fishing population of Tamil Nadu.[10] Such measures were implemented both by government as well as by ur panchayats and fisher organisations at various levels of operation. Not only were fishing operations impaired but migrant fishers were stranded in distant locations. Trade in fish products also suffered badly, with small-scale, female fish vendors probably experiencing the most serious effects. Relief measures have not always been adequate, and we have made several suggestions for their improvement.

We concluded this chapter with a series of measures that are necessary to improve the long-term health of the fisheries sector in Tamil Nadu. We emphasised the need for better and more participative governance, to restore the health of the inshore and offshore ecosystem and increase social legitimacy. We also noted the need for better protection of the rights of marine fish workers to marine and coastal space and resources. In conclusion, we are convinced that a combination of appropriate short- and medium-term response measures to disasters such as the present pandemic, plus long-term measures to improve the health of the fisheries sector as a whole, will revitalise the sector so that it can continue to make a major contribution to the economy and the public life of Tamil Nadu.

Acknowledgements

This chapter is based on a larger report authored by a wider collective. We thank Tara N. Lawrence, Prabhakar Jayaprakash, Kohila Senbagam, Bhagath Singh A., Arun Kumar A. S., Mehala S. A., Preetha K. V., Nicolas Bautès, Nitya Rao, and Senthil Babu for their valuable contributions. Sebastian Mathew provided useful comments on an earlier version of this chapter.

Notes

1. All further references to 'fishers' in this chapter are to marine fishers.
2. Different data sets, at different points of time, give different figures. The *Handbook on Fisheries Statistics 2018* (Department of Fisheries 2019) estimates that there are 12,36,567 engaged in fisheries, activities (harvest and post-harvest), but it is likely to be more. More important than exact numbers is that the fisheries sector is labour intensive and employs a large number of people.
3. According to the Food and Agriculture Organization of the United Nations, 'small-scale fisheries can be broadly characterised as a dynamic and evolving sub-sector of fisheries employing labour-intensive harvesting, processing and distribution technologies to exploit marine and inland water fishery resources' (FAO 2005).
4. While ur panchayats are village-based institutions, fisher organisations include different types of craft/vessel associations which include members from different villages.
5. We have not been able to access similar data for other months.
6. The fishing ban applies only to the mechanised sector.
7. Central Marine Fisheries Research Institute uses the term 'crafts', but the term 'vessels' is often used, especially to refer to larger mechanised crafts.
8. We build here on the final report (FIMSUL 2011a, 2011b) of a project jointly implemented in 2010 and 2011 by the governments of Tamil Nadu and Puducherry together with the FAO.
9. Estimates of the potential of the offshore and deep sea fisheries in India's exclusive economic zone vary significantly. The *National Policy on Marine Fisheries, 2017* suggests that 'While the fisheries resources from the near-shore waters are fully utilised, the deep sea and oceanic waters offer opportunities of increasing the catch' (Department of Animal Husbandry, Dairying and Fisheries 2017, p. 14. See also FIMSUL 2011a).

10. The health consequences of the pandemic for the fishing population can only be assessed in due course. Such assessment should include what specific public health measures are to be considered for fishing communities and fish workers.

References

Animal Husbandry, Dairying and Fisheries Department, *Fisheries: Policy note 2019–2020*. Government of Tamil Nadu, 2020a, available at http://cms.tn.gov.in/sites/default/files/documents/fish_e_2019_20_pn.pdf, accessed on 3 October 2021.

———, *Fisheries: Policy note 2020–2021*. Government of Tamil Nadu, 2020b, available at https://www.fisheries.tn.gov.in/includes/assets/cms_uploads/pdf/glance/Fisheries_-_Policy_Note_2020-21_-_English_4605.pdf, accessed on 3 October 2021.

Bavinck, M., 'Investigating poverty through the lens of riches—Immigration and segregation in Indian capture fisheries', *Development Policy Review*, 32(1), January 2014, pp. 33–52, available at https://doi.org/10.1111/dpr.12042, accessed on 3 October 2021.

Bennett, N. J., E. M. Finkbeiner, N. C. Ban, et al., 'The COVID-19 Pandemic, Small-Scale Fisheries and Coastal Fishing Communities', *Coastal Management*, vol 48, issue 4, 2020, pp. 336–347, available at https://doi.org/10.1080/08920753.2020.1766937, accessed on 3 October 2021.

Bhathal, B., and D. Pauly, '"Fishing down marine food webs" and spatial expansion of coastal fisheries in India, 1950–2000', *Fisheries Research*, 91(1), May 2008, pp. 26–34, available at https://doi.org/10.1016/j.fishres.2007.10.022, accessed on 3 October 2021.

Department of Animal Husbandry, Dairying and Fisheries, *National policy on marine fisheries, 2017*, Ministry of Agriculture and Farmers Welfare, Government of India, 28 April 2017, available at http://dahd.nic.in/sites/default/filess/National%20Policy%20on%20Marine%20Fisheries%202017_0.pdf, accessed on 3 October, 2021.

Department of Environment, *Draft Tamil Nadu State Action Plan On Climate Change – 2.0*, Government of Tamil Nadu, 2020, available at https://www.environment.tn.gov.in/tnsapcc-draft, accessed on 3 October 2021.

Department of Fisheries, *Handbook on Fisheries Statistics 2018*, Ministry of Fisheries, Animal Husbandry & Dairying, Government of India, September 2019, available at https://dof.gov.in/sites/default/files/2020-08/HandbookonFS2018.pdf, accessed on 3 October 2021.

Department of Fisheries, *Model standard operating procedures (SOPs) related to movement of fisherman and fishing boats in COVID-19 scenario*, Ministry of Fisheries, Animal Husbandry and Dairying, Government of India, 18 April 2020, available at http://dof.gov.in/sites/default/filess/Model%20SOPs%20for%20Marine%20Fishries%20dated%20 18.4.2020%20by%20DoF,%20GoI.pdf, accessed on 3 October 2021.

Fisheries Management for Sustainable Livelihoods (FIMSUL), *Fisheries Management for Sustainable Livelihoods (FIMSUL) project in Tamil Nadu and Puducherry, India: Final report, Volume I—Key findings and recommendations*, Food and Agriculture Organization of the United Nations, December 2011, available at https://sites.google.com/site/fimsulreports/home/reports/FinalReport1.pdf, accessed on 3 October 2021.

———, *Fisheries Management for Sustainable Livelihoods (FIMSUL) project in Tamil Nadu and Puducherry, India: Final report, Volume II—Summary of FIMSUL process and outcomes under each work package*, Food and Agriculture Organization of the United Nations, December 2011, available at https://sites.google.com/site/fimsulreports/home/reports/FinalReport2.pdf, accessed on 3 October 2011.

Food and Agriculture Organization of the United Nations (FAO), *Code of conduct for responsible fisheries*, 1995, available at http://www.fao.org/3/a-v9878e.pdf, accessed on 3 October 2021.

———, *Increasing the Contribution of Small-Scale Fisheries to Poverty Alleviation and Food Security*, FAO Technical Guidelines for Responsible Fisheries, 2005, available at http://www.fao.org/3/a0237e/A0237E00.htm, accessed on 3 October 2021.

———, *Voluntary Guidelines for Securing Sustainable Small-Scale Fisheries in the Context of Food Security and Poverty Eradication*, 2015, available at http://www.fao.org/3/a-i4356en.pdf, accessed on 3 October 2021.

Kumar, V. S., 'Covid-19 inflicts a daily loss of H224 crore to India's fishery sector', *The Hindu Business Line*, 20 April 2020, available at https://www.thehindubusinessline.com/economy/agri-business/covid-19-causes-a-daily-loss-of-224-crore-to-indias-fishery-sector/article31388582.ece, accessed on 3 October 2021.

Kurien, J., 'To make fishers "Atmanirbhar", India should re-vision small-scale harvesting post-lockdown', *On Manorama*, 20 May 2020, available at https://www.onmanorama.com/news/columns/straight-talk/2020/05/lockdown-crisis-india-should-re-vison-marine-fisheries-sector.html, accessed on 3 October 2021.

National Sample Survey Office, *Migration in India: 2007–2008 (NSS 64th round, July 2007–June 2008)*, Ministry of Statistics and Programme Implementation, Government of India, June 2010, available at http://mospi.nic.in/sites/default/files/publication_reports/533_final.pdf, accessed on 3 October 2021.

Ramachandran, A., D. Praveen, P. Radhapriya, S. K. Divya, K. Remya, and K. Palanivelu, 'Vulnerability and adaptation assessment a way forward for sustainable sectoral development in the purview of climate variability and change: insights from the coast of Tamil Nadu, India', *International Journal of Global Warming*, 10(1–3), 22 July 2016, pp. 307–331, available at http://doi.org/10.1504/ijgw.2016.077896, accessed on 3 October 2021.

Salim, S. S., M. R., Rahman, and N. R. Athira, 'Labour migration and alternate avocation in marine fisheries sector of Kerala', *Journal of the Marine Biological Association of India*, 59(2), July-December 2017, pp. 109–114, available at http://mbai.org.in/php/journaldload.php?id=2462&bkid=118, accessed on 3 October 2021.

Sivadas, M., P. U. Zacharia, P. T. Sarada, et al., *Management Plans for the Marine Fisheries of Tamil Nadu* (Marine Fisheries Policy Series No.11), Central Marine Fisheries Research Institute, 26 October 2019, available at http://eprints.cmfri.org.in/id/eprint/13913, accessed on 3 October 2021.

Sudhakara, N. S., V. Khader, R. Sathiadas, et al., 'Participation of women in post harvest fisheries sector', *Proceedings of the workshop on empowerment of fisher women in coastal ecosystem of Andhra Pradesh, Karnataka, Kerala and Tamilnadu*, Acharya N.G. Ranga Agricultural University, October 2003, pp. 69–75, available at https://core.ac.uk/download/pdf/33018711.pdf, accessed on 3 October 2021.

Vohra, S., 'India's fishers have been crushed by COVID-19', *Hakai Magazine*, 30 April 2020, available at https://www.hakaimagazine.com/news/indias-fishers-have-been-crushed-by-covid-19/, accessed on 3 October 2021.

Section IV

Trade and Industry

9

Why Assemble in Tamil Nadu?

Ideas from Trends in Global Trade

C. Veeramani and P. G. Babu

What should be our rationale for attracting new industrial investments to Tamil Nadu? Despite the global retreat away from free trade over the past few years, going by the old maxim, it might be good for Tamil Nadu to enter when all others are exiting. In the current context, with everyone focused inward, it is perhaps time for 'Assemble in Tamil Nadu for the World'.

The opportunities are particularly high in the current context of changing global geopolitics, in which China, the factory of the world, finds itself at the receiving end. There is a growing realisation among multinational enterprises (MNEs) that they need to diversify their supply chains in the future, instead of relying only on China (Javorcik 2020). Even before the Covid-19 pandemic, the US–China trade war had created incentives for some of the MNEs to relocate supply chains to other parts of Asia (Amiti et al. 2019). Potential realignment of global value chains (GVCs) provide an opportunity for India to replace China as the major assembly hub for manufactured exports, which can create millions of jobs for India's low-skilled labour. With appropriate policies, Tamil Nadu can try to maximise the available opportunities.

Why Tamil Nadu?

Tamil Nadu has all the necessary, social and economic factors in place to take advantage of this opportunity. The state has a huge demographic dividend with 70 per cent of the population in the age group of up-to-45 years. The gender divide is almost equal with 51 per cent males and 49 per cent females. About 53 per cent of the households live in rural areas.[1]

The literacy rate is around 86 per cent, and the female literacy rate is 80 per cent. Fifteen per cent of the population have completed a bachelor's or higher degree, four per cent have a diploma. Two-thirds of the population are either pursuing or have completed education up to high-school level.

The state's unemployment rate is around 3 per cent. While 45 per cent of the population are employed, 52 per cent are not in the workforce. Of all employed, 63 per cent of males and 27 per cent of females are employed. Private sector salaried employment has emerged as the major type of work with 21 per cent of population involved in it, followed by casual labour (agriculture) at 19 per cent and self-employment (non-agriculture) at 14 per cent. In rural areas, almost one-third of the population is involved in agricultural casual labour.

Speaking about aspirations, 50 per cent households in the state said that they expected their income to increase in the next 5 years. Urban households were more optimistic than rural households about the increase in their future income.

However, the wrinkle that has emerged from the analysis of the Centre for Monitoring Indian Economy data (CMIE) by Babu, Kumar, and Singh (see Chapter 3, this book) is that there has been a secular decline in labour force participation since at least January 2016. Tamil Nadu's unemployment rate worsened sharply during the strict lockdown in April 2020. It registered a large turnaround in May 2020 when lockdown was eased to some extent. However, labour force participation rate continued to decline, even though at a lesser rate, in May 2020.

The increase in unemployment rate is faster in the case of urban areas, males, and those with higher education. Persons with intermediate levels of schooling were affected more than college graduates, and recovery in employment is also slower in their case, even as their labour force participation continues to drop. There is an underlying need to pay special attention to bring women and those without college education back into the labour force.

Hence, the bottom line is not unemployment rate per se, as it is very low at 3 per cent to 4 per cent based on standard measures. The real issue is a lower labour force participation rate and a lower quality of employment. The majority of those employed are in casual jobs or are engaged in the informal sector, with low wages, low productivity, and low levels of job security. Given the demographic profile of the state, aspirations of higher income of its population, and lower labour force participation rate, particularly that of women, it is important to create quality jobs in the formal sector where wages are higher.

Assembly of network products can potentially create, for the youth and women, better jobs compared to that they are presently engaged in. East Asian countries did this in the early stages of their growth. The strategy helped these countries create a large number of jobs for relatively less-skilled people. Female labour force participation in East Asian countries is one of the highest (Fontana 2009). The same is true in Bangladesh, where garments account for more than 80 per cent of its exports. Within the value chain in garments, Bangladesh specialises in assembly; it gets raw materials from India and Pakistan. More than 80 per cent of the workers in garment factories in Bangladesh are women.

Network Goods

Network products are those for which production processes are globally fragmented and controlled by leading MNEs within their 'producer-driven' global production networks. It involves deliberate specialisation in labour-intensive 'network products', by importing components and assembling them in order to create jobs at a large scale. The basic idea can be understood from Figure 9.1 and Figure 9.2.

Within the iPod value chain, China specialises in assembly while parts and components are imported. The factory-gate price of an assembled iPod was estimated to be \$144 in 2008, but only \$4 of this constituted Chinese value added (3 per cent of factory-gate price). However, China assembled almost all of the 54.83 million iPods that Apple sold, which led to aggregate domestic value added of \$219 million.

Figure 9.1: Conceptual Framework for Gains from 'Assembling in India' as part of 'Make in India'

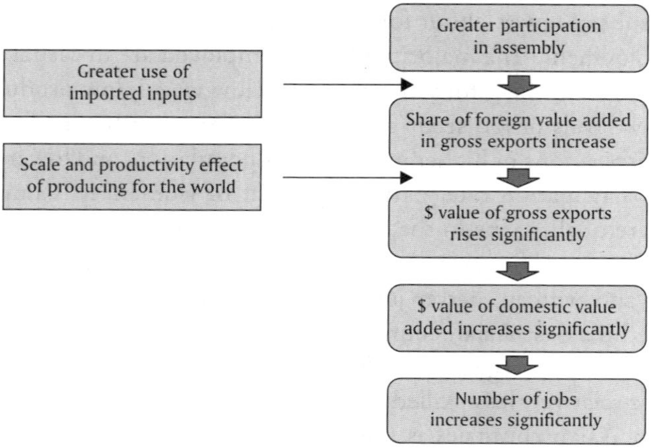

Sources: Ministry of Finance (2020b); Veeramani and Dhir (2019a).

Figure 9.2: Example of Gain from Assembly: Apple iPod and iPhone 7 Assembly in China

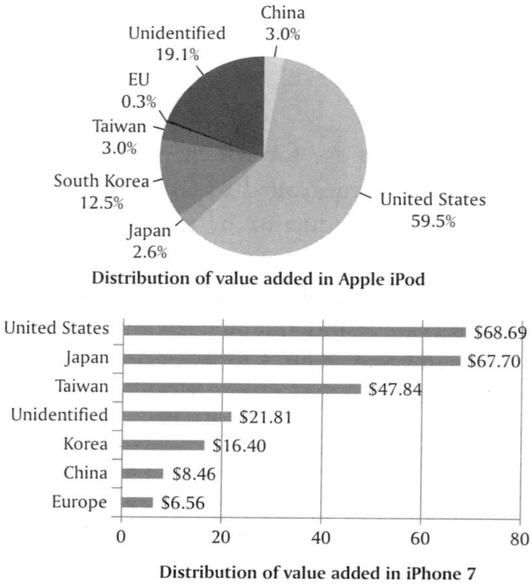

Sources: Ministry of Finance (2020b); Veeramani and Dhir (2019a).

China makes only US$ 8.46 from the assembly of an iPhone 7. However, total Chinese value added is very high ($8.46 × number of iPhones sold in the world). iPod and iPhone are just two examples. There are thousands of such products, where China has emerged as an assembly centre.

India already has two 'assemble in India' success stories, namely, automobiles and mobile handsets (Box 9.1 and Box 9.2). The country has a potential to expand its presence in electronics and electrical machinery. In the case of mobile handsets, there might be lessons for Tamil Nadu from the Nokia plant episode.[2]

Box 9.1: Success Story 1: Assembly of Mobile Phones in India

India toppled Vietnam to become the second largest manufacturer of mobile phones globally after China in 2018 with a world share of 11 per cent. India could manufacture around 1.25 billion handsets across various segments by 2025, firing up an industry worth around $230 billion (India Cellular and Electronics Association and McKinsey 2018). Between 2013 and 2017, while India's import of telecom handsets declined from US$ 4.47 billion to US$ 3.31 billion that of telecom parts increased steadily from US$ 1.34 billion to US$ 9.41 billion. At the same time exports of telecom handset increased significantly during the last three years. This pattern is consistent with the emergence of India as an assembly centre for telecom handsets.

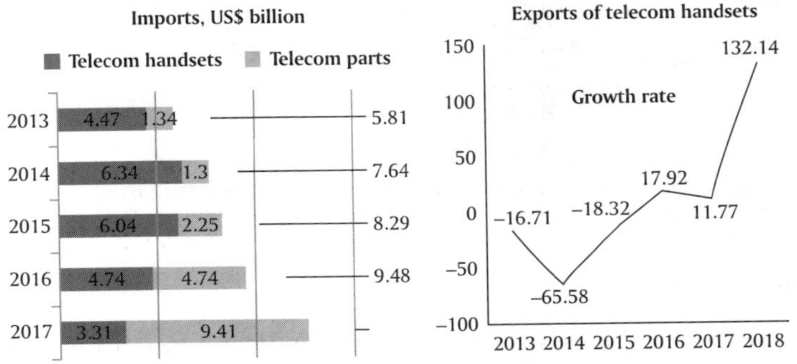

Sources: Ministry of Finance (2020b); India Cellular and Electronics Association and McKinsey (2018).

Box 9.2: Success Story 2: Learnings from Integration into GVCs by Indian Automobile Industry

From about the early 2000s, the Indian automobile industry has undergone a remarkable transformation from production for the domestic market, which remained its modus operandi for over a half century, to global integration. The country has emerged as a major assembly centre for compact cars (Athukorala and Veeramani 2019). India's exports of completely built units (CBUs) increased from about US$ 225 million in 2001 to US$ 8.8 billion in 2017, while exports of parts and components increased from US$ 408 million to US$ 5.5 billion between these two years (see panel (a) in Figure). The pattern is quite different on the import side with parts and accessories growing significantly faster than assembled vehicles during the same period (see panel (b) in Figure). In 2017, the import value of assembled vehicles stood below US$ 1 billion compared to about US$ 5.4 billion worth of imports of parts and accessories. While assembled motor vehicles constitute the bulk of India's automobile exports, parts and accessories account for the lion's share of total automobile imports. This pattern is consistent with the emergence of India as an assembly centre for automobiles.

Exports and imports of motor vehicles versus and parts & components (P&C)

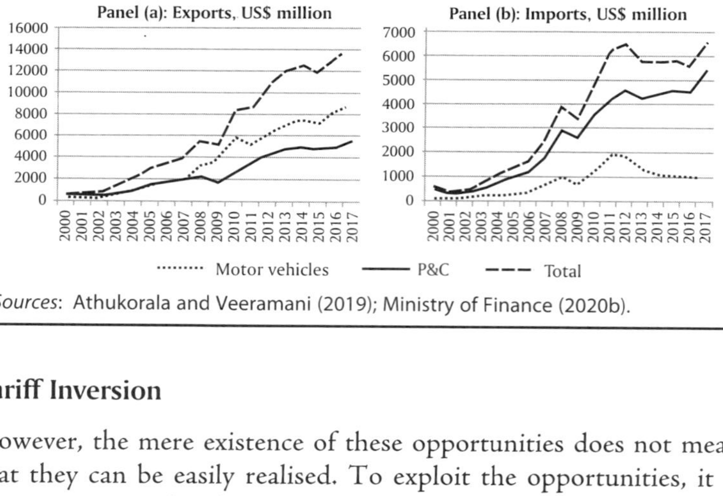

Sources: Athukorala and Veeramani (2019); Ministry of Finance (2020b).

Tariff Inversion

However, the mere existence of these opportunities does not mean that they can be easily realised. To exploit the opportunities, it is important to undertake a comprehensive set of reforms pertaining to factor market, trade policies and ease of doing business. In particular, the issue of inverted tariff and protectionism has to be addressed immediately. Inverted tariff exists when the import duty rate for the overall finished good is lower than the import duty rate of the component parts. Such a structure could render the relevant manufacturing process uncompetitive in the importing country. The presence of inverted tariff in India's network product industries is calculated as:

$$\textit{Tariff inversion in industry}_i = \frac{\textit{Weighted average of input tariff for industry}_i}{\textit{Weighted average of output tariff for industry}_i}$$

The tariff structure is inverted when this ratio is greater than 1. Table 9.1, constructed using input–output tables, shows the tariff inversion in different industries in India and how they have changed over the years. Figure 9.3 positions India in comparison with China, with regard to tariff inversion, to underline the issue.

Table 9.1: Inverted Tariff in Network Products

Product description	*Year*	*Output tariff*	*Input tariff*	*Tariff inversion*
Manufacture of communication equipment	2011	2.2	6.1	2.7
	2012	2.2	6.7	3.0
	2013	2.2	6.0	2.7
	2014	1.8	3.7	2.0
	2015	1.8	7.9	4.3
	2018	3.0	8.0	2.6
	2019–2020	9.0	11.3	1.3
Manufacture of electrical equipment	2011	8.0	8.1	1.0
	2012	8.0	8.4	1.1
	2013	8.0	8.1	1.0
	2014	8.0	8.1	1.0
	2015	8.0	8.4	1.0
	2018	8.6	8.4	1.0
	2019–2020	11.9	12.0	1.0
Manufacture of machinery and equipment n.e.c (i.e., not elsewhere classified)	2011	6.8	7.2	1.1
	2012	6.8	7.2	1.0
	2013	6.7	6.6	1.0
	2014	6.6	7.3	1.1
	2015	6.1	7.3	1.2
	2018	5.8	7.7	1.3
	2019–2020	10.7	12.2	1.1

(Contd)

Table 9.1 (Contd)

Product description	*Year*	*Output tariff*	*Input tariff*	*Tariff inversion*
Manufacture of transport equipment	2011	8.8	7.3	0.8
	2012	9.2	7.4	0.8
	2013	9.3	6.4	0.7
	2014	8.6	7.7	0.9
	2015	9.0	8.1	0.9
	2018	10.4	8.4	0.8
	2019–2020	9.8	12.2	1.2
Manufacture of electronic component, consumer electronics, magnetic and optical media, computer and peripheral equipment, optical and electronics products n.e.c.	2011	5.2	7.9	1.5
	2012	5.3	7.7	1.4
	2013	5.3	8.0	1.5
	2014	5.6	6.4	1.1
	2015	4.9	7.2	1.5
	2018	4.0	7.3	1.8
	2019–2020	6.6	10.6	1.6

Source: Veeramani and Basu (forthcoming).

Figure 9.3: Inverted Tariff for Network Products (Ratio of Weighted Average Input to Output Tariffs): Comparison with China

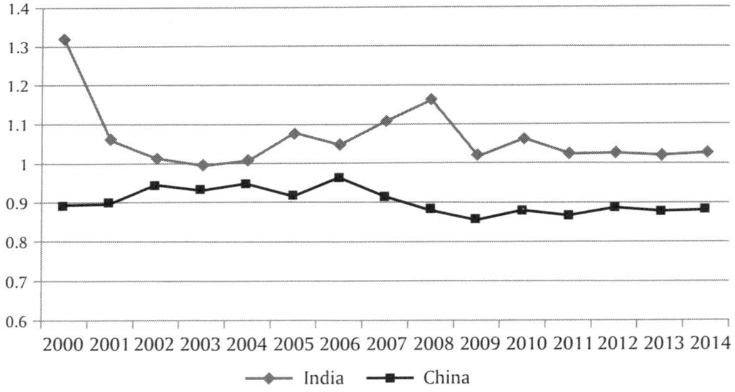

Source: Data from UN Comtrade and World Input Output Database.

The Way Forward for Tamil Nadu

Which industries should Tamil Nadu focus on? Given our comparative advantage in labour-intensive activities and the imperative of creating employment for a growing labour force, there are two groups of industries that hold the greatest potential, both for export growth and for job creation (Ministry of Finance 2020a; Veeramani and Dhir 2016).

First, there exists significant unexploited export potential in Tamil Nadu's traditional unskilled labour-intensive industries, such as textiles, clothing, toys, and leather products (including footwear). The GVCs in these industries are controlled by 'buyer-driven' networks wherein the lead firms that are based in developed countries concentrate in higher value-added activities, such as design, branding, and marketing. Physical production is carried out, through subcontracting arrangements, by firms in developing countries. Examples include the production networks of Walmart, Nike, and Karstadt.

Second, Tamil Nadu has huge potential to emerge as a major hub for final assembly in network products. The GVCs in these industries are controlled by leading MNEs, such as Apple, Samsung, and Sony, within 'producer-driven' networks. In general, these products are not produced from start to finish within a given country; instead, countries specialise in particular tasks or stages of the good's production sequence. Within the production network, each country specialises in a particular fragment of the production process; this specialisation is based on the country's comparative advantage. Labour-abundant countries, like China, specialise in low-skilled, labour-intensive stages of production, such as assembly, while the richer countries specialise in capital and skill-intensive stages, such as R&D. Thus, the lead firms retain skill and knowledge-intensive stages of production in high-income headquarters (e.g., the United States, European Union, and Japan) but locate assembly-related activities in low-wage countries (e.g., China and Vietnam). Researchers identified six groups of network products, based on Standard International Trade Classification (SITC) nomenclature, where global production sharing is most prevalent (Table 9.2).

Together, network products accounted for nearly 30 per cent of total world exports in 2018, with the share of Electrical Machinery (SITC 77) being the highest at 10.4 per cent. It is possible to disentangle total trade in these network products into two main subcategories—parts and components (P&C), and assembled end products (AEP).

Table 9.2: World Exports of Network Products, 2018

SITC code	*SITC description*	*World Exports, 2018 (trillion US$)*	*Share in Total World Exports, 2018*
75	Office machines and automatic data processing machines	0.83	4.37%
76	Telecommunication and sound recording equipment	0.65	3.42%
77	Electrical Machinery	1.97	10.44%
78	Road Vehicles	1.55	8.23%
87	Professional and scientific equipment	0.48	2.53%
88	Photographic Apparatus	0.12	0.66%
	Total Network Products	5.59	29.6%

Sources: Ministry of Finance (2020b); Veeramani and Dhir (2019b).

The world exports of network products increased steadily from US$ 2.01 trillion in 2000 to US$ 5.41 trillion in 2018. The increase was mainly driven by AEP, whose value rose from US$ 1.11 trillion to US$ 3.93 trillion. On an average, network products account for about 42 per cent of the world's manufactured exports during the period of 2000–2018. The average share of AEP exports in total network product exports increased from about 59 per cent during 2000 to 2016, to about 72 per cent during the last two years (2017–2018). Asia's share in world exports of network products increased phenomenally from about 37 per cent in 2000 to 51 per cent in 2018, while the shares of both Europe and America declined. East Asia accounted for the bulk of the total Asian exports and was followed by Southeast Asia. Rest of Asia (including South, Central, and West Asia) accounted for just 3 per cent of the total Asian exports.

The bottom line is that, given the young population profile, people looking for better-paying jobs, and global trade trends, one can explore the strategy of 'Assemble in Tamil Nadu for the World'. Indeed, trade policy being the domain of the central government, state governments are not in a position to change tariff rates to address the issue of inverted tariff. However, state governments can set up export processing zones (EPZs) with zero customs duties on imported intermediate goods for export purposes. The EPZs should also provide flexible labour laws.

With a huge coastline, Tamil Nadu is strategically located to integrate itself well with the production networks in East Asia and the ASEAN group of countries. Apart from creating well-functioning EPZs with the required facilities, Tamil Nadu should invest heavily on improving the connectivity of these zones with the rest of the state and the country. The state should also invest in reducing the service link cost—the cost of linking the assembly stage in Tamil Nadu with the P&C manufacturing stages in other countries, particularly in East and Southeast Asia.

Notes

1. The data cited in the first four paragraphs of this section derive from Census 2011 and MIDS–DES–SRC Tamil Nadu Household Panel Survey Pre-Baseline Summary, 2018–19, Draft Report submitted to Government of Tamil Nadu.
2. Nokia started its mobile phone manufacturing unit at Sriperumbudur in 2006, employing about 8,000 permanent workers. However, it had to shut its plant in 2014 due to a tax dispute with the Income Tax Department. When Microsoft took over the Nokia handset business in 2014, the plant was excluded from the deal. In October 2020, Salcomp, a Finnish electronics equipment manufacturer, brought Nokia's plant to make chargers and components for Apple.

References

Amiti, M., S. J. Redding, and D. Weinstein, *The impact of the 2018 trade war on U.S. prices and welfare* (NBER Working Paper No. 25672), National Bureau of Economic Research, available at https://www.nber.org/papers/w25672.pdf, accessed on 7 October 2021.

Athukorala, P-C., and C. Veeramani, 'From Import Substitution to Integration into Global Production Networks: The Case of the Indian Automobile Industry', *Asian Development Review*, 36(2), 2019, pp. 72–99, available at https://www.worldscientific.com/doi/full/10.1162/adev_a_00132, accessed on 7 October 2021.

Babu, P. G., V. Kumar, and P. Singh 'Employment and Covid-19: Trends and Issues in Tamil Nadu', Chapter 3, this book.

Fontana, M., 'The Gender Effects of Trade Liberalization in Developing Countries: A Review of the Literature', in M. Bussolo and R. E. De Hoyos (eds), *Gender Aspects of the Trade and Poverty Nexus: A Micro-Macro Approach*, Palgrave Macmillan, 2009, available at https://openknowledge.worldbank.org/bitstream/handle/10986/13264/48455.pdf?sequence=1&isAllowed=y, accessed on 7 October 2021.

India Cellular & Electronics Association and McKinsey, *Making India the Global Manufacturing Powerhouse for Mobile Handsets and Components* (Report), November 2018.

Javorcik, B., 'Global supply chains will not be the same in the post-COVID-19 world', in R. Baldwin and S. J. Evenett (eds), *COVID-19 and Trade Policy: Why Turning Inward Won't Work*, CEPR Press, 2020, available at https://voxeu.org/system/files/epublication/Covid-19_and_Trade_Policy.pdf, accessed on 7 October 2021.

Ministry of Finance, *Economic survey 2019–20*, Government of India, 2020, available at https://www.indiabudget.gov.in/budget2020-21/economicsurvey/index.php, accessed on 7 October 2021.

______, 'Creating Jobs and Growth by Specializing to Exports in Network Products', in *Economic survey 2019–20*, Government of India, 2020. Available at https://www.indiabudget.gov.in/economicsurvey/doc/vol1chapter/echap05_vol1.pdf, accessed on 7 October 2021.

Veeramani, C., and A. Basu, 'Protectionism, tariff inversion and assemble in India: Contradictions of trade policy' (IGIDR Working Paper), Indira Gandhi Institute of Development Research, (forthcoming).

Veeramani, C., and G. Dhir, 'India's export of unskilled labour-intensive products: A comparative analysis', in C. Veeramani and R. Nagaraj (eds), *International trade and industrial development in India: Emerging trends, patterns and issues*, Orient Blackswan, 2016.

______, 'Reaping gains from global production sharing: Domestic value addition and job creation by Indian exports' (IGIDR Working Paper No. WP-2019-024), Indira Gandhi Institute of Development Research, July 2019a, available at http://www.igidr.ac.in/pdf/publication/WP-2019-024.pdf, accessed on 7 October 2021.

______, 'Dynamics and determinants of fragmentation trade: Asian countries in comparative and long-term perspective' (IGIDR Working Paper No. WP-2019-040), December 2019b, available at http://www.igidr.ac.in/pdf/publication/WP-2019-040.pdf, accessed on 7 October 2021.

10

Sustaining Industrial Clusters in Tamil Nadu for Employment Generation

Some Policy Lessons from Tiruppur

M. Vijayabaskar

Industrial or economic dynamism tends to be a spatially differentiated phenomenon. Dense regional agglomerations of firms specialising in different segments of a sector and networked with one another are seen as engines of growth. As these agglomerations, also termed industrial clusters or districts, are critical for employment generation particularly in the Global South, policymaking to sustain them is important. According to the database hosted by the Ministry of Micro, Small and Medium Enterprises (MSME), Tamil Nadu is home to 28 modern MSME clusters apart from numerous artisanal ones (List of SME Clusters in India, n.d.). These clusters include those specialising in engineering goods that include castings and forgings, agricultural and textile machinery, auto components, machine tools, diesel engines, and kitchen equipment like wet grinders in Coimbatore, textiles and garments clusters including power loom, home furnishings, and spinning, spread across districts in western Tamil Nadu, such as Karur, Erode, Tiruppur, Coimbatore, and Salem. A readymade-garments cluster in Madurai and gauze cloth-making in Rajapalayam add to this list. There are also agro-processing clusters, like rice mills, starch and sago factories, and leather and leather goods in the Palar valley and Chennai, and the auto and auto-component cluster in the larger Chennai region. Many of the clusters are not only labour intensive but are also seen as dynamic in the sense that they have capabilities to diversify and move into new value-adding segments. To augment employment generation, it is therefore useful to understand the constraints that these clusters face in translating capabilities into improved dynamism and growth. Based on a recent study of the Tiruppur garments cluster,[1] arguably one of the most dynamic clusters in the state, and use of secondary material on other clusters, this chapter provides some directions for policy intervention to address the issue of employment generation in a post–Covid-19 future. To begin with, it is important to recognise that several of these clusters including Tiruppur have been in crisis even before the onset of the pandemic.

Elements of the Crisis: A Pre-Pandemic Map

As an article in the *Deccan Herald* indicates, the pandemic may well have been the last straw on the back of several factors that have affected enterprises in these clusters (Sivapriyan 2020). Some of the factors are sectoral, but some have to do with national and global-level factors that transcend sectors. Reports from Chennai, Coimbatore, and Tiruppur clusters map the crises that have affected several of the firms, particularly ones that occupy the lower end of the value chain of the specific clusters. Both demonetisation and the faulty implementation of Goods and Services Tax (GST) have affected their supply chains and access to working capital. While small firms are expected to pay GST every month, they invariably receive payments only after 3 months or so. As a result of the economic slowdown in the last couple of years, firms have been delaying payments even further, leading to a liquidity crunch and pushing suppliers to rely on informal credit to pay GST on time. Withdrawal of other incentives in the wake of implementation of GST has also affected firms in some sectors like garments. In addition, firms have also been left with unused stocks and inventories. Globally, there has been a shift to just-in-time production to cut costs of holding inventories. What this has meant is that firms pass the costs of maintaining inventories lower down the chain to different layers of suppliers. The fluctuations in demand, therefore, translate into unsold inventories for smaller suppliers, who also have to incur costs for storage of these inventories.

Apart from a crisis in profitability due to a decline in margins, small firms are also being impacted by the reduction in overall demand. Citing an interview with Mr. C. Sivakumar, the president of Coimbatore Tirupur District Micro and Cottage Entrepreneurs Association, *Livemint* (Ashok 2020) reported that at least 10,000 units in the Coimbatore–Tiruppur area had closed down, and that about 25,000 workers had lost their jobs due to slowdown, even before the spread of Covid-19 created new disruptions (Nidheesh 2020). Mr. Sivakumar also pointed out that there would be a shortfall of 60 per cent in the quantum of orders coming in. Tiruppur's garment exporters too have been facing similar challenges (Ashok 2020), which have been further compounded by preferential trade arrangements that exporters feel should be negated by formulating free trade agreements with the European Union.

What has the Pandemic Done?

Apart from contributing to a further fall in demand, the pandemic has also led to disruptions in the supply chain. Access to spares, raw materials, and other accessories have been affected. While this is true of the garments and leather goods sectors, it is much more visible in the auto-component sector, as China accounts for 27 per cent of the total auto imports into India (*The Economic Times Markets* 2020). On the demand side, it is estimated that 25 per cent to 30 per cent of export orders from Tiruppur have already been cancelled. Many buyers have asked the exporters to not ship their orders on account of a shortfall in demand. Outstanding payments were reported to be delayed. The leather industry too expects a fall of 20 per cent in export orders, with buyers asking exporters to hold on to shipping their consignments. Many auto majors too stopped production, and since they are primarily assemblers, it is likely to have led to considerable job losses in the component supplier firms as well. Loss of jobs and inability to get back home, especially with concerns of contracting the virus, created considerable anxiety among migrant workers. This added to further supply chain disruptions, as workers were reluctant to return in the short run. The pandemic has, therefore, aggravated the problems faced by MSMEs, even as many firms had been hoping to be able to move out of the demand slump by the middle of 2020. While this chapter does not engage with policy measures to address the question of demand directly, it offers some pointers on what should be done to ensure that revival in demand translates into better employment and production linkages in these clusters.

Two Premises

While all factors cannot be addressed at the level of the state government, there are some possible entry points for interventions, including strong negotiations with the union government on issues that come under the latter's domain. Some of them may be feasible in the short term, but others are likely to have an impact in the medium term.

There are two premises that inform this chapter. First, for labour-intensive manufacturing to sustain in an open environment, policy focus on expansion of volume of output alone is not sufficient. Wage-led competition may lead to a situation where returns to labour and capital may continue to fall even as output and employment expand, described in literature as 'immiserizing' growth (Bhagwati 1958). It is, therefore, important to ensure that firms diversify into segments that have more barriers to entry, through skill, quality, technology, and design intensity. This will allow them to appropriate more returns, and generate new employment and production linkages. Appropriation of more value also enables producers to improve the quality of employment, which is particularly important in the context of states like Tamil Nadu, characterised by a substantial availability of skilled labour. Emphasis must, therefore, be on the quality of employment rather than on mere employment generation, given the relatively higher levels of economic and human development in the state.

Second, a key principle that the chapter relies on is the recognition that the state can no longer be a mere facilitator for private actors as it has been in recent decades. It has to also be an 'entrepreneur'. Mazzucato (2013) established that economic dynamism has taken place globally only when the state has been an entrepreneurial actor, playing a key role in setting up institutions for innovation and being a market for such innovations. She points out that even in the apparently most pro-market of economies like the United States, the public sector—in partnership with universities, and at times with private firms—has been at the forefront of generating innovations and economic dynamism.

Based on these two premises, this chapter seeks to identify key domains for policy intervention. While the focus is primarily on textiles and garments, the chapter also identifies some principles for intervention across sectors.

Need to 'Upgrade': Innovations, Labour Intensity and Price Realisation

The textiles and clothing sector accounts for 2 per cent of gross domestic product, 7 per cent of industrial output, and 15 per cent of India's export earnings, and employs more than 45 million workers. The Tiruppur knitwear cluster is the largest source of garment exports from India and is a major source of employment in Tamil Nadu, especially for semi- and low-skilled labour exiting agriculture. Though India's share in global garment exports has only marginally increased from around 3.5 per cent to 4.2 per cent after the removal of export quotas in 2005, the share of knitwear within apparel exports has nevertheless increased. Firms in Tiruppur have also diversified from low-volume semi-fashion segment into standardised, large-volume production and, to a limited extent, into niche segments.

Due to growing levels of automation demanded by improved quality standards, labour absorption per unit of output has reduced in the spinning, knitting, and processing segments, such as dyeing, bleaching, printing, and embroidery. Garment-making, however, continues to be labour intensive. Growth in the size of firms has led to emergence of human resource departments and managerial staff, which constitute new employment avenues. Overall, though employment intensity has decreased with time, expansion in output has ensured an increase in demand for labour and new skill-sets for non-manual labour.

Despite firms investing on improving the quality of processing, the average price realisation per piece has stagnated at less than US$ 2.5 per piece for the last seven to eight years. This has squeezed margins for exporters. Many firms have responded by diversifying into the domestic market, where demand for knitwear has expanded during this period. While the learning from exporting has helped firms to cater to domestic demand, there are constraints that firms face. Vendors in several segments of the auto sector too report poor price realisation despite improvements in quality and technologies. This makes diversification and entry into more value-adding segments critical to generation of better quality employment.

Oligopolistic Control and Weak Capacities in Man-Made-Fibre Textiles

Indian export of garments, including from Tiruppur, continues to be dominated by cotton, whereas the global markets are dominated by man-made fibre (MMF) and blended fabrics. To address this bias, both the National Textile Policy of 2000 and the National Fibre Policy of 2010 encouraged MMF-based textiles and a shift to fibre consumption and production. Despite such measures, producers have been unable to access quality fabrics at competitive prices. Oligopolistic control over fibre production has rendered domestic fibre prices higher than that prevailing in the global market (Nair and Dhanuraj 2016). Even after taking on board transit costs, imported yarn is reported to be cheaper by 3 per cent to 5 per cent. Some also cite lack of access to duty-free imports of synthetic fibres due to lobbying by domestic producers. While the issue has been addressed to some extent, this is a domain that requires immediate attention. The recent emphasis on 'make in India' may reverse such tariff reductions, and such a policy shift may well affect competitiveness of the employment-generating garment industry. This requires re-orientation of policy measures to ensure competitive pricing and product competitiveness of the domestic fibre industry, and to direct garment-makers to move into high-end textiles that make use of such fibres. Apart from demanding appropriate trade policies, the state government may also facilitate interactions between medical service providers (who are major users of technical textiles) and textile firms. Tamil Nadu being a major centre for medical services, such interactions are likely to be useful.

Price Fluctuations for Intermediate Goods

A factor which constrains exporters from taking on large-scale orders of relatively high value is the risk posed by currency and input-price fluctuations (the latter particularly in the case of yarn). Yarn accounts for the bulk of production costs. Since contracts and prices are fixed before the commencement of production, any increase in yarn prices after signing of the contract will affect the profit margins of exporters. The same holds true for exchange rates. While insurance instruments are available to address this risk, high transaction costs deter small- and medium-sized firms from relying on these mechanisms for risk mitigation. Yarn producers and traders tend to view these products merely as a commodity rather than as a critical input to an industry with strong employment linkages. Policymaking cannot afford such a perspective given the linkages involved. This is true of other inputs, supply of which are shaped by oligopolistic practices. Governing production and distribution of intermediate goods so as to ensure assured cost-effective supply for final goods production is, therefore, critical for employment generation.

Declining State Support for R&D

There has been a steady decline in public research and development (R&D) support for various sectors. To give an example, the union government supports only 10 per cent of the annual budget of South India Textile Research Association, one of the government-supported R&D organisations for the textiles sector. This decline has not been accompanied by any step up in R&D investments by large private actors as it had been expected. Consequently, the number of scientists employed has declined from around 300 scientists in the 1980s to less than 50 at present. There is also a reported policy bias against long-term R&D investments and a preference for short-term research projects that have immediate (but not substantial) results. This is worrisome in a context where innovation in fabrics, such as diversification into new natural fibres and technical textiles are emerging as major sources of rents globally.

While the start-up ecosystem is reasonably good in Tamil Nadu, the role of the state government in providing resources and appropriate directions for this important activity has been inadequate. Identifying crucial employment-generating sectors and ensuring adequate R&D support to help firms diversify into more value-adding segments are, therefore, critical. The role played by the Central Leather Research Institute in Chennai may serve as a model in providing support for the leather sector.

Tapping into the capabilities of technical colleges and universities too has been weak. Given the substantial investments made in engineering and science education in the state, there is a potential to devise and implement incentives for local university–industry collaborations in innovation. Interventions cannot, therefore, merely be by way of resource allocation but require reorientation of the direction of technical education in the state.

Productivity

It is generally said that productivity in India is lower than in competing countries like Vietnam and China. But the difference may lie in industrial and process engineering than merely the skill levels of workers. The extent to which industrial engineering departments in colleges in the state can support initiatives to increase productivity is worth exploring. Industrial engineering solutions to improve productivity have to also recognise the organisational peculiarities of production in specific clusters, given the competitiveness in certain segments. Tiruppur specialises in multiple kinds of garments, with the same firm producing different styles and for different markets simultaneously. The skill demands are, therefore, more for multi-skilling as opposed to specialisation in competing countries. Though cluster-level training initiatives have been launched, issues of poor standards of training and lack of incentives for workers and firms to avail of such options persist. Certifications based on proper evaluation are therefore critical. In addition, the extent to which such skilling feeds into a dynamic production system needs to be studied before advocating expansion of these measures.

Absence of User–Producer Networks

A key source of innovation and learning for firms is through non-market networks forged with other firms and institutions in the value chain. While networks like these already exist between exporters, processors, and subcontracting firms within the cluster; collaborative networks between material suppliers and users, textile machinery producers and users, and between designers and exporters are negligible. These networks transcend cluster-level ties, and firms are often not in a position to forge such trans-local ties. Cotton yarn trade and exports, for example, are controlled by a traders' lobby that seldom interacts with garment producers. Furthermore, machines are largely imported at present despite the presence of spinning machinery capabilities in the neighbouring Coimbatore region. This has weakened both learning and employment generation potential. Similarly in the Chennai region, vibrant auto-component and software services segments coexist but with hardly any interactions between actors in the two sectors. Given the growing role of software in manufacturing, a strong case exists for fostering productive linkages between the two sectors. Inputs from the software services segments will be useful for several MSME clusters as well. This would also require a move away from a sectoral approach towards an inter-sectoral and a regional approach to employment generation.

Neglect of Social Infrastructure

While real wages matter for labour, enterprise profitability depends on nominal wages. Public provisioning of housing, education, and healthcare may, therefore, help firms access a pool of skilled labour at relatively lower costs. There is evidence to show that more and more households are relying on private schooling, and on private healthcare providers (albeit to a lesser extent when compared to the former), despite a relatively robust public education and healthcare system in Tamil Nadu. At present, households are of the impression that public institutions (e.g., Employees' State Insurance Scheme Hospitals or Government Schools) do not deliver quality healthcare or education. As a result, labour households spend a considerable amount on health and education, leading to an erosion of their real wages. Rising land costs and the large-scale presence of migrant workers also imply substantial outgo on housing rentals. The absence of a long-term career path undermines incentives for workers to make claims for better conditions of work or to invest in their own training.

Given the likelihood of a fall in land prices because of the economic slowdown, the state government can consider initiating a new venture to build worker hostels. Furthermore, the universal public distribution system, which has contributed substantially in providing social protection to labouring households in the state, needs to be sustained and extended to interstate migrant labourers in these industrial clusters.

Physical Infrastructure

For many enterprises, especially at the lower end of the value chain, outflow of income due to high rentals for factory space leads to lowering of the viability of the firm. The state government can potentially intervene in this domain. Similarly, building infrastructure for storage of raw materials or inventories, and channelising input supplies, could help individual small enterprises reduce costs. But creating such an infrastructure needs to take on board the nature of inter-firm linkages and the ecosystems that specific clusters operate in.

Clustering and Ecological Diseconomies

Most industrial clusters extract large quantities of water and often generate polluting effluents that undermine the health and livelihoods in the region. In the case of Tiruppur, though zero liquid discharge technology is available in the cluster, firms are not able to pass on the higher costs—of using it for ecologically sustainable production—to the buyers. Firms report lack of institutional support in using this technology as well as to use 'eco-labels' to upgrade. Due to lack of such support, firms in the cluster are often forced to take the 'low road' by moving dyeing operations to new locations where monitoring of pollution is poor and hence processing costs are lower. The importance of state intervention in enforcing environmental regulations cannot be overstated.

Summing Up

Though most issues that constrain cluster dynamism have been drawn from the experience of Tiruppur, many of these factors operate in other clusters and other sectors as well. There is a need for a shift away from a mode of intervention that has primarily been by way of incentivising capital through lower taxes or provision of subsidised land or other inputs. Instead, emphasis should be on the extent of employment and production linkages that can be created through entry of new firms or new firm-level strategies, and the nature of state intervention to ensure realisation of such linkages. Apart from the need for investments in social infrastructure, these interventions clearly call for additional resources for the state government. This, in turn, will require a move away from centralisation of resource mobilisation and a move towards a more equitable sharing of resources mobilised between the union and state governments. More crucially, recent policy shifts have further eroded the ability and incentives for state governments to intervene to chart growth paths that are responsive to local conditions and institutions. Such shifts also undermine the sources of regional dynamism of MSME clusters (Magazine 2020). Effective intervention at the state level to improve the quality of employment cannot, therefore, be disengaged from negotiations with the union government to secure space for greater policy autonomy.

Acknowledgements

A number of stakeholders in the Tiruppur knitwear cluster took time off to share their valuable insights on the issues confronting them. J. Jeyaranjan offered useful comments on an earlier draft. The author is extremely thankful to them.

Notes

1. This was undertaken as part of a larger study titled 'Manufacturing Matters', coordinated by the Indira Gandhi Institute of Development Research (Mumbai), to look into constraints to employment generation through industrialisation across key sectors in India.

References

Ashok, S., 'A tense textile hub spins out of control', *Livemint*, 1 May 2020, available at https://www.livemint.com/news/india/a-tense-textile-hub-spins-out-of-control-11588261831485.html, accessed on 8 October 2021.

Bhagwati, J., 'Immiserizing Growth: A Geometrical Note', *Review of Economic Studies*, 25(3), June 1958, pp. 201–205, available at https://academic.oup.com/restud/article-abstract/25/3/201/1552362?redirectedFrom=fulltext, accessed on 9 October 2021.

List of SME Clusters in India, UNIDO, n.d., available at http://laghu-udyog.gov.in/clusters/clus/smelist.htm#clus, accessed on 8 October 2021.

Magazine, A., 'One in three small businesses close to winding up, says survey', *The Indian Express*, 2 June 2020, available at https://indianexpress.com/article/business/coronavirus-lockdown-msme-businesses-winding-up-6438024/, accessed on 8 October 2021.

Mazzucato, M., *The Entrepreneurial State: Debunking Public vs. Private Sector Myths*, Anthem Press, 2013.

Nair, Lakshmi R. and D. Dhanuraj, *Common Man's Clothing: Effects of Taxes and Tariffs*, Elamkulam: Centre for Public Policy Research, 2016, available at www.cppr.in, accessed on 25 June 2019.

Nidheesh, M. K., 'Fear and loathing in India's small factories', *Livemint*, 29 January 2020, available at https://www.livemint.com/industry/manufacturing/fear-and-loathing-in-india-s-small-factories-11580232448058.html, accessed on 8 October 2021.

Sivapriyan, E. T. B., 'Tiruppur knitwear hub in doldrums', *Deccan Herald*, 23 February 2020, available at https://www.deccanherald.com/business/business-news/tiruppur-knitwear-hub-in-doldrums-807457.html, accessed on 8 October 2021.

The Economic Times Markets, 'Coronavirus' impact on India's auto sector', 10 April 2020, available at https://economictimes.indiatimes.com/markets/stocks/news/coronavirus-whats-its-impact-on-indias-auto-sector/articleshow/75078607.cms, accessed on 8 October 2021.

11

The Tamil Book-Publishing Industry and the Impact of Covid-19 Pandemic

A Note

A. R. Venkatachalapathy

The popular Tamil proverb '*Nitya kandam, poorna ayusu*' ('A full life; but a crisis everyday!') aptly captures the general situation of Tamil trade publishing. (Trade publishing refers to general books meant for the public as distinct from textbook publishing catering to the pedagogic needs of schools and colleges.) Even in the best of times, Tamil trade publishing is a precarious profession with low turnover and narrow profit margins. The Covid-19 pandemic has dealt the industry a severe blow, and the immediate, short-term, and long-term future looks grim.

However, even though the Tamil publishing industry is rather small, its cultural importance cannot be overstated and hence is deserving of special attention.

This chapter provides an overview of Tamil trade publishing and offers some suggestions to help tide over the present crisis.

Historical Background

Tamil was the first non-European language to deploy moveable type to produce printed books, as early as 1577. Among Indian languages, Tamil publishing claims many 'firsts', including the first complete translation of the New Testament in 1714–15, the first full translation of the Bible in 1796, the first extended lexicon in 1912–36, and the first modern encyclopaedia in 1954–68.

In 2004, Tamil was the first to be given the status of a classical language by the Government of India. In 1956, the Government of Tamil Nadu was the first state to pass the Official Language Act. *Tirukkural* has the honour of being the most translated secular book. The Government of Tamil Nadu is unique in bringing the works of many cultural figures into the public domain through the process of 'nationalisation'.

Tamil publishing draws its strength from this rich historical legacy.

Contemporary Importance

It is widely accepted that along with Hindi, Bengali, Marathi, and Malayalam, the Tamil language publishes the largest number of trade books. Until even a few decades ago, Chennai was also the centre of Telugu book publishing. The Chennai Book Fair is now in its 45th year and—along with the Delhi International Book Fair and the Kolkata Book Fair—one of the three largest book fairs in India. (However, it should be noted that while the Delhi and Kolkata book fairs are heavily funded and subsidised by the government, the Chennai Book Fair receives no such largesse.) India's modern library movement, despite many problems plaguing it, had its origins in Chennai (S. R. Ranganathan, the famed librarian and bibliographer, was a founding member of the Madras Library Association), and the Tamil Nadu Directorate of Public Libraries (DPL) is a robust organisation. Since the 1960s, the Government of Tamil Nadu has invested significantly in creating a state-wide network of public libraries.

However, for an industry with such historical depth and cultural richness, hard data on its extent and magnitude are scarce, if not non-existent. Even basic data, such as the number of publishers, the number of titles published annually, annual turnover, or number of employees, are unavailable. While this is true of publishing in other Indian languages and in English as well, that is small consolation for an industry struggling to survive.

Evolution of the Tamil Publishing Industry

In the pre-Independence period, publishing was driven by ideals inspired by the freedom struggle, the Dravidian movement, and the Communist movement. During World War II, Nattukkottai Chettiar capital fleeing from South East Asia was invested in publishing, and the 1940s saw independent India's first bloom in Tamil publishing. Firms such as Pari Nilayam, Star Prasuram, Tamil Puthakalayam, Palaniappa Bros., Mullai Pathippagam and the now defunct Sakthi Karyalayam date from this period. The nationalisation of textbook publishing in 1971 (and the creation of the Tamil Nadu Textbook Corporation that had a monopoly over textbook publishing) was a body blow to the industry. The second wave of publishing can be dated to the 1970s when avant-garde publishing houses, such as Cre-A: and Annam, were started. The 1990s was a period of crisis when the industry floundered. In the new millennium—in the wake of economic and social processes triggered by globalisation—there was a quantum leap in the number of publishing houses and the number of titles published.

Organisation of the Industry

The Tamil publishing industry is loosely organised. Though the very first public limited company in Indian language publishing was a Tamil firm, the South India Saiva Siddhanta Works Publishing Society, which celebrated its centenary year in 2020; Tamil publishing houses are mostly individual- or family-owned, or partnership firms. Fewer than a dozen firms are private limited companies, such as New Century Book House, Annam Publications, New Horizon Media (Kizhakku), Kalachuvadu Publications, and Amudha Nilayam. Most firms operate like a cottage industry. Typically, a Tamil publishing firm is managed by its owner, with help from family members. With most of the functions outsourced, publishing houses directly employ only a handful of staff for coordinating production, maintaining accounts, and dispatch of books.

Even though publishing is covered under Micro, Small & Medium Enterprises (MSME), and Udyog Aadhaar, very few publishers are registered under these. Given the informal nature of their operation, most firms are unable to provide the paperwork to avail bank loans. As a result, they rely on informal sources of credit at high rates of interest. Inputs, such as paper, are purchased on credit, thereby adding to costs.

Booksellers and Publishers Association of South India (BAPASI), the only industry association of publishers, has 570 members, of which an overwhelming 450 are Tamil publishers and booksellers; English publishing accounts for the rest. After a gap of a nearly ten years, about eighty new members were admitted in late 2021; still many applications for membership are said to be pending. It is believed that the current membership may also include bogus members. Industry estimates range between 800 and 1,000 firms, though the actual number may be lower. One-third of these may be part-time publishers, who publish books primarily for propagating their ideas and cultural values. Idealism is an important element in Tamil publishing—it provides the drive to develop new content and therefore, the importance of such publishers should not be discounted.

More than 80 per cent of the publishers are based in Chennai. A few major publishers are located in Coimbatore, Madurai, Tiruchirappalli, and Nagercoil.

Production

With the advent of new digital technology and methods of production, book production has become highly decentralised. As a result, publishing firms do not have more than a handful of full-time employees. It is estimated that the entire Tamil publishing industry may employ about 2,000 people directly. Only a small fraction is on regular payroll, and even fewer are covered by Provident Fund and the Employees' State Insurance Scheme. The bulk of the employment generated by the publishing firms is through outsourced, rather than in-house, services.

With the obsolescence of the letterpress and composition using moveable type (as well as hot metal technologies, such as monotype and linotype), desktop publishing (DTP) has become universal over the past decade. As a result, printing presses do not use moveable metal types and instead utilise DTP services provided by individuals usually working from their homes. Typically, such operators charge as low as Rs. 10 per page (crown octavo size). They also do not use licensed software as it adds to costs.

There are a number of printing presses in Chennai which service Tamil publishing almost exclusively. Printing presses have become capital intensive, using advanced technology for printing. But as the rates are low, printers rely on volume to recoup capital investment and running expenses. This puts an enormous strain on the presses. The advent of print on demand (POD), which enables the printing of even a single copy of a book, has further affected the economic health of printing presses. Given high input costs and slow sales, many publishers are now turning to POD and, as a result, print runs have now come down to as low as 50 or 100. When manual binding was the norm, there were a number of small binding units. With the mechanisation of the bookbinding process, this service is now mostly provided by the printers themselves, who also do multicolour work of printing wrappers, lamination, and shrink-wrapping. Thus a range of production services are now provided by the printing presses.

Proofreading is no longer done in-house and is farmed out to retired teachers and part-time employees. Rates for proofreading are abysmally low (as little as Rs. 4 per crown octavo page). A few honourable exceptions apart, most firms do not employ copy editors. Designing of wrappers is done by independent designers, and the rates may be as low as Rs. 750 per cover design (though some standard publishers pay up to Rs. 1,500). Private courier companies are the major channel for distribution, and they provide preferential rates for publishers.

Production costs have increased in the wake of the implementation of goods and services tax (GST). While the publishers pay GST on paper (an expensive component of production, where about 50 per cent of the costs may go into purchasing paper), no input credit can be claimed as books are not covered by GST.

In all, it is estimated that about 10,000 people may be indirectly employed by Tamil trade book publishing. This count does not include writers and authors. There are few writers whose livelihood is writing, as it is not an option for a sustainable livelihood. Only a few publishers offer written contracts to their authors. Agreements are oral and informal, leading to bickering, heartburn, and intense distrust. Royalties, if and when they are disbursed, are ad hoc payments. For a majority of authors, writing is a passion and a treacherous path to name and fame.

Number of Titles

As both the premier national deposit library (The National Library, Kolkata) and the state deposit library (The Connemara Public Library, Chennai) have stopped producing the *Indian National Bibliography* and *Tamil Nuttrogai*, respectively, there are no figures available for the number of titles published every year. The DPL typically receives purchase applications for about 8,000 titles every year. However, a good number of these titles are fake (meant to elicit orders), and the figures are therefore unreliable.

Dial for Books, an online web portal for sale of Tamil books, has 28,000 titles available for sale; based on this, it is estimated that about 5,000 Tamil titles are published every year. An overwhelming number of titles are never reprinted, and few publishers have successful backlists. This has a big impact on profitability, as there is no incentive for publishers to invest in developing and nurturing books and authors.

Distribution and Sales

The biggest problem plaguing the Tamil publishing industry is the extremely weak distribution network. There are no reliable conduits for linking the publisher and the reader. Bookshops are few. Even Chennai has fewer than a dozen bookshops catering to Tamil books. Chain stores, such as Starmark and Odyssey, focus on English books, allocating only a few shelves to Tamil titles. While major cities have a few dedicated Tamil bookshops, most second- and third-tier cities and towns have no bookshops worth the name. Furthermore, the terms of sale are weighed against the publisher. Books are sent on sale or return basis, and the credit period is about a year, and sometimes even longer. So, a publisher cannot expect any revenue for about a year—an unfortunate situation. As commercial rents are high, bookshops do not have adequate shelf space to display titles. Total revenue through across-the-counter sales and through bookshops is estimated at Rs. 30 crore annually. In the past few years, organisations like Amazon, Flipkart and Dial for Books have started generating online sales of Tamil books, and this is slowly expanding, benefitting both publishers and readers. The market for e-books and audio books is extremely limited as there is hesitancy on the part of readers to pay for virtual books. The market share for e-books is practically non-existent.

A significant number of Tamil books emanating from India are sold in Sri Lanka, Malaysia, Singapore, United Kingdom, France, and Canada. But there are no estimates, reliable or unreliable, for these overseas sales.

In the absence of a network of bookshops, most publishers rely on book fairs to distribute their books and generate revenue. Chennai Book Fair is the largest book fair, with over 850 stalls. Organised annually during the time of Pongal (mid-January), the Chennai Book Fair receives about 5,00,000 footfalls every season, according to BAPASI office-bearers. Total sale is about Rs. 15 crore. Many publishers state that about 25 per cent of their annual revenue comes from the Chennai Book Fair. The other major book fairs—at Madurai, Erode, Tiruppur, and Coimbatore—generate sales of about Rs. 8 crore. Book fairs in smaller towns generate sales of about Rs. 7 crore. In all, sales at various book fairs yield about Rs. 30 crore.

Library Orders

A major chunk of revenue is through acquisition by the DPL, which has a strong network of 4,300 public libraries under it. It follows a three-tier system with a district central library, circle libraries, and branch libraries. The consultation and borrowing of books are practically free, and it can be said without exaggeration that these libraries have created a veritable revolution in the reading habits in the rural hinterland of Tamil Nadu. A library cess of Rs. 0.50 for every ten rupees of property tax is collected to fund the libraries.

Unfortunately, the complaint by the publishing industry is that the cess thus collected is not transferred to the DPL.

Annual acquisition by DPL is about Rs. 30 crore. The titles are chosen by a committee drawn from various walks of life, though, in reality, choice of members is dictated by the party in power. The rate for purchase is fixed by the DPL. Rates are low and do not take into account either production costs or marked price. Despite this, publishers make an effort to get DPL orders as this involves bulk purchase, which was earlier 600 copies of every title, but has now been increased to 1,000 copies, though numbers vary. As a result, a publisher can recoup costs and make a modest profit on each title without selling a single copy to the reader. This inevitably leads to corruption, and a huge shadow network of publishers, officials, and touts work together to ruin the library system and the book trade.

Apart from the budget provided by the Government of Tamil Nadu, DPL is also the nodal agency for the Raja Rammohun Roy Library Foundation, which provides about Rs. 3 crore every year for purchase of Tamil books.

Other Government Schemes

Many earlier schemes, such as Operation Blackboard and Anna Marumalarchi Thittam, have been discontinued. It is whispered in the industry that there are government schemes (for example, Rashtriya Madhyamik Shiksha Abhiyan), to the tune of about Rs. 30 crore, which are tapped only by a few publishers, as there is no transparency in the acquisition. It is a consistent demand of the industry that such schemes should be advertised prominently in newspapers and on government websites to create a level playing field for all publishers.

Magnitude of the Trade

Based on these estimates, the size of the Tamil trade book publishing is likely to be about Rs. 150 crore. Considering the size of the state, and the richness of its cultural and intellectual traditions, this figure leaves much to be desired.

Impact of the Covid-19 Pandemic and Its Mitigation

The lockdown following the Covid-19 pandemic has had a devastating effect on Tamil trade book publishing. With all bookshops closed and the postal and courier services functioning only minimally, sales had virtually come to a halt. There has been virtually no revenue for 2020. As 31st March is the closing date for accounts (when annual settlements are made), the timing of the lockdown further exacerbated revenue issues. Most publishers were unable to pay salaries to their staff, or to draw even their own salaries, or account for their running expenses. Printing presses came to a grinding halt. DTP operators, proof-readers, translators, wrapper designers, and binders were thrown out of work. Sales of printing paper purchases and print implements (such as ink) plummeted to zero.

The immediate and longer-term future looks bleak. Book publishing is the bedrock of any developed society with a cultural depth and rich intellectual tradition, and no monetary value can be put on it. Immediate steps are required to bail out the industry if it is to survive. Towards this end, the following recommendations are proposed.

1. Interest-free loan may be extended to publishers for three years, without collateral security. The maximum loan extended may be 25 per cent of the total turnover as reflected in the last financial year's income tax filing.
2. Reverse GST on royalty may be waived permanently. GST on paper purchase and printing bills may be waived for publishers for two years.
3. Many bills are still pending with the DPL for as long as a year. Clearing these bills will immediately infuse money into the publishing trade.
4. About 25 small book fairs across the state, with large space and limited book stalls at subsidised rates, may be organised.
5. Run a publicity campaign to encourage book reading.
6. Propose to the central government a lowering of book post rate for two years.
7. Create a Tamil Nadu state book policy. Declare books as an essential commodity.

8. A systematic study of the Tamil book industry must be commissioned.
9. BAPASI may be reorganised in a more democratic manner to reflect the interests of all stakeholders.
10. The Welfare Board for publishers, printers, and booksellers, created by the Government of Tamil Nadu in 2009, is practically defunct. The Board may be rejuvenated, and funds lying unused (said to be to the tune of Rs. 3 crore) may be immediately released to publishers and booksellers as interim relief.

Acknowledgements

Grateful thanks are due to K. S. Pugalendi (Sixthsense Publications), Kannan Sundaram (Kalachuvadu Pathippagam), Marudhan Gangadharan (Kizhakku Pathippagam), 'Parisal' Senthilnathan (independent bookseller), M. Palaniappan (Mullai Pathippagam), and B. S. Shunmugasundaram (Mani Offset) for providing information and insights. However, I alone am responsible for all statements of fact and interpretation made in this chapter.

12

Measures to Revive the Tourism Sector in Tamil Nadu after the Covid-19 Pandemic

Krishanu Pradhan

The consequences of the Covid-19 pandemic and the ongoing lockdown have been severe and unprecedented for the tourism sector in Tamil Nadu. Suspension of all types of surface transport as well as domestic and international air travel, closure of hotels and restaurants, and the complete shutdown of places of worship, beaches, sports facilities, tourist spots, and recreational sites have dealt a body blow to this sector. Rebooting the sector is challenging because the lockdown has substantially weakened the financial health of tourism and its allied activities. Job and income losses to people due to economic slowdown have also affected their ability to take up tourism-related activities. In addition, fear of uncertainty, enforcement of social distancing norms, and unwillingness of tourists to come out from self-containment is expected to continue to prevail in the coming months.

Importance of Tourism Sector

Expenditure by visiting tourists creates significant backward and forward effects on the economy. Although tourism activities come under the service sector, they also contribute positively to the primary and secondary sectors. According to Kshitiz Sharma, the income multiplier effect of tourism activities in India is estimated to be 3.2; that is, for every one rupee spent by visiting tourists, more than three rupees of income are created in India (Sharma 2014). More than 70 per cent of these income multiplier effects are captured by local final demand. The tourism industry is also the third-largest foreign exchange earner (US$ 240 billion in 2018) in India. It is also highly labour intensive and provides significant scope for local employment. According to the International Labour Organization (ILO), the employment elasticity of tourism sector (1.8) is far greater than that of the manufacturing sector (0.57), mining and quarrying (0.45), and construction (1.14) (International Labour Organization 2009).

Tourism Sector of Tamil Nadu

The tourism industry in Tamil Nadu is the largest in India. The Tamil Nadu Tourism Development Corporation's (TTDC) 'Enchanting Tamil Nadu—Experience Yourself' campaign, launched in 2003, yielded significant positive results, making the state, since 2014, the most popular destination for domestic and foreign tourists in India. In 2018, close to one-fourth (over 385 million) of India's domestic tourists and one-fifth (over 6 million) of foreign tourists visited Tamil Nadu. Considering the importance of the sector, the Tamil Nadu government's *Vision 2023* put significant emphasis on it, estimating Rs. 100 billion investment requirement, on public–private partnership (PPP) basis by 2023 for the development and renovation of amusement parks, sports complexes, science museums, training institutes, and infrastructure (iMaCS 2012).

Pre– and Post–Covid-19 Scenarios

Table 12.1 shows that there was hardly any growth in tourist flow in Tamil Nadu in 2019. The slowdown of the domestic economy and the nationwide stir—against the Citizenship Amendment Act (CAA) and the National Register of Citizens (NRC)—caused a significant decline in domestic tourist flows in 2019 (Kaushik 2019). Another major reason for tepid growth in tourist arrivals in the state was the overall decline in foreign tourist arrivals in India in 2019 (9.6 million) as compared to 2018 (10.56 million). The major causes of deceleration of foreign tourist arrivals in 2019 were the India–Pakistan border tensions in early 2019, travel advisories issued by the European Union (EU) and the United States over the abrogation of Article 370 and Article 35A of the Indian Constitution, Government of India advisories for tourists visiting undivided Jammu and Kashmir (J&K) after the revocation of special status of J&K, overall recessionary fears in the EU and the United States, and Brexit (Narayanan 2019). The spread of Covid-19 virus in China from late-November 2019, which triggered travel and visa restrictions by the Government of India, also contributed to the deceleration in foreign tourist arrivals.

Table 12.1: Tourist Footfall in Tamil Nadu (2015–2019)

Year	*Tourist arrivals (in lakh)*			*Growth in tourist arrivals (in per cent)*		
	Domestic	*International*	*Total*	*Domestic*	*International*	*Total*
2015	3,334.60	46.90	3,384.20	N.A.	N.A.	N.A.
2016	3,438.10	47.20	3,485.30	3.10	0.64	2.99
2017	3,450.60	48.60	3,499.20	0.36	2.97	0.40
2018	3,859.10	60.70	3,919.80	11.84	24.90	12.02
2019*	3,900.00	61.00	3961.00	1.06	0.49	1.50

Note: *Provisional
Sources: Kabirdoss and Ayyappan (2020); Government of India (2019).

According to the United Nations World Tourism Organization, international tourist arrivals could decline by 60 per cent–80 per cent due to the Covid-19 crisis, and the resultant revenue loss would be anything between US$ 910 billion to US$ 1.2 trillion. Asia and Pacific regions, especially India, could experience the steepest fall in international tourist arrivals (UNWTO 2020).

Tourist arrivals in 2020 and the near future will register a significant decline due to the Covid-19 pandemic and the subsequent lockdowns. The extent of the decline in tourism activities after the nationwide lockdown can be gauged by comparing the figures of all-India tourism revenue earned in December 2019 (US$ 3.2 billion) versus March 2020 (US$ 0.785 billion) (CEIC 2020). Also, foreign tourist arrivals in India from January to March 2020 registered a 23 per cent decline compared to the same period in 2019, due to the spread of Covid-19 in China and Europe and the subsequent restrictions on foreign travellers by the Government of India (Government of India 2020a). Five countries—the USA (13.83 per cent), the UK (9.15 per cent), Australia (3.36 per cent), Canada (3.22 per cent), and China

(3.11 per cent)—that contribute up to one-third of foreign tourist arrivals in India have also been significantly affected by the Covid-19 pandemic (Government of India 2020b).

As per the update on 6 July 2020 by Government of India, Tamil Nadu, which attracts one-fourth of foreign tourist arrivals in India was the second-worst Covid-19-affected state, after Maharashtra. Therefore, the crisis in the tourism and allied sectors in the state has been acute.

Impact of Lockdown on Tourism Sector in Tamil Nadu

According to a report by the Federation of Indian Chambers of Commerce & Industry (FICCI) and Grant Thornton, India is staring at an overall income loss of US$ 17 billion and a loss of 40 million jobs from the travel and tourism sector in 2020 alone. The report also highlighted that the cancellation of over 90 per cent of bookings of hotels and flights from March–May 2020 caused a loss of US$ 1.2 billion to the hotel, aviation, and travel sectors. The report also mentions that, according to the Indian Association of Tour Operators, average losses in the income of tour operators and travel agents would be in the range of 50 per cent–80 per cent of the previous year's income (FICCI and Thornton 2020).

State-wise estimates on income and job losses in the tourism sector due to the lockdown are absent. The derived income loss of the tourism sector in Tamil Nadu would be over US$ 4 billion and a direct or indirect loss of around 10 million jobs. The state has suffered a significant decline in arrivals of both domestic and foreign tourists and a considerable contraction of the sector. According to the Nilgiris Hotel and Restaurant Association, close to one lakh people have lost jobs in hotels and restaurants in The Nilgiris District alone during the lockdown period. Since the lockdown period coincided with the peak season of tourism in the district (April to June), hotel and restaurant owners were unable to pay salaries to the staff (Premkumar 2020). Without cash flow, the liquidity crisis in the sector has been severe, and as a result, bankruptcies, business closures, and job losses have been unavoidable. Taxis, private bus and tour operators, small business owners and street vendors, who depended on tourism activities, have suffered significant income losses.

Since the state is home to 60 per cent of all places of worship in India (around 33,000 temples alone), the lockdown and ban on religious gatherings have caused a loss of livelihood for priests, workers, flower sellers, and small eateries in pilgrimage centres. Similarly, the closure of beaches, hill stations, botanical gardens, and zoos have adversely affected local hotels, restaurants, and street vendors.

Short-Term Measures (Less Than 1 Year)

Need for Immediate Fiscal Support

The amount of immediate fiscal and financial support as derived from the estimates of the FICCI and Grant Thornton report, to the aviation sector, hoteliers, tour operators, travel agents, taxi drivers, and workers in hotels and restaurants, would not be less than US$ 5 billion (Rs. 375 billion)(FICCI and Grant Thornton 2020). Fiscal support is required to meet some of the pandemic-inflicted losses of the sector and to repair the broken financial health of the businesses. Since the ongoing lockdown has paralysed the sector, a portion of the Rs. 100 billion investment proposed in *Vision 2023* should be earmarked for immediate relief and support to the sector. The immediate need is the survival of the sector. Revival can follow the lifting of the lockdown.

Liquidity Crisis and Credit Support

To address the liquidity crisis of hotels, restaurants, small business shops, and tour operators due to the Covid-19 pandemic and lockdown, banks should come forward to extend credit facility to help them remain functional. Apart from credit support, an urgent need is for banks to not restructure the outstanding loans (or to not treat them as non-performing assets) extended to the aviation sector, hospitality sector, hoteliers, and travel agents. Once the sector revives after the lifting of the lockdown, banks can recover their dues. The FICCI and Grant Thornton report also suggested to the Government of India a minimum 12 months' moratorium on all working capital, principal, interest payments, loans, and overdrafts (FICCI and Thornton 2020).

Need for Waiver of Taxes and Establishment Charges

Apart from the support of bank loans, the government should also waive all property taxes, trade license fees, renewal fees, and other establishment charges like power tariffs and water charges for hotels, restaurants, accommodation service providers, small business owners, and tour operators. The amount saved on account of such waivers may not be huge but would give the ailing industry a cushion to overcome the immediate liquidity crisis. Also, there is a need for the deferment of all previous goods and services tax dues, at least until the pandemic ends. Any new compliance that involves payment of fees should be exempted. Such waivers would minimise the outflow of liquidity and strengthen their working capital position (Agarwal 2020).

Strategy to Increase Footfall

Owners of hotels, guest houses, recreational clubs, and restaurants should offer packages of discounts and staycations to woo tourists and visitors once the restrictions are eased and the lockdown is lifted. Government support alone cannot solve their crisis. The immediate objective of private firms engaged in the hospitality sector should be to increase footfall to reduce their liquidity crisis. Free cancellations or reschedule facilities, and no advance deposits, would gain the confidence of customers. Similarly, all air carriers should allow the rescheduling of itineraries without any charges as long as the lockdowns persist.

Need for Improvement in Basic Services

Tamil Nadu has been the most attractive destination for domestic and foreign tourists, but lack of basic, hygienic and sanitation facilities in tourist spots is a serious concern, especially because of the Covid-19 crisis. For example, the famous Meenakshi Temple in Madurai, which attracts thousands of visitors every month, does not have good quality washrooms and drinking water facilities in the vicinity. The government would be required to put in maximum effort for provisioning and maintenance of such essential services and facilities to woo the tourists. Upgradation of basic infrastructure facilities, like parking facilities for cars,[1] hygienic rest rooms, hand sanitisers, face masks, and clean drinking water facility will help to protect tourists from getting infected by the virus. Similarly, the government should ensure that private tour operators, hotels, restaurants, and accommodation facilities are fully equipped to follow the norms that would minimise the spread of Covid-19.

How to Recreate Tourism Demand

To recreate the demand for tourism, the first step is to create a few model tourism activities at a few important sites, where all forms of safety, hygiene, and social distancing norms are practised. Standard operating procedures where direct human contacts are minimised should be in place for the visitors and should be shared via social media. Well-publicised implementation of these practices would generate confidence among tourists. Tour operators or the tourism agencies should create customised videos and pictures of the model tourist sites where ideal safety, hygiene, and social distancing norms are adopted. Social media platforms should be used to tap the targeted audience.

The second step is to encourage domestic tourism at the local level. Since domestic tourists contribute 83 per cent of the total tourism expenditure (FICCI and Thornton 2020), the government should use this leverage to promote more intra-state (inter- and intra-district) tourism activities. Since the resumption of international flights would take time and the government will put restrictions on international tourists, it is desirable to focus more on domestic and local tourism activities. To encourage domestic and local tourism, resumption of public transport with proper care is required. Therefore, wherever possible, the government should resume public transport services, especially in the districts where Covid-19 cases are very few or non-existent.

Medium-Term Policy Responses for Tourism Sector (3 to 5 Years)

Potential for Pilgrim Tourism

Tamil Nadu has immense potential to exploit opportunities from religious (pilgrimage) tourism. The government should promote the tourism potentials in small towns and rural areas by connecting them with proper roads and other infrastructural facilities. This would decongest the already overexploited tourist spots and help small towns and rural areas to gain economically from tourism. The state already has four international and three domestic airports (Government of India 2020c), more than 70,000 km of highways and over 2.7 lakh km of extensive road network (Government of Tamil Nadu 2021) and more than 4,000 km of railway routes (Government of India 2020d).Therefore, the issue is how to connect small towns and lesser-known tourist destinations of immense potential with the existing infrastructure network. Also, Tamil Nadu's tourism agencies should partner with the Indian Railways and state transport agencies of other states to facilitate special trains or bus services to connect famous tourist spots like temples, heritage sites and hill stations.

Information Dissemination about Potential Tourist Spots

One of the areas where the government should put greater focus is on providing adequate information about potential tourist spots located close to the major ones. At present, tourists visiting the major spots do not have any information about neighbouring tourist attractions that they could easily visit on the same trip. So, providing this information to tourists plays a major role in tourism benefits trickling down to areas neighbouring the major spots. Information about local or rural tourism sites should be available at major tourist destinations in the form of booklets and handbills in two or three languages. Since the language barrier is a significant impediment to disseminate tourism-related information to visitors from outside the state, in the age of mobile technology, the TTDC should develop a mobile app that will provide all kinds of information, hospitality services, and logistics support about the existing major tourism sites as well as for the potential tourist attractions. In this way, income and employment can be generated at a much greater decentralised level.

Role of the Private Sector in Maintaining Tourism Infrastructures

Private sector investment should be encouraged for the operation, maintenance, and interior design of government-provided idle tourist infrastructure, like forest bungalows, guest houses, hotels, and restaurants. For example, although the TTDC has been earning a modest profit in recent years, it has been incurring losses from running hotels. Already there has been a spurt in the availability of hotel rooms and restaurants in various tourist spots from the private sector (Press Trust of India 2018). Therefore, it does not augur well for TTDC to run such high-cost hotels in a highly competitive market and incur losses. The government should either privatise all hotels and restaurants of TTDC, or franchise them out to private operators through open bidding. The process of franchising the loss-making hotels to private operators started in 2010, but it did not gain much momentum due to opposition from employees. It may help strengthen the process of privatisation if the employees can be transferred to other departments or offered a voluntary retirement scheme.

Development of Modern Tourism

The state has immense potential for the development of modern forms of tourism like sports tourism and adventure tourism. Considering the investment requirement and marketing strategies, the development of modern tourism activities may be left to the private sector or by PPP. The government can identify the proposed land or the project area for the development of modern tourism sites and give them to private operators on a long-term lease. The most competent operator would be identified through proper bidding on the principle of build, own, operate, and share a certain percentage of revenue with the government. After the development of the core projects, provision of other infrastructural facilities and services—like lodging, hotels, and shopping malls—may be left to the private sector. What the government needs to provide is the supply of water, electricity and public transport facilities to the core project and surrounding areas.

Development of Ecotourism

To promote the sustainability of the tourism sector, the government should promote ecotourism in the state. Ecotourism involves using the local communities in tourism-related activities so that a significant amount of tourism benefits are shared by the local communities. Out of the 25 destinations identified for ecotourism in 2014, only 13 ecotourism sites are operational in the state; that is, half of the potential for ecotourism in the state has not been exploited. Considering the potential for tourism in the state, the government should encourage private sector investment to develop and operate ecotourism sites. The promotion of ecotourism also requires better marketing strategies, which private players generally do better than government agencies.

Importance of Medical Tourism and its Relocation

Tamil Nadu is also a pioneer in medical tourism in the country. Close to 40 per cent of the country's medical tourism takes place in the state due to better facilities and low-cost treatment compared to other states and metro cities. Chennai has emerged as a health tourism hub. A substantial proportion of patients from abroad come to Chennai for good quality, yet inexpensive, health care facilities. Close to 45 per cent of foreign health tourists and 40 per cent of domestic health tourists visit Chennai for medical care (Asian News International 2019). However, such a distinct success has not been unblemished. For example, the city has more than 4,000 hospitals and clinics which generate an estimated 60 tonnes of toxic biomedical waste every day (TNN 2019). Such huge quantities of biomedical waste would generate serious public health hazards in the future. Therefore, the government should not encourage more hospitals and clinics in Chennai. Rather, to exploit the opportunities from medical tourism, the state should incentivise the opening of new hospitals and clinics in other parts of the state, such as Coimbatore, Madurai,

Tiruchirappalli and Salem, which are well connected by air, railways, and surface transport.

Private Investment in Tourism-Related Logistics and Infrastructure

The sector needs a significant amount of investment to upgrade and maintain the existing tourism infrastructure, seamlessly provide logistics and hospitality services to tourists, and create new tourism avenues like adventure tourism and ecotourism. Considering the poor fiscal health, the government expected significant support from the private sector through the second Global Investors' Summit (GIM-II) in 2019. However, the response from the private sector was not impressive. The actual worth of MoUs (Memorandum of Understanding) signed was just Rs. 6.42 billion (*The Hindu Business Line* 2019) as compared to the government's expectation of Rs. 30 billion to Rs. 40 billion (Mehra 2018). Though the tourism sector was included for the first time in GIM-II, the main foci of GIMs in the past had been on manufacturing, information technology (IT) and IT-enabled services, real estate, and energy sectors. Therefore, the state's tourism agencies should organise a special investors' summit exclusively for the tourism sector. The tourism department should do the groundwork for identification of tourism sites and required investment, negotiations with investors, and setting up of a single-window clearance system to make the summit effective.

Need for Priority-Sector-Lending Status to the Tourism Sector

Considering the importance of the tourism sector in generating employment, local demand, foreign exchange earnings, and overall income multiplier effects to the economy, the government should include the tourism sector under priority sector lending (PSL) category by banks. The inclusion of the sector under PSL would result in more credit and investment flow required for the upgradation and expansion of the sector.

Need for Reliable Databases

One of the major problems of the tourism sector in India in general, and in Tamil Nadu in particular, is the lack of a comprehensive database about the tourists. For example, the absence of databases about the age, gender, and place of residence of tourists, the frequency of their visits, their preferences for various types of tourism activities, and the problems they face in accessing logistics, facilities and information, significantly constrain the planning, coordination, and marketing activities among various stakeholders. Private sector participation in the creation and maintenance of tourists' databases may be required for better planning and coordination. Private sector participation is also required for the preparation of investment guidelines and marketing strategies for various types of tourism activities and travel-related products and services.

There is also no proper database about the workers, street vendors, small-business owner (of small shops and eateries) who earn their livelihood in the neighbourhoods of temples or beaches or tourist spots. In the absence of such a database, relief and rehabilitation works would be challenging. Therefore, the responsibility to create and maintain the required database may be entrusted either to the local government, the management of the place of worship, or the authority of the particular tourist spot.

Note

1. Since most tourists would prefer to avoid public transportation and instead travel by private vehicles during post–Covid-19 period, there will be a steep increase in the demand for parking facilities.

References

Agarwal, V, 'Covid-19 and Tourism', *KPMG*, 30 March 2020, available at https://home.kpmg/in/en/blogs/home/posts/2020/03/covid-19-and-tourism-travel-hospitality-and-civil-aviation.html, accessed on 21 October 2021.

Asian News International, 'Chennai: India witnessing influx of medical tourists from Arab nations', *The Economic Times*, 30 June 2019,

available at https://health.economictimes.indiatimes.com/news/industry/chennai-india-witnessing-influx-of-medical-tourists-from-arab-nations/70016821, accessed on 21 October 2021.

CEIC, 'India Tourism Revenue', *CEIC Data base*, 2020, available at https://www.ceicdata.com/en/indicator/india/tourism-revenue, accessed on 21 October 2021.

FICCI and Grant Thornton, *Travel and Tourism: Survive, revive and thrive in times of COVID-19*, June 2020, available at https://www.grantthornton.in/globalassets/1.-member-firms/india/assets/pdfs/travel-and-tourism-in-times-of-covid-19.pdf, accessed on 21 October 2021.

Government of India, 'India Tourism Statistics at Glance 2019', 2019, Ministry of Tourism, available at: https://tourism.gov.in/sites/default/files/2020-04/India%20Tourism%20Statistics%20at%20a%20Glance%202019.pdf, accessed on 7 January 2022.

______, '*eNewsletter January—March 2020*', 2020a, Ministry of Tourism, available at https://tourism.gov.in/sites/default/files/2020-06/Newsletter%20Jan-Mar%2020-01062020.pdf, accessed on 7 January 2022.

______, 'India Tourism Statistics at a Glance – 2020', 2020b, Ministry of Tourism, available at https://tourism.gov.in/sites/default/files/2020-09/ITS%20at%20a%20glance_Book%20%282%29.pdf, accessed on 7 January 2022.

______, 'The Lists of Indian Airports', 2020c, Airport Authority of India, Ministry of Civil Aviation, available at https://www.aai.aero/sites/default/files/basic_page_files/list%20of%20airport%20bilingual.pdf, accessed on 7 January 2022.

______, 'Indian Railways Year Book 2019-20', 2020d, Ministry of Railways, available at https://indianrailways.gov.in/railwayboard/uploads/directorate/stat_econ/Annual-Reports-2019-2020/Year-Book-2019-20-English_Final_Web.pdf, accessed on 7 January 2022.

Government of Tamil Nadu, 'Policy Note 2021–2022, Demand No.21', 2021, Highways and Minor Ports Department, available at https://cms.tn.gov.in/sites/default/files/documents/hw_e_pn_2021_2022.pdf, accessed on 7 January 2022.

ICRA Management Consulting Services (iMaCS), *Vision Tamil Nadu 2023: Strategic plan for Infrastructure Development in Tamil Nadu*, Government of Tamil Nadu and Asian Development Bank, March 2012, available at http://www.spc.tn.gov.in/pdfs/TN_Vision_2023.pdf, accessed on 21 October 2021.

International Labour Organization, *Towards an Employment Strategy for India*, 2009, available at https://www.ilo.org/wcmsp5/groups/public/---asia/---ro-bangkok/---sro-new_delhi/documents/genericdocument/wcms_177078.pdf, accessed on 21 October 2021.

Kabirdoss, Y., and V. Ayyappan, 'For the Tourism Business, it's Time to Think Local', *The Times of India*, 15 May 2020, available at https://timesofindia.indiatimes.com/india/for-the-tourism-business-its-time-to-think-local/articleshow/75466408.cms, accessed on 21 October 2021.

Kaushik, M., 'Economic slowdown and CAA stir hit holiday plans', *India Today*, 26 December 2019, available at https://www.indiatoday.in/mail-today/story/economic-slowdow-caa-stir-hit-holiday-plans-1631492-2019-12-26, accessed on 21 October 2021.

Mehra, P., 'Tamil Nadu Aims Rs. 4000 Cr Investment in Tourism During Investor Summit 2019', *Travel Trends Today*, 17 December 2018, available at https://www.traveltrendstoday.in/news/states/item/6620-tamil-nadu-aims-rs-4000-cr-investment-in-tourism-during-investor-summit-2019, accessed on 21 October 2021.

Narayanan, V., 'Now, slowdown bug bites tourism sector', *The Hindu Business Line*, 14 September 2019, available at https://www.thehindubusinessline.com/economy/now-slowdown-bug-bites-tourism-sector/article29411118.ece, accessed on 21 October 2021.

Press Trust of India, 'ITDC incurred losses of around Rs. 20 cr in 3 yrs in running 7 hotels', *Business Standard*, 2 April 2018, available at https://www.business-standard.com/article/pti-stories/itdc-incurred-losses-of-around-rs-20-cr-in-3-yrs-in-running-7-hotels-118040201215_1.html, accessed on 21 October 2021.

Premkumar, R., 'Hospitality sector in the Nilgiris may see 70% slide in revenue', *The Hindu*, 28 May 2020, available at https://www.thehindu.com/news/national/tamil-nadu/hospitality-sector-in-the-nilgiris-may-see-70-slide-in-revenue/article31690066.ece, accessed on 21 October 2021.

Sharma, K., *Introduction to Tourism Management*, McGraw Hill Education (India) Private Limited, 2014.

Times News Network (TNN), '75% biomedical waste in Chennai left to rot in- open', 17 December 2019.

The Times of India, 17 December 2019, available at https://timesofindia.indiatimes.com/city/chennai/75-biomedical-waste-in-city-left-to-rot-in-open/articleshow/72782344.cms, accessed on 21 October 2021.

The Hindu Business Line, 'TN's 3-pronged investment strategy pays off', 24 January 2019, available at https://www.thehindubusinessline.com/news/tns-3-pronged-investment-strategy-pays-off/article26082599.ece, accessed on 21 October 2021.

United Nations World Tourism Organization (UNWTO), 'International tourist numbers could fall 60–80% in 2020, UNWTO Reports', 7 May 2020, available at https://www.unwto.org/news/covid-19-international-tourist-numbers-could-fall-60-80-in-2020, accessed on 21 October 2021.

Section V

Labour

13

Covid-19 and Migration

The Experience of Tamil Nadu

K. Jafar and A. Kalaiyarasan

Compared to any other occasion, issues faced by interstate migrants due to the Covid-19 outbreak, and the nationwide lockdown announced on 24 March 2020, were widely covered in the national and international media. Facing job losses and unable to obtain basic necessities, the migrants started walking towards their homes located hundreds of kilometres away. This unprecedented and large-scale movement of people from one end of the country to the other, without adequate support for transportation, food, and other essentials, was compared with the mass migration that took place after the Partition in 1947 (Biswas 2020). Vignettes from various parts of north India—of long treks by harried families, children crying out in hunger, disinfectants being sprayed on human beings, and so on—not only touched the collective conscience of many people but also made them wonder why migrant labourers were compelled to move when there was no work for them in their place of origin. Compared to this, the discussion on adverse effects of the pandemic on international migration, inflow of remittances, and the concerns of diaspora was limited to specific regions.

Tamil Nadu, being both one of the destinations and suppliers of interstate migrants in India, witnessed a large number of migrants leaving the state and many coming back to their homes after the Covid-19 outbreak. With a long history of international migration and inflow of remittances, the state expected to face an impact on international migration due to the pandemic. This chapter highlights the nature of migration, post-pandemic challenges, and policy suggestions to address these challenges while formulating a post-pandemic development strategy at the national and state levels.

Dynamics of Migration: Pre–Covid-19 Trends

We still do not have a comprehensive database or precise estimates of the number of workers moving across the states and districts of India. The cause of the movement can be traced back to the distress prevailing in India's rural and agrarian sector. Although the share of agriculture in India's GDP has declined sharply over the decades, the share of the workforce dependent on agriculture (mostly seasonal or marginal workers) remains high. This prompts millions of cultivators and agricultural labourers to rely on non-agricultural activities. Given the limited options available in rural areas, many of them move out of their villages in search of work. Their social capital endowments and access to informal social networks may help some of them in reducing the vulnerability and uncertainty while moving out. For various reasons, measures like the Mahatma Gandhi National Rural Employment Guarantee Act (MGNREGA) and skill-development programmes have failed in retaining them in rural areas and reducing the risk involved in this transition.

Along with the distress in rural areas, factors like higher wages and better opportunities at the destination, as well as personal reasons (e.g., marriage, education) also contribute to migration. Geographically, internal migrants are mostly from low-population-density rural areas, but the concentration and nature of the urban context open migrants' lives in cities to fresh challenges and opportunities.

Interstate migration has seen two broad patterns—large-scale migration from high-income states to low-income states, observed during the 1980s and 1990s, and, in the recent period, movement from the northern and eastern states to the western and southern states. In Chhattisgarh, Bihar, Jharkhand, Odisha, and West Bengal, a significant share of the total number of workers are marginal workers. These states are also known for severe distress in the rural and farm sectors. Mass migration from Bihar and Uttar Pradesh to Delhi, Haryana, Punjab, and Maharashtra, and from Odisha,

West Bengal and other eastern states to southern states, indicate the formation of conspicuous migration corridors within the country.

The *Economic Survey 2016–17* estimated that on an average, around 9 million people migrate between states every year (Ministry of Finance 2017). Delhi, Maharashtra, Tamil Nadu, and Gujarat attract a large number of migrants from the northern states (Uttar Pradesh, Bihar, and Madhya Pradesh). According to the *Survey*, the emerging pattern was of Tamil Nadu and Kerala experiencing a surge in the inflow of internal migrants, while there was a decline in some of the earlier popular destinations.

The Census of India 2011 (Office of the Registrar General & Census Commissioner 2011) identified about 54 million interstate migrants (by place of residence). There were about 4.6 million short-term migrants (less than a year) and they were largely concentrated in Maharashtra (17 per cent), Delhi (13 per cent), Gujarat (9 per cent), and Haryana (8.6 per cent). Nearly 60 per cent of the interstate migrants lived in seven states—Maharashtra, Delhi, Uttar Pradesh, Gujarat, Haryana, Karnataka, and Madhya Pradesh (Figure 13.1). Uttar Pradesh, Bihar, Rajasthan, Maharashtra, Madhya Pradesh, Karnataka, and West Bengal sent nearly 64 per cent of the total interstate migrants, and except for Karnataka, were net suppliers in 2011 (Figure 13.2).

Figure 13.1: Distribution of Migrants by State of Destination, 2011 (Share in per cent)

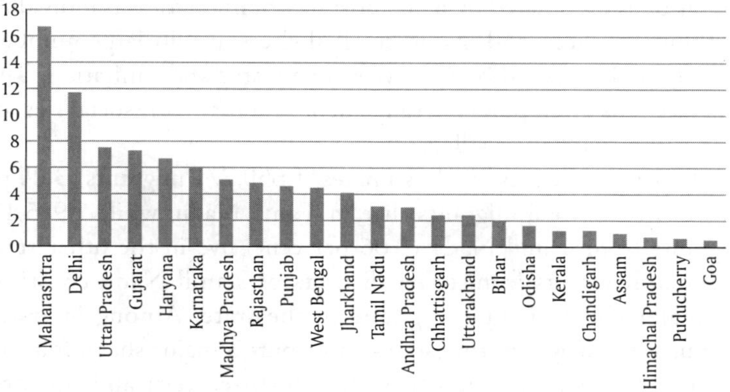

Source: Census of India 2011.

Figure 13.2: Distribution of Migrants by State of Origin, 2011
(Share in per cent)

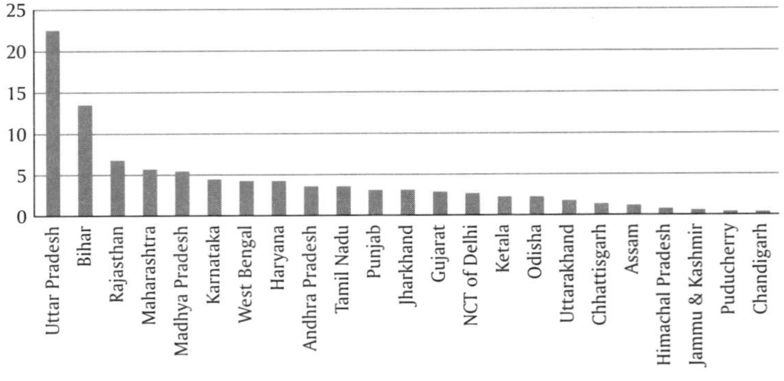

Source: Census of India 2011.

Interstate migrants are vulnerable at their destinations. They face difficulties in accessing food and healthcare, and go through conflicts and disputes (e.g., non-payment of wages, physical abuse, accidents) at worksites and outside. Most of them are casual workers engaged in low-paying, hazardous, and informal market jobs like in construction, hotels, textiles, manufacturing, transportation services, and domestic and care work, which offer hardly any social or economic safety nets. Compared to men, women tend to be more active in short-distance migration and engage in domestic work, care services, and other wage works which make them vulnerable to many issues. Long-distance migration is dominated by men, most of whom migrate as individuals (without families), and live in small shelters and in large numbers, with limited access to basic services like water and sanitation. They consider it as a temporary arrangement and maintain social ties and connections with their villages.

As per the Census 2011 estimates, 1,650,771 migrants (3.04 per cent of India's total migrants) live in Tamil Nadu, while 1,985,157 migrants from Tamil Nadu (3.66 per cent) live in the other states of India. Migrants from other districts of Tamil Nadu constitute the major share of total migrants in the state. Among interstate migrants, the neighbouring states contribute a major share, followed by long-distance migrants from the north-eastern and northern states. Compared to other states, Tamil Nadu experienced a steady growth of urbanisation and the emergence of manufacturing-based urban centres across the state, resulting in the distribution of migrant workers across these industrial centres. Initially, migrants from other districts of Tamil Nadu, and later migrants from other states, migrated to these cities.

A survey conducted in 2014 estimated a total of 1.067 million migrant workers in Tamil Nadu. About 27 per cent of them were engaged in the manufacturing sector, 14 per cent in textiles, and 11.4 per cent in construction. They were concentrated in Kancheepuram, Chennai, and Tiruvallur, which together hosted about 51 per cent of total migrant workers in Tamil Nadu. Two other districts, Coimbatore and Tiruppur, known for textile industries, attracted the remaining migrants—12 per cent and 9 per cent, respectively (Philip 2016). A more recent survey of interstate migrants in Kancheepuram, Tiruvallur, and Chennai districts indicated that 85 per cent of the migrants were from Bihar, Uttar Pradesh, Odisha, Assam, West Bengal, and Jharkhand. Nearly 90 per cent of them reported rural and agrarian distress as the key reason for migration. They also reported issues related to the workplace and outside, such as housing and other basic services (Jayapathy et al. 2016). Another survey, conducted in 2013, among migrant workers in Chennai had indicated a concentration of migrants from the north-eastern and eastern states (together accounting for 60 per cent) compared to the northern and southern states. Interestingly, a majority (60 per cent) reported the requirement of lump sum money, and 23 per cent reported better opportunities as reasons for migrating to the destination (Jeyaranjan 2013).

In 2018, India was identified as the country of origin for the largest number (17.5 million) of international migrants and the top recipient of foreign remittance (US$ 78.6 billion) in the world (International Organization for Migration 2019). The pattern of international migration varies significantly across states. The Tamil Nadu Migration Survey 2015 estimated around 2.2 million Tamil migrants living in different countries and nearly 1.3 million return emigrants in the state. In terms of destination, Singapore (0.41 million), United Arab Emirates (0.4 million), and Saudi Arabia (0.35 million) host the highest number of emigrants from Tamil

Nadu. The United States has been the favourite destination for high-skilled emigrants from the state (0.3 million). In Tamil Nadu, one out of ten households has one or more emigrants while 6.1 return emigrants were estimated for every 100 households. Emigration is limited among the men; women constitute only 15 per cent of the emigrants (0.33 million), and most of them live in Gulf countries, Singapore, and Malaysia (engaged as domestic helpers, cleaners, and so on). In 2015, Tamil Nadu received a total remittance of Rs. 618.43 billion (with Rs. 8,500 average per capita remittance) (Rajan et al. 2017). This amount is equivalent to 14 per cent of the state's domestic product, 6.8 times of central government's revenue transfer to the state, and 1.8 times the entire state government expenditure.

Post-Pandemic Challenges

During the pandemic, migrants became more vulnerable due to loss of jobs, the public health crisis, and the unavailability of essentials like food and care. This brought thousands of migrants out into the streets and their precarious lives into mainstream consciousness. Hunger made them pack their bags and take to the road during the lockdown. For migrant workers, access to food matters as much as combating the pandemic.

Reverse migration—migrants returning from cities to villages—had serious implications for India's efforts in controlling the pandemic. Returnees from megacities (the worst-affected areas in the country) ran the high risk of being carriers of the disease to villages in the northern and eastern states, which otherwise had reported only a few cases of infection in the early phase. Allowing millions of migrants living in different parts of the country to reach their home safely (instead of resorting to a sudden, nationwide lockdown) would have avoided exposing them to the virus as well as having to resort to desperate measures such as walking home all the way.

The post-lockdown events highlighted the importance of mobility and the magnitude of the crisis. Many of them highlight the critical role of state governments in managing the crisis effectively. States such as Odisha, West Bengal, and Bihar took some measures to protect migrants (e.g., ensure their safety in the destination states) or initiated efforts to safely bring back their workers. Some migrants remained in the destinations due to the long distance they would have to travel or because adequate support was available during the lockdown period. Kerala opened a large number of community kitchens in the state and arranged supply of essentials and support for migrants to stay back safely.

Tamil Nadu too coordinated with states of origin in arranging transportation for migrant workers stranded in the state. Supply of free food through Amma canteens, supply of essential items, and healthcare support during the lockdown helped those migrants who stayed back in Tamil Nadu. Special trains arranged for transferring migrant workers to the northern and north-eastern states helped a large number of workers in reaching their homes. However, these interventions were not adequate to address the high demand. Hundreds of migrant workers continued to hang out at the transit points, especially in major railway stations, hoping to find some travelling arrangements to reach their homes.

Reverse migration may change the nature of seasonal migration and has implications for both states of destination and of origin. Many of the returned migrants may stay back in their villages for an extended period or avoid long-distance migration in the short run. This may add to the distress in the villages due to excess supply of labour. In the destination states, the sudden withdrawal of migrant workers is likely to result in a shortage of workers. (Shortage of farm workers for harvesting wheat has been already reported in Punjab and Haryana). Presently, the movement of interstate migrants to distant origins has been limited through special trains. However, reverse migration from cities and other destinations is likely to increase once the regular, long-distance train services become operational. This flow will depend on many factors, including the responses of the states of destination and origin, policies of the central government, responses of employers in the destination, and the experience of the migrants.

The excess supply of labour in rural areas of origin states and the shortage of labour in the destinations are likely to worsen the situation in the labour market. At the national level, farm sector growth has been very poor vis-à-vis non-farm sectors. During 2013–2019, the average growth rate of the agricultural gross domestic product (GDP) was 3.1 per cent, which is much lower than the average GDP growth rate of 6.7 per cent. Even this growth in agriculture was driven by non-crop sectors, chiefly livestock. The average growth of the crop sector, which accounts for two thirds of agricultural GDP, was 0.3 per cent, the lowest in two decades. According to the recent (2017–2018) Periodic Labour Force Survey, farm employment fell from 231 million in 2012 to 205 million in 2018, while the construction sector—which used to absorb farm labourers and offer jobs to seasonal small cultivators in the off-season—grew at a meagre rate from 55 million to 59 million (Mehrotra and Parida 2019). These signal the crisis which migrant workers and workers in informal sectors in India are likely to face in the future.

As a state that depends on migrant workers in its key sectors and has witnessed large-scale reverse migration, Tamil Nadu may face shortages of workers in some sectors and interruptions in the production cycle of industries (Shivakumar 2020). For instance, the Tiruppur industrial cluster has been facing severe labour shortage in resuming production after the state announced an end of the lockdown. Even when economic activities and transport systems have been fully restored in the state, the smooth recovery of business will depend on whether the migrants return to their destinations immediately or stay back in their villages for a longer period.

Being also a supplier of interstate migrants (to other states), Tamil Nadu will also see a large number of people returning to the state. On the health front, this may result in specific challenges, especially once regular public transportation is restored. On partial relaxation in air and train services (special services for stranded/emergency care), many people came back to Tamil Nadu. Till 13 June 2020, 1,906 persons who travelled to Tamil Nadu had tested positive for Covid-19, and many of them came from containment areas in other states (Government of Tamil Nadu 2020). Once travel restrictions are withdrawn, the state may face new challenges in managing the large inflow of passengers and the higher risk of infection.

Due to the Covid-19 outbreak, a large number of Indians living in other countries have lost their jobs or face issues in continuing in their jobs or businesses. Once regular air travel is restored, a large number of them—facing challenges to life and livelihood—are likely to return to India, putting more stress on the state. In the short run, people coming from highly infected countries may be potential carriers of the virus. States, including Tamil Nadu, will have the additional responsibility of arranging adequate facilities for quarantine, isolation, containment, and the treatment of suspected and infected persons.

Tamil Nadu reported a large number of Covid-19 positive cases among those who returned from other countries. Even during the restricted period (since 9 May), 200 persons who came in various international flights (till 13 June 2020) were reported as Covid-19 positive in the state (Government of Tamil Nadu 2020). With regular air travel restored, the number of passengers and reported cases is likely to increase. The government will also have to arrange immediate healthcare as well as rehabilitation of returnees who lost their jobs and business.

Policy Implications and Suggestions

The state's transformation—from a predominantly agrarian state into a rapidly growing economy based on competitive manufacturing and services—opened up new opportunities, and it will continue to attract migrants to the state. However, a comprehensive policy on migrants is needed to deal with economic shocks, including the current one. While it is important to make quick humanitarian interventions and take measures to address the emergency, the state should also look for medium- and long-term solutions to shocks like the pandemic, to address the key issues highlighted in this chapter.

Short-Term Measures (Immediate)

1. The absence of a comprehensive and updated database on migrants continues to be a key challenge in addressing migrants' issues at various levels. Lack of adequate identity and residential proofs often result in denial of access to basic services and specific welfare measures introduced for migrants. Therefore, an immediate measure should be to focus on identifying migrants and developing a comprehensive database of migrant workers in Tamil Nadu. The existing registration process may

be supplemented through mobile applications, helpdesks, and volunteers to speed up the process of self-registration.

2. The state can set up a labour helpline, as the Government of Rajasthan did, to be run by civil society organisations, to coordinate and address the concerns of migrants at origin and destination.
3. Once registration is completed, the migrant workers' needs can be addressed. The state can use this database to identify migrants who have decided to stay back, and focus on ensuring adequate supply of essentials (food and basic amenities at residence or camps/shelters) by following the guidelines issued in the context of the pandemic, and providing income support and healthcare (including mental healthcare) during the crisis. The support of civil society organisations and volunteers may complement government's efforts.
4. On the health front, the government's efforts in different parts of the state, to arrange separate places for maintaining physical distance, isolation, and health check-up camps for migrant workers, have been helpful. The government may widen its coverage to new locations and ensure regularity till the pandemic comes under control.
5. The virtual queue and registration system (E-Pass) for facilitating interstate and inter-district movements has been effective in regulating the movement of migrants and short-term visitors stranded in the state. This has also helped people from Tamil Nadu stranded in other states of India, and in other districts within the state, to come back to their homes. Given the alarming rate of infection reported in Chennai and specific areas of the state, the E-Pass system can be used more effectively to regulate movements in high-risk areas to control further spread.
6. The information collected through the virtual queue established for issuing E-Pass can be used for understanding the pattern of migration from Tamil Nadu to other states of India, and the pattern of post-pandemic reverse migration. The government may use this to prepare the economy's key sectors to adjust with the shift in demand and supply of local and migrant workers.

7. The government can consider identifying the key sectors where reverse migration has resulted in shortage of labour and adopt measures to minimise the disruption. The recent announcement of unlock allowed resumption of manufacturing, but industrial clusters, such as Tiruppur, face a shortage of labour. The state can facilitate intra-state movement of labour where necessary.
8. Following the Covid-19 outbreak, a large number of international migrants face issues with their lives and livelihoods, and many have been forced to return to India. Collecting information about them, supporting their return journey, and arranging healthcare support (including quarantine and treatment, as many of them come from highly infected countries) need to be done effectively.

Medium-Term Measures (2–5 Years)

As the current pattern of migration and the disruption caused by the pandemic may continue for a while, states should prioritise their long-term strategies to improve the preparedness to survive such shocks in future, and develop a comprehensive policy to regulate and support interstate migration.

1. The state may focus on developing migrant-friendly social policies that ensure affordable housing, access to social protection and basic services like the public distribution system (PDS), public health, and education), legal and technical support, and financial inclusion. In addition, the state should ensure the portability of access to universal basic services. This could be achieved either through the scheme of 'one-nation, one ration card' or by issuing duplicate ration cards for migrants. The central government has already initiated a 'One Nation One Card' scheme, and its realisation may resolve some of these issues.
2. At the national level, there has been some progress in introducing portability of public services, including access to the PDS. The report of the working group on migration submitted in 2017 recommended that short-term migrants or migrants who move without their household should have access to PDS (Ministry of Housing and Urban Poverty Alleviation 2017).

Since the major portion of the PDS is covered under the National Food Security Act, 2013, the state should not feel a financial burden for the additional cards. If necessary, the state can issue duplicate/temporary ration cards to migrants. Also, the recent relief package announced by the central government puts a conditionality on the state to ensure portability of PDS (Mishra 2020).

3. Tamil Nadu has proposed portable ration cards (family cards) which would allow cardholders to access subsidised food items from PDS outlets anywhere in the state (Jesudasan 2020). In response to the Covid-19 outbreak, the government rolled out this on an experimental basis, but also distributed essentials—both subsidised and free items—to households without ration cards, benefiting many migrants living in the state. The government can extend this portable card facility to other essential services.
4. Like portability in access to services, the state should also ensure the protection and welfare attached to the identity of migrants. Caste is one such social identity. Besides protection from caste discrimination, caste certificates will help migrants enjoy the welfare schemes that flow from central and state governments.
5. The Building and Other Construction Workers Welfare Cess Act, 1996, which mandated a cess (at one per cent of the cost of construction incurred) became the basis for the formation of Tamil Nadu's Construction Workers Welfare Board. While the board has been active in offering relief to its members, its coverage of migrant workers has been very limited. The board may be directed to ensure compulsory registration of migrants who work in the construction sector. A recent news report revealed that the board has spent only 13 per cent of the total fund (Shanmughasundaram 2020). It is imperative to increase not only its coverage but also the content of welfare offered to its members. Similarly, the government should also direct other 16 welfare boards affiliated to the Department of Labour to encourage registration in their respective sectors.
6. Continuing wage differential and better opportunities attract migrants to cities. Therefore, it is equally important to deal with the crisis of rural Tamil Nadu, since many migrants,

particularly intra-state, would have returned to villages in the state. Enhancing MGNREGA and other forms of support through the Tamil Nadu Rural Transformation project may address the concerns of returnee migrants in villages.

7. In the long run, the state should be prepared to face the cost of disruption in the emigration of workers and the inflow of remittances. A policy framework has to be prepared to address the issues connected to a steady increase in the number of returning migrants and their long-term rehabilitation. As many emigrants would have lost their jobs, the government may explore the possibilities of initiating new programmes to absorb these workers, utilising their experience and promoting entrepreneurship among them.

References

Biswas, S., 'Coronavirus: India's pandemic lockdown turns into a human tragedy', *BBC,* 30 March 2020, available at https://www.bbc.com/news/world-asia-india-52086274, accessed on 2 November 2021.

Government of Tamil Nadu, *Media Bulletin,* 14 June 2020.

International Organization for Migration, *World migration report 2020,* 15 October 2019, available at https://publications.iom.int/books/world-migration-report-2020, accessed on 2 November 2021.

Jayapathy, F., S. Crossian, P. O. Martin, and B. D' Sami, *A survey on Inter-State Migrants in Tamil Nadu (Kancheepuram, Thiruvallur and Chennai districts),* Loyola Institute of Social Science Training and Research, and Indian Social Institute, 2016, available at https://tnlabour.in/wp-content/uploads/2018/08/A-Survey-on-Inter-State-Migrants.pdf, accessed on 2 November 2021.

Jesudasan, D. S., 'Tamil Nadu rolls out ration card portability', *The Hindu,* 24 January, 2020, available at https://www.thehindu.com/news/national/tamil-nadu/tn-rolls-out-ration-card-portability/article30637836.ece, accessed on 2 November 2021.

Jeyaranjan, J., *The Life and Times of Migrant Workers in Chennai,* National Institute of Rural Development and Panchayati Raj, 2013, available at http://www.nirdpr.org.in/nird_docs/srsc/srsc-rr-090518-7.pdf, accessed on 2 November 2021.

Mehrotra, S., and J. K. Parida, *India's Employment Crisis: Rising Education Levels and Falling Non-agricultural Job Growth* (CSE Working

Paper 2019–04), Centre for Sustainable Environment, Azim Premji University, October 2019, available at https://cse.azimpremjiuniversity.edu.in/wp-content/uploads/2019/10/Mehrotra_Parida_India_Employment_Crisis.pdf, accessed on 2 November 2021.

Ministry of Finance, *Economic survey 2016–17*, Government of India, 2017, available at https://www.indiabudget.gov.in/budget2017-2018/survey.asp, accessed on 2 November 2021.

Ministry of Housing and Urban Poverty Alleviation, *Report of the Working Group on Migration*, Government of India, January 2017, available at http://mohua.gov.in/upload/uploadfiles/files/1566.pdf, accessed on 2 November 2021.

Mishra, A. R., 'PDS ration cards to be made portable, says Nirmala Sitharaman', *Livemint*, 14 May 2020, available at https://www.livemint.com/news/india/pds-ration-cards-to-be-made-portable-says-nirmala-sitharaman-11589455267628.html, accessed on 2 November 2021.

Office of the Registrar General & Census Commissioner, India, *Data on Migration 2011*, Ministry of Home Affairs, Government of India, 2011, available at https://censusindia.gov.in/2011census/migration.html, accessed on 7 March 2022.

Philip, C. M., 'Tamil Nadu now home to 1 million migrant workers: Study', *Times of India*, 7 February 2018, available at https://timesofindia.indiatimes.com/city/chennai/Tamil-Nadu-now-home-to-1-million-migrant-workers-Study/articleshow/50861647.cms, accessed on 2 November 2021.

Rajan, S. I., B. D' Sami, and S. S. A. Raj, *Tamil Nadu Migration Survey 2015* (CDS Working Paper No. 472), Centre for Development Studies, February 2017, available at http://14.139.171.199:8080/xmlui/bitstream/handle/123456789/94/WP472.pdf?sequence=1&isAllowed=y, accessed on 2 November 2021.

Shanmughasundaram, J., 'Tamil Nadu spent only 13 per cent of workers' welfare funds', *Times of India*, 25 May 2020, available at https://timesofindia.indiatimes.com/city/chennai/tamil-nadu-spent-only-13-per-cent-of-workers-welfare-funds/articleshow/75969817.cms, accessed on 2 November 2021.

Shivakumar, C., 'With business reopening post-COVID lockdown, need of Tamil Nadu's migrant labourers arises', *The New Indian Express*, 31 May 2020, available at https://www.newindianexpress.com/states/tamil-nadu/2020/may/31/with-business-reopening-post-covid-lockdown-need-of-tamil-nadus-migrant-labourers-arises-2150257.html, accessed on 2 November 2021.

14

Protecting Livelihood, Health, and Decency of Work

Paid Domestic Workers in the Time of Covid-19

S. Anandhi and E. Deepa

Covid-19, combined with measures by the government to contain it through lockdowns, has severely affected one of Chennai's indomitable informal workforces—paid domestic workers. Roughly about 1.8 million poor women in Tamil Nadu work as paid domestic workers. Their work is primarily, dually informalised since it is performed in the private informal sphere of the domestic by women who are often invisible as 'workers', in addition to the work being contractual with no employment protection or worker benefits, such as Provident Fund, health insurance, or old-age pension. Paid domestic workers are not covered by the Workmen's Compensation Act, 1923, or by the Contract Labour (Regulation and Abolition) Act, 1970,[1] and therefore they are not entitled to weekly holidays, sick leave, or maternity leave. The minimum wage fixed by the state for these workers is woefully inadequate and has not taken into account the specific nature of vulnerabilities and the intense physical labour involved in this work.[2] Working part-time or full time, or as live-in for 8–10 hours a day, either in one house or in multiple houses, these workers are subjected to various forms of gendered exploitation, with their labour being expropriated without adequate compensation or any work security.

Since the onset of the pandemic, paid domestic workers face crises of employment and non-payment of salary, in addition to pre-existing social stigmas against them. Some of them are forced to go to work amidst the health crisis, risking their life, with no health security. The largest contingent of these women workers belongs to the slums of Chennai—known for inadequate housing and sanitation facilities—and lack the income to meet any health crisis. Under these abject living conditions, they also share an undue burden of the social distancing policy of the state. Keeping in mind the many woes and challenges faced by domestic workers during the pandemic, we suggest, in this chapter, various measures for social and health protection of these workers along with other labour welfare measures that have been on the books for many decades without being strictly implemented.

Challenges Faced by Paid Domestic Workers in the Context of Covid-19

Crisis of Employment

The impact of Covid-19 on women domestic workers has been profound and immeasurable. The first major problem faced by these workers was sudden unemployment, which is no less a threat to their lives than the virus itself. In compliance with the lockdown, many employers requested their domestic workers not to come for work until they were called back (ILO 2020c).This created an enormous uncertainty for paid domestic workers, who began to fear job loss. A domestic worker from north Chennai, expressing this anxiety in her interview with us, said, 'If I stay at home without work, my family will starve. If I leave home defying the lockdown, corona will get me. I dread to think what will happen, but dared to go for work' ('*Uyirai panayam vechuthan velaikku pogiren*').[3]

Some employers shrewdly dismissed these workers just before the lockdown and promised to take them back once the lockdown was eased. However, some of them were not convinced about getting their jobs back. After 21 days of lockdown, a worker in her interview said that much of her trepidation was about her employers who might get used to doing their housework by themselves and not call her back, and what if they too get only half pay, and therefore not pay her salary during the lockdown. 'I am not sure if they will call me back' ('*Yenna velaikku vetchipaangalaanu theriyala*'), was her remark on the plight of unemployment. Several domestic workers in Chennai city did not receive their monthly wages for the 2 months of lockdown. Some of them received only half pay for the month of March and nothing for the following months (Ramakrishnan 2020). A woman who works for bachelors said that her employers paid only half the salary for three months and were also demanding that she be present for work even when she faced the problem of transport. According to her, they were also unwilling to advance a loan for any health contingency. Some workers risked police vigilance, and—putting their own health at risk—went to work so that they did not lose their jobs. They also undertook more work in these households, where the demands of care work as well as sanitation work had increased due to the Covid-19 crisis.[4]

Reverse migration of families, in search of rural livelihood, had forced some of these domestic workers to leave Chennai without a hope of getting back to their work in the city. Our prediction is that due to job loss in other sectors of informal work, with no employment guarantee scheme for urban workers, there could be a huge supply of domestic workers, mainly poor women, seeking jobs for survival. This would not only increase competition among workers but will also reduce their bargaining capacity in terms of wages and other benefits, including their capacity to negotiate their demands for toilet facilities within employer's home or for any other health security.

Low Pay, Liquidity Crunch, and Welfare Crisis

A large proportion of domestic workers are middle-aged, married women—among whom a substantial number are widowed, divorced, or living with abusive alcoholic husbands—with financial instability in the family. These women workers are the main providers for their family, and therefore, encounter the worst situation of liquidity crunch in their homes at a time when prices of essential commodities have gone up and their familiar neighbourhood stores (where they have monthly accounts or loans to purchase household items) are shut for a while. Some of them told us that they could not venture out to borrow money from their employers, or get money transferred though phone banking since they are not familiar with such technologies.

Often, divorced or separated women workers do not have a ration card or a bank account to avail of government welfare schemes during the pandemic.

Pressure to pay rent on time, despite the government order not to collect rent for these months (Revenue and Disaster Management (DM-II) Department, 2020; see also *The News Minute* 2020), had forced many of them to borrow money at high interest. One single woman worker narrated her experience of being harassed by her landlord, 'I am living in a hut, paying Rs. 2,500 per month in rent. The owner has been harassing me to pay the rent, and I had to fight with him for two days, reminding him of the government order not to collect rent by force. Finally, he relented, but it is still like a dagger at my neck.' The state welfare provisions, as many pointed out, are not adequate to meet the needs of the entire family.[5]

Although the Tamil Nadu Domestic Workers Welfare Board has been allocated special relief funds to manage the crisis of the workers during the pandemic, the Board suffers from long years of inactivity, with no proper registration of domestic workers to deliver the welfare schemes. It is estimated that Greater Chennai alone would have 5.5 lakh domestic workers, whereas by 2009, only 64,825 women workers had been registered with the Board. Among the registered, only 17,066 members have received any benefits from the welfare board, and many of them are not even aware of the manual workers' welfare schemes (Tamil Nadu Manual Workers Welfare Board and 13 Other Boards n.d.).

Return to Work: New Challenges

Ever since the slum-dwellers in Chennai were relocated to faraway Kannagi Nagar and Perumbakkam, paid domestic workers living in these resettlement colonies have had to travel a long distance to work at the central parts of the city, spending a huge amount on transport. With the easing of lockdown, these workers were expected to return to work, but many of them have not been able to do so, since their mobility is severely hampered by a lack of transportation facilities. A young worker who lives in Perumbakkam and works in Mylapore expressed his anxiety of losing work due to lack of transportation: 'I do not know what to do. If I do not take up the work when called, the employers might go for other workers, and I stand to lose these houses to work in. I cannot walk such a long distance for work. I am caught in a dilemma' ('*En nilamai, iruthalaikollierumbu madhiri*').

Care Workers or Carriers of Virus?

'Will we go to work with the virus when we care for them?' ('*Avangala paathukira nanga noiyoda velaikku varuvama?*'), asked a worker during our interview with her. With the spread of the virus, the stigma attached to domestic work and workers are reinforced by identifying these workers as carriers of virus (Viswanath 2020). In Chennai, taking into consideration the upper caste–class anxiety about manual workers as being the carriers of disease, many resident associations have barred entry of domestic workers and drivers into their premises. This continues despite the government relaxation of lockdown rules (Radhakrishnan 2020). In cases where they have been called back to work, severe restrictions and surveillance have been put in place, to the extent of denying dignity to the workers. One worker confided that after the lockdown, new kinds of surveillance practices have been put in place at her employer's house, making her feel uneasy and self-conscious about her hygiene status. 'Interrogating me as to whether I keep my house clean and whether everyone at home bathed etc., in addition to the routine washing of my feet with turmeric water before entering their house, have become a new routine, making me feel conscious of my working class status.' Another worker felt that although maintaining hygiene and self-distancing are good to keep the virus away, it should not be used to stigmatise or cast aspersions on the workers. In some residential apartments, domestic workers have been prohibited from using the lift to reach houses. So far, it appears that instructions on maintaining social distancing given to these workers have been used in subtle ways to reinforce pre-existing stigmas against workers who have to risk their own lives, for want of adequate provisions for handwashing, self-isolation, and wearing of masks or any other personal protective gear.

Paid Domestic Workers and Unpaid Care Work

The Covid-19 pandemic has worsened the persistent inequality in the gender distribution of unpaid care work, with all interviewed workers indicating the unusual burden of domestic responsibilities and no assistance from men in doing household chores.[6] This is more so in the case of poor domestic workers, whose low pay and temporary employment have always undermined their capacity to hire paid labour to care for their families, thus adding to their responsibilities of doing paid care work. During lockdown and due to the pandemic, such unpaid care work in their own houses has intensified for paid domestic workers. The absence of day-care centres and schools, and the permanent presence of unemployed men demanding care, along with care for the elderly and increasing attention to sanitation have added to the woes of domestic workers doing unpaid work for their family. In addition, these workers face the everyday ordeals of erratic water supply, lack of transportation, and lack of time to access ration shops, public hospitals, and municipal corporation dispensaries.

Altogether, Covid-19 has exacerbated the crisis of existence for women domestic workers, with their lack of access to labour and social protection, including healthcare and maternity protection, especially when many of them, with reduced immunity, are forced to work even under such life-threatening conditions. Therefore, these women workers are, as ILO observes, likely to be more impoverished and marginalised from income replacement, and from social protection schemes than formal workers (ILO 2020a).

Need for a Coordinated Social and Health Policy for Domestic Workers

More than ever before, in the context of the pandemic, it has become important to recognise the economic productivity of domestic workers and their right to a safe and healthy working environment. The state must take effective measures in this direction. Incidentally, India has not even ratified the ILO Convention on Domestic Workers, which mandates nations to ensure occupational safety and health of these workers.[7]

Given the vulnerability of paid domestic workers, prioritising monetary and health support along with meeting their immediate needs become the responsibility of the state. In particular, the state has to attend to their special needs of sanitation and healthcare, and evolve specific social protection schemes. About ten central trade unions in India have demanded immediate measures from the state to protect the livelihood of vulnerable workers in the informal sector, including migrant workers, and for the inclusion of trade unions in the Covid-19 response task force.[8]

Rethinking the Role of the Tamil Nadu Domestic Workers Welfare Board

In consonance with the demands of trade unions, the Tamil Nadu Domestic Workers Welfare Board may initiate a few consultative processes with trade unions that work for the welfare of domestic workers and include them as part of the task force to address the specific needs of domestic workers. The Board must recognise the specific, gendered nature of discriminations and exclusions faced by these workers during the pandemic, in order to prioritise their occupational health and livelihood issues (ILO 2020b).

Treating domestic workers as essential service workers, supplying them with necessary personal protective equipment, and providing them with reliable and accessible information and affordable health services, are the responsibility of the Tamil Nadu Domestic Workers Welfare Board. Simple measures, like having mobile Covid-19 testing centres placed in various public places where the workers can easily get tested, will help them and the state contain the spread of the virus.[9] In this endeavour they can be helped by domestic workers' unions.

Established in 2007, the Tamil Nadu Domestic Workers Welfare Board offers a range of financial assistance to registered domestic workers, including for children's education, for marriage and maternal health expenses of the workers, death-related benefits for the workers' heirs, and a nominal pension amount. If the Board effectively carries out these welfare measures with the focus on providing affordable or free public health care facilities to these workers, this can enable them to tide through the present virus crisis.

Unfortunately, the welfare board has not paid attention to the compulsory registration of all domestic workers to help them benefit from these schemes. Many domestic workers are not even aware of the existence of the Board. Non-availability of data in the public domain on the actual number of registered paid domestic workers makes it difficult to assess the working of these welfare schemes that would have provided a buffer to the domestic workers who have suffered a wage loss in the midst of shouldering various financial crises at home.

The Board needs to adequately publicise its activities and schemes and evolve new norms and rules for compulsory registration of the workers. At this moment, the Board, with the help of labour organisations and research institutes, can conduct a census for quick reference to ascertain the number of these workers and their well-being. Compulsory registration of domestic workers, employers, and the placement agency have to be made mandatory by the welfare board.

In fixing the minimum wages for domestic workers, the state has overlooked the problem of fixing the categories of domestic work as unskilled labour, leading to low pay for these essential care workers. For example, in a recent minimum-wage notification, cooking, childcare, and elderly care have been categorised as 'unskilled work', leading to low pay for such arduous care work. All these have serious implications for the dignity and decency of work of domestic workers.

Engaged in informalised work, domestic workers are not legally entitled to sickness leave benefits. During disasters or a pandemic, these workers are forced to work, even when they are sick, to maintain their jobs and incomes. Thus, they place their own and others' health at risk. As the ILO has pointed out, in the context of Covid-19, there is a need for a coordinated health and social welfare response to the crisis so that the state can ensure occupational safety, and better working environments for these workers, without discriminations and exclusions (ILO 2020a). To address specific health needs of the workers in times of a pandemic, employers could be made to pay a nominal amount towards an insurance scheme or other benefits for the workers. If the data is used effectively, the welfare board can also facilitate the process of placement for workers and fulfil the need of the employers.

The 'Work from Home' policy, mainly for private sector employees, affects paid domestic workers who work in such employees' houses. Some workers anticipate increasing workloads, with houses multiplying as office space, but with no additional wage for doing any extra cleaning or sanitation work. Some workers expressed their anxiety about working in houses where only bachelors would be working from home.[10] These fears and anxiety of the workers need to be addressed. Extending the laws related to sexual harassment at work to the domestic work sphere, and improving wages for the higher workload would enable these workers to feel safe at work.[11]

With the postponement of school education, the likelihood of young girls being induced into paid domestic work in small towns and in rural Tamil Nadu is worrisome as this amounts to child labour (Kundu 2020).To overcome such a crisis, as suggested by the ILO, providing accessible technology-based educational solutions for vulnerable families could become an important solution to mitigate the problem of child labour (ILO 2020a).

As long-term measures to mitigate the vulnerability of paid domestic workers,[12] the following steps can be taken by the state through the Domestic Workers Welfare Board:

1. Formalise the domestic work sector through mandatory registration of domestic workers with the municipal corporation's divisions or wards.
2. Employers should be made to employ only registered domestic workers, and punitive measures should be taken for violating such norms. As the trade unions perceive such registration to benefit both the employer and the domestic worker, there would be no hindrance for this proposal to gain acceptance in society and not require too much surveillance, either.
3. The registered workers should be entitled to the following:
    - living wage (time-rated or work-specific wages) to be fixed by the labour department;
    - clearly laid out working conditions;
    - guidelines for treatment of domestic workers (most of who are from the lowest strata of society) to prevent abuse, mistreatment, and unsafe work;

- leave, annual bonus, transport, etc. as part of the contract;
- right to associate and freedom to participate in union activities;
- right of access to good public health centres near their homes; and
- right to information related to their welfare provided by the government through the Domestic Workers Welfare Board.

4. The state government could additionally levy tax through municipal corporations to cover the cost of social security and insurance. The money collected from workers, employers, and the additional levies, could form part of a Domestic Workers' Fund. The existing Domestic Workers Welfare Board could be the nodal body for welfare and oversight.
5. Forced savings are to be introduced through cooperative efforts which might enable domestic workers to utilise, borrow, and lend to other women during this kind of a crisis.
6. Housing security should be provided for women workers to avoid eviction threats by landlords, state, and lenders. This is especially important for rural migrant workers who sell their small-sized *patta* lands in the village to buy non-patta land in the city, for a permanent dwelling with little housing security.
7. Displacement of workers within the city—which has huge social, economic, and health costs for the workers—should be stopped. Their social mobility is constrained due to such displacement, which means losing the previous employment and having to commute a long distance for work in the absence of an efficient transport system in the city.

The Domestic Workers Welfare Board can collaborate with Pen Thozhilalar Sangam, Centre for Women's Development and Research (Chennai) and ILO's Decent Work Programme (New Delhi), to

- carry out these welfare measures;
- create a framework or guidelines in the light of the present crisis; and
- look into aspects of laws and their implementation.

Acknowledgements

This chapter offered information and recommendations to enable government and organisations working with domestic workers to ensure dignity of labour and protection to the workers. Some of the suggestions are ad hoc in nature and can be improved along with the changing conditions related to the pandemic. We thank Sujatha Modi (Pen Thozilalar Sangam, Chennai) and Renuka Bala (Centre for Women's Development Research, Chennai) for their valuable inputs on current conditions of domestic workers.

Notes

1. Applying the Contract Labour Act to paid domestic work would have helped regulate this contractual work, since the regulatory requirements under this statute include registration of the principal employer and the issue of licence to recruitment agencies as contractors.
2. In 2018, the Government of Tamil Nadu fixed their minimum wage at Rs. 37 per hour and the monthly minimum wage at Rs. 6,836 for 8 hours of work per day.
3. We carried out tele-interviews with a small number of domestic workers from north, south, and central Chennai, and received notes, on challenges faced by domestic workers during Covid-19, from domestic workers' forum led by Pen Thozhilalar Sangam (for north Chennai) and Manushi workers' union associated with Centre for Women's Development Research (for Greater Chennai Corporation area).
4. The facts provided here are based on our telephone interviews with women domestic workers living in various parts of Chennai.
5. Those with a ration card have received an allowance of Rs. 1,000 along with substandard rice and lentils. This is not adequate for even a small family.
6. ILO observes that prior to the Covid-19 crisis, over two thirds of 16.4 billion hours were spent by women in unpaid care work every day across the world. This has now increased manifold. See ILO (2020d).
7. Article 13, ILO *Domestic Workers Convention, 2011 (No. 189)*, available at https://www.ilo.org/dyn/normlex/en/f?p=NORMLEXPUB:12100:0::NO::P12100_INSTRUMENT_ID:2551460, accessed on 3 November 2021.
8. At the time of writing, the central government has not responded to these demands. See ILO (n.d.).

9. Similar demands have been placed by the International Domestic Workers Federation (2020).
10. One worker who works for bachelor IT workers enters their house after they have left for work, and therefore, she felt comfortable. She expressed her fear that they might make it inconvenient for her to work when they are present without any other woman around in the house.
11. Two legislations concerning domestic workers (Unorganised Workers Act, 2008, and Sexual Harassment of Women at Workplace Act, 2013) are inadequate in addressing specific forms of exploitation peculiar to this work. See Rajkotwala and Mehta (2020).
12. The ILO labour standards on employment, social protection, wage protection, and workplace cooperation already contain specific guidance on policy measures for various sets of workers, such as paid domestic workers affected by Covid-19–related crisis. We have kept that in mind while drawing up our specific suggestions. See ILO (2020e).

References

International Domestic Workers Federation, *Statement on Protecting Domestic Workers Rights and Fighting the Coronavirus Pandemic*, 18 March 2020, available at https://idwfed.org/en/updates/global-idwf-statement-on-protecting-domestic-workers-rights-and-fighting-the-coronavirus-pandemic, accessed on 3 November 2021.

International Labour Organization (ILO), *COVID-19 and the world of work: Country policy responses*, n.d., available at https://www.ilo.org/global/topics/coronavirus/country-responses/lang--en/index.htm#IN, accessed on 3 November 2021.

———, 'Pillar 3: Protecting workers in the workplace', in *A policy framework for tackling the economic and social impact of the COVID-19 crisis* (ILO Brief), May 2020a, available at https://www.ilo.org/wcmsp5/groups/public/@dgreports/@dcomm/documents/briefingnote/wcms_745337.pdf, accessed on 3 November 2021.

———, *COVID-19 crisis and the informal economy: Immediate responses and policy challenges* (ILO Brief), 5 May 2020b, available at https://www.ilo.org/global/topics/employment-promotion/informal-economy/publications/WCMS_743623/lang--en/index.htm, accessed on 3 November 2021.

International Labour Organization (ILO), *Contagion or starvation, the dilemma facing informal workers during the COVID-19 pandemic*, 7 May 2020c, available at https://www.ilo.org/global/about-the-ilo/

newsroom/news/WCMS_744005/lang--en/index.htm, accessed on 3 November 2021.

———, *The Covid-19 response: Getting gender equality right for a better future of women at work* (ILO Brief), 11 May 2020d, available at https://www.ilo.org/global/topics/coronavirus/WCMS_744685/lang--en/index.htm, accessed on 3 November 2021.

———, *ILO Standards and COVID-19 (coronavirus): FAQ—Key provisions of international labour standards relevant to the evolving COVID-19 outbreak*, 29 May 2020e, available at https://www.ilo.org/wcmsp5/groups/public/---ed_norm/---normes/documents/genericdocument/wcms_739937.pdf, accessed on 3 November 2021.

Kundu, P., 'COVID-19 Crisis Will Push Millions of Vulnerable Children Into Child Labour', *The Wire*, 21 April 2020, available at https://thewire.in/rights/covid-19-crisis-will-push-millions-of-vulnerable-children-into-child-labour, accessed on 3 November 2021.

Radhakrishnan, S., 'Residential colonies debate on allowing domestic helps to enter', *DT Next*, 4 May 2020, available at https://www.dtnext.in/News/City/2020/05/04065718/1228201/Residential-colonies-debate-on-allowing-domestic-helps-.vpf, accessed on 3 November 2021.

Rajkotwala, M., and R. Mehta, 'Lockdown woes: The dismal state of domestic workers in India', *The Jurist*, 6 May 2020, available at https://www.jurist.org/commentary/2020/05/rajkotwala-mehta-domestic-workers-covid-19/, accessed on 3 November 2021.

Ramakrishnan, S., 'With no pay, hopes dry up for domestic helps in Chennai', *The New Indian Express*, 18 May 2020, available at https://www.newindianexpress.com/cities/chennai/2020/may/18/with-no-pay-hopes-dry-up-for-domestic-helps-in-chennai-2144681.html, accessed on 3 November 2021.

Revenue & Disaster Management (DM-II) Department, *Government Order G.O. (D) No. 195*, Government of Tamil Nadu, 30 March 2020, available at https://tnsdma.tn.gov.in/app/webroot/img/covid_19/gos/lockdown/G.O.195.pdf, accessed on 3 November 2021.

The News Minute, 'TN govt announces one month rent freeze for workers, including migrants', 31 March 2020, available at https://www.thenewsminute.com/article/tn-govt-announces-one-month-rent-freeze-action-can-be-taken-if-house-owners-disobey-121552, accessed on 3 November 2021.

Tamil Nadu Manual Workers Welfare Board and 13 Other Boards, 'Information Handbook Under "Right to Information Act 2005" (Section 4 of the Act)', n. d., pp. 29–30, available at https://www.

tn.gov.in/rti/proactive/labour/handbook_welfareboards.pdf, accessed February 2022.

Viswanath, K.,'It is time to stop seeing domestic workers as Covid-19 "carriers"', *The Wire*, 27 May 2020, available at https://thewire.in/labour/covid-19-lockdown-domestic-workers, accessed on 3 November 2021.

Section VI

Infrastructure Development

15

Infrastructure Development Post Covid-19

PPP Contracts and Design Issues

P. G. Babu and Chandan Kumar

Infrastructure plays a critical role in the growth and development of any economy. That is why, infrastructure development is necessary, but not sufficient, to sustain a growth path in the long run. Infrastructure development, however, has an immediate effect in the short run too, by generating employment through construction activities. Income generation through employment and backward linkages can lead to higher consumption demand that, in turn, can boost the overall demand.

The literature highlights the following two key empirical observations based on the projections for worldwide consumption and its components, grounded in microeconomic estimates of how spending patterns change as total consumption rises:

- There is a linear relationship between the logarithm of total individual consumption and the share of spending on food; and
- There is a nonlinear relationship between individual incomes and the share of spending on transportation, which along with associated energy requirements, forms a major component of infrastructure.

Given that the first estimated relationship is in line with the received wisdom, let us focus on the second. The relationship is S-shaped; initially it is convex, signifying that the share of spending on transportation increases steeply as income increases, and then it becomes concave, implying that the share of spending on transportation rises less steeply as satiation sets in (See Figure 15.1).

Figure 15.1: Share of Income Spent on Transportation Versus Logarithm of Per Capita Total Consumption

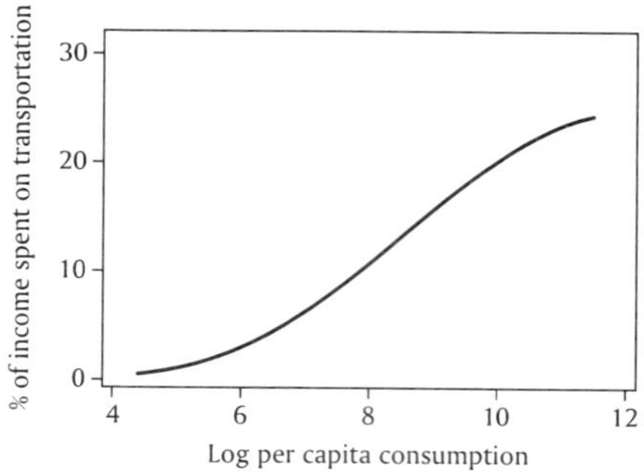

Source: Based on Hellebrandt and Mauro (2015).

One can broadly conclude that developing countries exhibit convexity while richer countries exhibit concavity. Turning to India, in particular, the spending on transportation is projected to increase by a factor of four (compared to factor of three for China). In numbers, that cumulative increase in transportation, as a share of total initial consumption, between 2013 and 2035, is 46.3 per cent (Hellebrandt and Mauro 2015). The expected high growth in transportation expenditure in India for the next two decades would need to be complemented by developing the requisite infrastructure in order to have a larger economic impact.

Within India, Tamil Nadu is among the fastest growing states in the transportation sector. Such a massive increase in transportation would necessitate huge investment in infrastructure.[1] Financing of physical infrastructure has its own issues. It usually requires substantial investments with a high fixed capital and large sunk costs, which gives rise to a 'natural monopoly' and requires economies of scale. Investments in this type of infrastructure usually have long gestation periods, non-recourse or limited recourse to lending, along with various kinds of risks, and are in the nature of a public good (Grimsey and Lewis 2004).

Tamil Nadu's *Vision 2023* for infrastructure development (Government of Tamil Nadu 2012) acknowledges the fiscal limitations of the state, and therefore, encourages private investment through the public–private partnership (PPP) model. The vision plan expects a major contribution of more than 40 per cent from private participation, which is more than the state contribution (i.e., less than 30 per cent) in the total investment on infrastructure. To overcome the recessionary mode of the economy due to the Covid-19 pandemic, Tamil Nadu may immediately focus on restarting construction in the infrastructure sector to complete all the remaining projects under the vision plan.

Challenges of Private Investment in Infrastructure

Relying on private investment for infrastructure development through the PPP model has its own challenges. The PPP model is complex in nature, and the success of this model depends on many factors. Hence, the designing of the PPP programme is crucial for its successful implementation. It needs a supportive institutional system and has to balance various aspects, such as risk sharing, selection of suitable partners, risk pricing or risk premium, government guarantees, incomplete contracts, governance and regulation (a new role for the government under PPP), and contract renegotiations. This chapter discusses a few issues that have been faced by the Indian PPP programme on its highways development, and the lessons from the Indian experience, which can help to improve the designing of an overall PPP framework for Tamil Nadu.

Institutional Support

An effective institutional framework designed to support the PPP model is a prerequisite for its successful implementation. Institutional framework includes laws and policies, transparency and competition in the selection process, and political support and acceptability. Public agencies involved in PPP should have the requisite capabilities of planning and executing PPP projects, along with an effective dispute resolution system in place. Financial markets should also be flexible enough to fulfil the requirements of PPP project financing (Li et al. 2005).

Understanding the Risks

Achieving 'value for money'[2] in the PPP model depends on the identification and allocation of risks appropriately. Who bears the bulk of risks—government or private parties—makes the PPP model different from the traditional procurement method of infrastructure. Allocating risks to the private party, who can manage it better than the other partner, is the sign of better risk management. Failure to do so translates into financial costs, because lower the capacity to manage the risk, higher the cost to handle it and thus lesser the value for money (Organisation for Economic Co-operation and Development [OECD] 2008). However, bearing these risks can have social costs in terms of loss in overall social welfare. These costs can be compensated by better risk allocation that carries powerful incentives to generate substantial benefits through technical efficiency (Moore, Boardman, and Vining 2017).

PPP projects carry a number of risks. These can be classified into two broad categories.

- Some risks are related to projects, and these 'endogenous' risks can be controlled by the project promoters. These risks are considered the driver to achieve efficiency in the PPP model.
- Some risks, like legal, political, regulatory, and environment risks, are 'exogenous' risks (or global in nature), as these risks are beyond the control of the project sponsors or promoters. Improper risk sharing may result in disputes that, in turn, can lead to project failures.

The case of Delhi Airport Metro Express is, perhaps, a suitable example to illustrate it, where the improper risk allocation (along with other factors as well) steered the project into dispute, and later on, led to the cancellation of the project partnership. Therefore, understanding the risks effectively is paramount for the success of private participation in infrastructure (Pratap 2013).

Government Guarantees

A government guarantee is a legal obligation for the government to pay out a known or unknown payment in the case of a specific event.

PPPs often need the support of government guarantees, which carry considerable uncertainty for the government because it remains unclear how much the government will have to pay for the services provided. This uncertainty largely depends on the risk allocation, as more the risk taken by the government, higher the obligations, guarantees, or contingent liabilities the government will have (Mody and Patro 1996; OECD 2008). As the PPP model differs from the traditional method of procurement on the range of risks assumed by government, it would be prudent for the government to take only global (exogenous) risks.

Failure to do so can result in serious implications, both financial and otherwise, as was the case in the Delhi–Noida Toll Bridge project. Here, the government, the sponsoring agency, guaranteed 20 per cent annual returns to the concessionaire over and above its actual costs. That left little incentive for the private partner to control its construction and maintenance costs. As a result, the initial project tenure of 30 years has been increasing—currently over 70 years and may increase further—to recover its complete costs and the guaranteed profit (Pargal 2007).

In the PPP model, guarantees have been seen as one of the modes of government intervention, but it often carries significant fiscal consequences in terms of contingent liabilities arising from assuming the risks (Hemming et al. 2006). Another major issue is the accounting of these guarantees, as it is difficult to measure the exact payment obligations under these contingent liabilities for the government (Grimsey and Lewis 2005).

Contract Design or Choice

The PPP is, in simple terms, a contractual relationship between the government and the private player, and the contract plays a central role in drawing the best out of this partnership. The contract design, therefore, needs special attention to deliver the expected outcomes. PPP contracts are usually long term, which span periods of 15–30 years, and it involves many complexities and uncertainties. It is hard to foresee the future conditions and requirements of a particular service[3] at the time of contract awarding, which makes it difficult to develop fully specified contracts. Hence, PPP contracts, by nature, are incomplete contracts.

In the case of PPP, where each project is stand-alone, private players remain under tight budget schedules of the independent project. Profit-seeking promoters would compel their managers to bring in efficient methods to increase the probability and quantum of profit (Fourie and Burger 2000). It, however, can lead to compromise on quality. A well-specified contract with all the required quality parameters can reduce the possibility of quality compromise. It, however, makes these long-term contracts inflexible. Requisite quality and quantity of service need to be specified in the contract, and payment to the private partner is conditioned to the delivery of that service. Since the contracted specifications (including both quality and quantity) are subject to changes overtime, in such circumstances, the inflexibility and the long-term nature of PPP contracts may bind the government to follow a cost-ineffective way to achieve the desired services (OECD 2008). Or, if it goes for renegotiation, then post-negotiation distribution of benefits depend on the power relation designed into the contract (Lonsdale 2005).

Uncertainties and complexities make incomplete contracts prone to opportunism and hold-ups. Contract theory suggests many implicit and explicit ways to prevent such behaviour. Cases of the Chennai–Tada or the Panipat–Jalandhar highways projects under the National Highways Authority of India highlight the possibilities of opportunism or hold-up–like situation using the complex nature of the contract. Both the projects went through lengthy litigation to force the concessionaires to complete the projects but could not fetch the desired results. Finally, the court passed an order to terminate the Chennai–Tada project. The Panipat–Jalandhar project is still work-in-progress, even after completing two thirds of its contract tenure and taking its share of revenue (Kumar 2018a).

Selecting the Right Private Partner

For the success of the PPP model, selection of the right private partner is as important as appropriate risk allocation. The selection of the private partner usually takes place through an evaluation criterion (also called the bidding criterion). The bidding criterion could be the project cost, contract tenure, subsidy grant, revenue sharing, or something else. To attract the best private players, the bidding criterion and bidding process should be transparent, competitive, and innovative so as to select the most efficient player among the bidders. The synergy between bidding criterion, contract agreement, and institutional set-up is also crucial in order to bring the best out of the contractual relationship.

Lessons from Indian Highways Contracts

In the 1990s, when India was one of the fastest growing economies of the world, it needed strong infrastructure support to maintain high economic growth. Owing to the huge infrastructure investment requirement, Indian policies moved swiftly towards the PPP model to attract private investment into infrastructure development. Its recent plan—Bharatmala Pariyojana—too expects private investment in highways development, though with a relatively lower share of private investment (around 15 per cent) due to issues in the implementation of the PPP programme.

Under its PPP programme (before the Bharatmala Pariyojana), India adopted three different contract models: Toll, Annuity, and Operations & Maintenance (O&M) contracts. However, if one looks at actual numbers with regard to the share of these contracts, Toll is close to 75 per cent of total projects, whereas Annuity accounts for around 20 per cent, and O&M projects are roughly 5–6 per cent.

For the first two (Toll and Annuity[4]) contract models, the contractor is responsible for the engineering, procurement of materials, construction, and maintenance of the project. The key difference between Toll and Annuity is that in the case of Toll, the traffic/commercial risks are borne by the concessionaire, and the investment is sustained by toll revenues, while in Annuity projects, all costs are borne by the government in the form of deferred budgetary payments. In the case of Toll, government budgetary support, if any, is restricted to an upfront grant, while in some cases the concessionaire may even pay the granting authority a one-off fee as part of the concession grant. In the case of Annuity, the concessionaire relies on annuity payments determined by competitive bidding and made out of budgetary allocations spread over time. The third type of contract (O&M) involves only operation and maintenance of the project, and here the contractor bears the traffic or commercial risk; the contractor does not have the responsibility of road construction.

Effect of the Highways Contract Choice

Two sets of contracts (Toll and Annuity), which are designed for the same task and implemented under similar conditions, are different in the contract governance attributes. Under Toll contracts, private players recover their cost from user (toll) charges, hence they bear the demand or commercial risk of the project, whereas in Annuity contracts, the government pays pre-determined annuity payments to recover the investment without any payment risk for the private partner. Another major difference between these contracts is the incentives and penalty given for timely completion. In addition to that, an extra support to mitigate the demand risk (up to an extent) for the Toll contracts is built in. A performance comparison between Toll and Annuity contracts highlights that Annuity contracts that have relatively better incentive structure and stringent administrative controls are better performing than Toll contracts in terms of timely delivery of the projects and minimising the cost overruns. The probabilities of time overrun and cost overrun—and their magnitudes too—are relatively higher in Toll contracts as compared to Annuity contracts, due to tighter budget constraints in the latter contracts (Kumar 2018b).

Impact of Contractual Checks and Balances

Within the Toll type of contracts, India followed two subtypes of contracts. The incentive structure to deliver the project on time differs in both subtypes of contracts. In other words, the risk of delaying the project delivery and its impact on project revenue are allocated differently, but with the same level of penalty. In the one set of contracts, this risk is directly linked to the duration of toll collection, whereas, it is disconnected in the other set of contracts. So, they are called Linked and Delinked projects, respectively. The risk disconnection in Delinked projects increases the scope of opportunism of not delivering the project on time.

Comparing the contract designs of the two subtypes of the toll projects, and analysing the strengths and weaknesses to avoid opportunism or hold-up, it has been observed that the same level of penalty may not be suitable for all types of contracts. Each type of contract should have its own self-enforcing range to make it incentive-compatible, where contracting parties would lose if they breach or disrespect the contractual commitments.

Results from the empirical exercise confirm these findings from an analytical framework. The delinked contracts were adopted majorly for financial reasons, without incorporating much checks and balances in the contract, while giving the rights to collect revenue from the beginning. The low probability of timely completion and longer time overruns in the Delinked projects indicate the possibility of opportunism. A further analysis of Delinked contracts shows how the same set of companies (which have both types of contracts in their portfolio) could exploit the incorrectly-specified Delinked contract to create a hold-up–like situation. It leaves us with an important lesson, as contract theory suggests, that the state should ensure extra leverage for more accountability and better checks (Kumar 2018a).

Winner's Curse and Alternative Bidding Method

The selection of the right partner depends on the selection or evaluation criterion. For Toll model contracts, India followed a premium/subsidy-based method. This bidding method coupled with the incentive structure of the concession agreement can result in overvaluing the projects due to an optimism bias. In this method, bidders have to bid on the basis of long-term expectations, where uncertainties in many parameters are high. By design, only the most optimistic bidder (not necessarily the most efficient bidder) wins, and as the optimism fades away, the winner starts facing trouble, which is called winner's curse. This can put the projects under stress or cause a failure, which is quite visible in the Indian PPP Toll projects.

Compared to the existing bidding method, an alternative method, Least Present Value of Revenue (LPVR), is based on the parameter of total revenue. In this method, bids are invited for the present value of the total revenue calculated on the basis of a discount rate predefined by the authority. The project gets awarded to the least value quoting bidder. The bid winner gets the responsibility of building, financing, and maintenance of the road, against the rights of collecting the toll fee from the users. In this method, the duration of contract is variable. If the traffic growth rate is slower than expected, then the contract period is usually for a longer time than the expected duration and vice-versa. However, the total revenue from the project remains constant. As soon as the concessionaire collects the total revenue (in present value terms) equal to its bid, the contract gets over. It avoids many problems which are quite common and crucial in infrastructure projects. It also helps reduce the complexity of the contract (Kumar 2018c).

Takeaway

Infrastructure development can help Tamil Nadu move on to a faster recovery path by generating employment, and in turn, boost the demand in the short run and also provide the requisite support for its medium- and long-run development goals. With limited public resources competing to fulfil other equally compelling social and economic objectives, the state government may have to look for alternatives for financing its infrastructure. Private financing through PPP model can fill this space, but the state government will have to pay sufficient attention to the checks and balances highlighted here—that are equally relevant to all infrastructure sectors (roads, urban infrastructure, education, health, or others)—in order to draw the maximum out of the PPP option, without compromising on social welfare.

For comprehensive infrastructure development, Tamil Nadu needs to focus on several sectors within infrastructure and prioritise them. Each sector differs from the other in inherent risk characteristics, and hence, one set of policies or framework may not be suitable to all. This would necessitate evaluation of sector-specific risk profiles, because improper risk allocation can result in disputes or project failures. Moreover, the government should be wary of assuming unnecessary risks, as they can translate into long-term contingent liabilities, either for the government or to be borne by the end users. Government guarantees must also be limited to those risks related to government policies.

While deliberating on the institutional framework for the PPP model, contract design or choice is a critical parameter for the successful implementation of the PPP programme for Tamil Nadu. Given the varying requirements of the different infrastructure sectors, one contract choice may not fit all sectors and projects. Hence, each sector would need careful deliberation while designing the contract with sufficient checks and balances in order to make it incentive compatible, where private partners are sufficiently incentivised to carry out the project more efficiently. The contract must have the internal enforcement strength to avoid any opportunism or a hold-up problem. The evaluation criterion for selecting the private partner would also be crucial for Tamil Nadu to execute the projects through capable and suitable private partners. The lessons discussed here from the Indian experience of PPP projects can be educative for Tamil Nadu for better design of PPP framework and its infrastructure projects.

Notes

1. Infrastructure is of two types: (i) human or social infrastructure; and (ii) physical or economic infrastructure. Human infrastructure comprises sectors like education and health, whereas physical infrastructure consists of various sectors, like roads, ports, airports, telecommunications, power, water, and sanitation. Each sector has its own peculiarities and specific challenges.
2. 'Value for money' is the concept used by several public agencies or organisations (such as World Bank, OECD, and government departments) to judge the suitability of the PPP model to provide public infrastructure. Value for money calculates the expected benefits and costs during the life cycle of the project under the PPP model vis-à-vis the traditional methods of procuring the public infrastructure (Grimsey and Lewis, 2005; OECD, 2008). However, there is no uniformity across

the countries or organisations to measure it (Burger and Hawkesworth 2011).

3. For example, it was very difficult to predict in early 1990s about the uses of computerised electronic equipment for toll collections on roads, which helped to reduce congestions and improve operational efficiency. In all the upcoming projects of national highways, the use of these techniques is mandatory.
4. Recently, India experimented with the Annuity contract by modifying its financing structure. In the modified contracts—called Hybrid Annuity Model— the government supports the private partner with the upfront 40 per cent financial contribution of the total project cost during the construction phase, and the rest 60 per cent paid in terms of annuity payments while the project is under the operation period. As this modified model is at its nascent stage, the performance and outcomes of this model will unfold in the future.

References

Burger, P. and I. Hawkesworth, 'How To Attain Value for Money: Comparing PPP and Traditional Infrastructure Public Procurement', *OECD Journal on Budgeting*, 2011(1), January 2011, pp. 1-56, available at https://www.oecd.org/gov/budgeting/49070709.pdf, accessed on 3 November 2021.

Fourie, F. CvN. and P. Burger, 'An Economic Analysis and Assessment of Public-Private partnerships (PPPs)', *South African Journal of Economics*, 68(4), December 2000, pp. 305–316, available at https://doi.org/10.1111/j.1813-6982.2000.tb01274.x, accessed on 3 November 2021.

Government of Tamil Nadu, *Vision Tamil Nadu 2023: Strategic Plan for Infrastructure Development in Tamil Nadu*, March 2012, available at http://www.spc.tn.gov.in/pdfs/TN_Vision_2023.pdf, accessed on 3 November 2021.

Grimsey, D. and M. K. Lewis, *Public Private Partnerships: The Worldwide Revolution in Infrastructure Provision and Project finance*, Edward Elgar, 2004, available at https://www.elgaronline.com/view/9781840647112.xml, accessed on 3 November 2021.

———, 'Are Public Private Partnerships value for money?', *Accounting Forum*, 29(4), 2005, pp. 345–378, available at https://doi.org/10.1016/j.accfor.2005.01.001, accessed on 3 November 2021.

Hellebrandt, T. and P. Mauro, *World on the Move: The Changing Global Income Distribution and Its Implications for Consumption Patterns and Public Policies* (Policy Brief 15-21), Peterson Institute for International Economics, November 2015, available at https://www.piie.com/sites/default/files/publications/pb/pb15-21.pdf, accessed on 3 November 2021.

Kumar, C., *Opportunism and Hold-up in the Incomplete Public Private Partnership (PPP) Contracts* (Working Paper 2018-012), Indira Gandhi Institute of Development Research, March 2018, available at http://www.igidr.ac.in/pdf/publication/WP-2018-012.pdf, accessed on 3 November 2021.

______, *Effects of Contract Governance on Public Private Partnership (PPP) Performance* (Working Paper 2018-014), Indira Gandhi Institute of Development Research, March 2018, available at http://www.igidr.ac.in/pdf/publication/WP-2018-014.pdf, accessed on 3 November 2021.

______, *Role of Bidding Method and Risk Allocation in the Performance of Public Private Partnership (PPP) Projects* (Working Paper 2018-013), Indira Gandhi Institute of Development Research, March 2021, available at http://www.igidr.ac.in/pdf/publication/WP-2018-013.pdf, accessed on 3 November 2021.

Li, B., A. Akintoye, P. J. Edwards, and C. Hardcastle, 'Critical success factors for PPP/PFI projects in the UK construction industry', *Construction Management and Economics*, 23(5), 2005, pp. 459–471, available at https://doi.org/10.1080/01446190500041537, accessed on 3 November 2021.

Lonsdale, C., 'Contractual Uncertainty, Power and Public Contracting', *Journal of Public Policy*, 25(2), pp. 219–240, 2005, available at https://doi.org/10.1017/S0143814X05000334, accessed on 3 November 2021.

Mody, A. and D. K. Patro, 'Valuing and accounting for loan guarantees', *The World Bank Research Observer*, 11(1), 1996, pp. 119–142, available at https://doi.org/10.1093/wbro/11.1.119, accessed February 2022.

Moore, M. A., A. E. Boardman, and A. R. Vining, 'Analyzing risk in PPP provision of utility services: A social welfare perspective', *Utilities Policy*, 48, October 2017, pp. 210–218, available at https://doi.org/10.1016/j.jup.2017.08.008, accessed on 3 November 2021.

Organisation for Economic Co-operation and Development (OECD), *Public-private partnerships: In pursuit of risk sharing and value for money*, June 2008, available at https://www.oecd.org/gov/budgeting/public-priva

tepartnershipsinpursuitofrisksharingandvalueformoney.htm, accessed on 3 November 2021.

Pargal, S., *Concession for the Delhi Noida Bridge* (Case Study), Planning Commission, Government of India, August 2007, available at https://ppp.worldbank.org/public-private-partnership/sites/ppp.worldbank.org/files/documents/Concession%20for%20Delhi%20Noida%20Bridge_EN.pdf, accessed on 3 November 2021.

Pratap, K. V., 'Delhi Airport Metro Fiasco: What Can Be Done to Redeem the Project?', *Economic and Political Weekly*, 48(49), 07 December 2013, pp. 18–20, available at https://www.epw.in/journal/2013/49/commentary/delhi-airport-metro-fiasco.html, accessed on 3 November 2021.

Staff Team Led by Richard Hemming, *Public-Private Partnerships, Government Guarantees, and Fiscal Risk*, International Monetary Fund, 2006, available at https://www.imf.org/External/Pubs/NFT/2006/ppp/eng/ppp.pdf, accessed on 3 November 2021.

16

Affordable Housing in Chennai and Some Notes on Post-Pandemic Prospects*

Karen Coelho and A. Srivathsan

This chapter outlines the dynamics and determinants of affordable housing in the Chennai Metropolitan Area (CMA), drawing on data from a five-year period (2013–2018). It estimates Chennai's housing shortage and housing affordability, outlines the role of state and private players in supplying affordable housing, and discusses builders' responses to state incentives aimed at increasing the supply of low-cost housing. It ends with some comments on the post-pandemic market for affordable housing.

Housing Demand and Shortage

Housing demand and shortage need to be distinguished. Housing demand, often used by housing agencies, such as the Tamil Nadu Slum Clearance Board (TNSCB), to determine the quantum of housing stock to be built under supply-driven schemes, such as the Pradhan Mantri Awas Yojana (PMAY), captures subjectively defined demand for new housing, including by the middle- and high-income households. Shortage, on the other hand, is an indicator more sharply targeted toward need, gaps, and affordability. As per the Technical Group on Urban Housing Shortage, housing shortage comprises four categories of inadequate housing, namely, congested houses, obsolescent houses, non-serviceable *kuccha* houses, and homeless households (Ministry of Housing and Urban Poverty Alleviation 2011). We calculated the housing shortage for Chennai, employing these parameters and using data from the Census 2011 and from the most recent NSSO Housing and Amenities survey (69th Round). Using this approach, the total housing shortage in the Greater Corporation of Chennai (GCC) area was estimated to be 2.99 lakh households, comprising 2.96 lakh congested and 0.03 lakh homeless households. For the CMA, the housing shortage was 8.85 lakh households.[1]

Housing Affordability

Housing affordability is defined by how much a household can spend on housing without compromising on other essential needs. The broadly accepted parameters of housing affordability range from four to five times a household's annual income, as established by the Deepak Parekh Committee Report and the KPMG report, respectively (High Level Task Force of Ministry of Housing and Urban Poverty Alleviation 2008; KPMG 2010). Assuming that for economically weaker section (EWS) and low-income group (LIG) households, the monthly income is equal to expenditure due to a low savings ratio, and using expenditure data from the NSSO's (National Sample Survey Office) 66th Round, we calculated the affordability threshold in Chennai at Rs. 8 lakh to Rs. 10.2 lakh for EWS households and Rs. 16 lakh to Rs. 20 lakh for LIG. In practice, however, state agencies as well as private builders tend to define 'affordable housing' by size, referring to units ranging from 300 square feet to 600 square feet. As we show below, this approach has made most 'affordable housing' produced by the state Housing Board as well as the private sector unaffordable to EWS and LIG households.

Housing Supply

In Chennai, affordable housing is supplied through both the public and private sectors. Public sector affordable housing supply is generated through two state agencies, the TNSCB, which focuses on EWS sections, and the Tamil Nadu Housing Board (TNHB), which provides for LIG, middle-income group (MIG), and high-income group (HIG) households. Over the last five years, the two agencies together have created around 1.2 lakh units of 'affordable housing' in Chennai, of which TNSCB accounts for 1.16 lakh units and TNHB for 4,000 units. TNHB has built 6,045 units of LIG housing (including non-'affordable' units) over the past five years. The prices of these units range from Rs. 13 lakh to Rs. 49.5 lakh, falling far outside the LIG affordability threshold. TNHB no longer offers subsidised housing—the square foot prices of LIG and HIG houses are the same, and are comparable with what the private sector provides. TNSCB housing is the only category that fits the affordability parameters for EWS households. The TNSCB housing stock was created through a variety of schemes, such as the Jawaharlal Nehru National Urban Renewal Mission, the Rajiv Awas Yojana, State Funds for tenement construction and reconstruction of dilapidated tenements, State-specific grants (13th Finance Commission), the Emergency Tsunami Reconstruction Project, and the Housing for All (HFA) scheme under the PMAY.

To estimate the affordable housing stock supplied by the private sector, we have relied on building approvals issued by the Chennai Metropolitan Development Authority (CMDA) and by local bodies in the CMA. The private-sector affordable housing stock is produced predominantly through state regulations. The CMDA, through the previous Development Control Regulations (DCR), mandated that ten per cent of the area in residential projects greater than one hectare be reserved for LIG housing units, with unit sizes not to exceed 45 square metres. Over the past five years, these development regulations have resulted in the production of around 12,200 units in the categories of Special Buildings, Multi-Storeyed Buildings, and Layouts, amounting to around 9 per cent of the total stock. However, since the median price of these units is Rs. 30.2 lakh, a large proportion falls outside Chennai's affordability ceiling. The majority of these residential developments are located on the outskirts of the city, where land prices are lower.

The bulk of residential development happens in the form of 'Ordinary Buildings' (floor area under 300 square metres and height no more than G+1). Although this category does not have a regulatory mandate to provide units for LIG households, it generates a substantial number of small-sized residential units. Our study of approvals from the GCC and three municipalities indicates that small units comprise 22 per cent to 45 per cent of the total stock in these jurisdictions.[2] These figures suggest that a bulk of affordable housing is produced on small plots of land, that is, less than 300 square metres in size.

Private Sector Perspectives on Supplying Affordable Housing

To private builders, the meaning of affordable housing is determined by size, usually under 600 square feet. The private supply of affordable housing, thus, comprises units sold in the Rs. 15 lakh to Rs. 25 lakh range (typically located at the outer peripheries of the city) with an upper limit of Rs. 40 lakh, in sizes ranging from 300 to 600 square feet. Developers note that the goods and services tax's (GST) upper threshold for affordable housing, Rs. 45 lakh, is too high for Chennai where land costs are particularly high, making this price more a base than a ceiling.

Developers identify two categories of affordable housing buyers—income-based buyers who seek low-priced housing for their residential use, and speculative buyers, who invest in an affordable second home at a slightly higher price range, to maintain an income stream from rentals, or for their higher potential for property appreciation. The latter accounts for over 50 per cent of the affordable housing market.

Developers who have succeeded in providing housing in the sub-Rs. 20-lakh range tend to control all operations internally to lower costs. However, this is possible only for larger players who have the capacity to invest the time, energy, and finance to sustain these allied activities. Smaller builders can deliver housing only in the range of Rs. 30 lakh to Rs. 50 lakh.

Affordable housing projects are edging away from the city centre, as land is cheaper on the peripheries. Figure 16.1 and Figure 16.2 provide a picture of the distribution of the stock of affordable housing across different providers and across the CMA geography. Projects have developed along the two key industrial corridors—the Grand Southern Trunk Road and the Old Mahabalipuram Road—to lure homebuyers and renters with the dual benefit of connectivity and proximity to the workplace. Developers also believe that the expansion of the CMA boundaries will lead to an escalation in property prices, and that having a first-mover advantage in this situation is necessary. Finally, developers feel that current state policies and regulations are reactive and myopic in nature with no real consideration for ensuring the long-term supply of affordable housing.

Figure 16.1: Contour Map of Property Prices in CMA (Based on Residential Guideline Values)

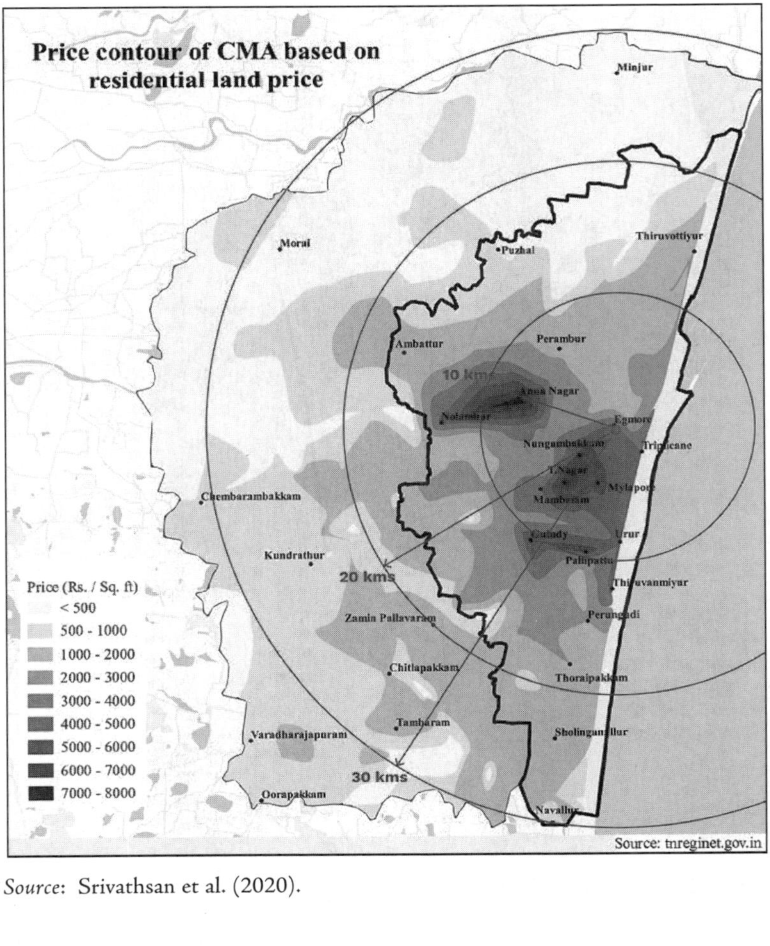

Source: Srivathsan et al. (2020).

Figure 16.2: Affordable Housing Stock (Public and Private Sectors) Mapped onto Price Contours

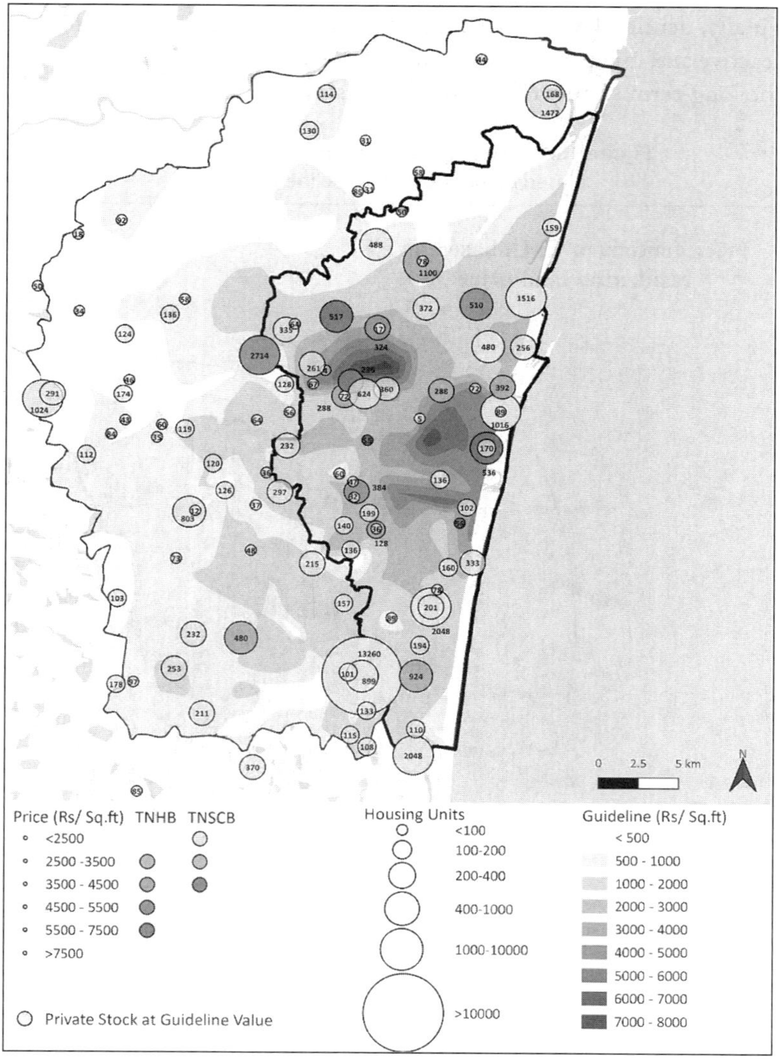

Source: Srivathsan et al. (2020).

Effectiveness of State Incentives to Private Builders

Increased Floor Space Index

Increasing the Floor Space Index (FSI) has had a limited impact on selling price. Although it is widely believed that additional FSI can reduce the cost of land, builders reveal that this measure has had only a small impact on the sale price since land costs are only one component of the total cost. Construction and approval costs and market dynamics significantly impact the sale price. After a certain height, the cost of construction exceeds the cost of land, minimising the benefit of additional FSI. In the case of Special Buildings, developers state that they have been unable to utilise the additional FSI fully due to building-height regulations. Small builders have not utilised the additional FSI as they prefer to concentrate their offerings on units that have a high demand, that is, units sized 700 to 1,000 square feet, with a selling price of Rs. 30 lakh to Rs. 50 lakh.

The Credit Linked Subsidy Scheme

The Credit Linked Subsidy Scheme (CLSS), a component of the PMAY, lowers the financing burden of households by providing a subsidy on the housing loan interest and is potentially an important demand-side incentive. However, developers find that it has had a limited impact in terms of enabling low-income households to purchase a house, for several reasons. First, formal finance is inaccessible to many low-income households as they do not have formal employment and lack the necessary documentation. Second, the current housing market does not cater to EWS households as affordable housing prices start at Rs. 15 lakh. EWS households cannot finance the 10 per cent down payments at these prices. Even with the CLSS benefit, the Equated Monthly Instalment (EMI) to Income ratio amounts to around 54 per cent, which is much higher than the recommended 30–40 per cent. Third, banks and financial institutions charge low-income households a higher interest rate of 14 per cent due to the perceived threat of default and delinquency. Finally, according to developers, banks are typically not interested in providing loans of lower ticket size due to lower commission and interest earnings.

Land Reservation for EWS housing

The previous DCR mandated the reservation of 10 per cent of land in projects over one hectare for the development of 'lower-income housing', defined as units below 45 square metres in size. This ruling has been a failure, as these units have largely been sold to those who could afford to pay for these small units, or have been amalgamated into larger units, rather than being allotted to lower-income households. Developers categorically asserted that a reduction in size does not translate to affordability, especially when projects are located in affluent areas.

Reduction in GST

In March 2019, the GST on affordable housing projects under construction was reduced from 8 per cent to 1 per cent. Although this was hailed as a positive move, developers claim that it would not have a large effect on house prices, as the input tax credit benefit was withdrawn at the same time. Developers state that this would raise the costs of raw materials and construction and would neutralise any price reduction for the buyer.

Challenges Faced by the Private Sector

Private developers listed the following as factors constraining them from providing more affordable housing in Chennai:

Supply of Serviced Land

In the absence of serviced land, developers either incur substantial costs in developing road networks, or purchase higher-priced land along main roads. The provision of deep road networks is particularly important for small builders and developers, as this facilitates access to smaller plots of land, allowing builders or households with limited capital to develop these plots. This in turn can lead to a multi-fold increase in the supply of small and affordable housing units.

Construction Costs

Construction costs form a major component of the sale price. The cost of construction per sq. ft. is Rs. 1,600–Rs. 1,800 for special buildings, and can go up to Rs. 2,200 or more for multi-storeyed buildings, due to requirements for higher quality steel and other raw materials, deeper pilings, and stronger foundations. Developers claim that the poor regulation of the raw materials market has resulted in monopolies, leading to an escalation in prices.

Other Costs

Other costs include costs of approvals, infrastructure, marketing, administrative overheads, and maintenance. All these together form a major component of the sale price. Developers claim that delays in receiving approvals lead to a significant increase in interest costs, as they are forced to pay interest charges even before commencement of construction. Kickbacks also increase the cost of approvals, and these charges are ultimately built into the price of the house. Additionally, developers incur heavy expenses in providing civic infrastructure, as this is not provided by the government on the outskirts. These costs are also transferred to the customers, which alone can account for 10 per cent of the total project costs. Developers also call for a reduction in stamp duty, registration and other mandatory charges for affordable housing projects, as these inflate the price of the housing units.

Incremental Self-Built Housing in Chennai

A third source of affordable housing supply in Chennai is through auto-constructed, 'self-help' housing. The World Bank's interventions in Chennai in the 1980s enabled the large-scale production of these houses through the provision of tenure security, basic services, and loans. They heavily influenced Chennai's housing landscape, creating and upgrading many neighbourhoods through incremental investments by beneficiary households. We studied these processes and their outcomes in three sample neighbourhoods in Chennai.

We found a strong level of overall satisfaction with housing conditions among households in all three neighbourhoods. This derived from three major factors—longevity of residence and spatial inclusion within the city, enhancement and expansion of basic housing in line with household needs over time, and finally, a sense of personal achievement about housing improvements and a long-term commitment to the neighbourhood.

Self-built housing facilitates the emergence of diverse built forms, economies, and cultures of urban settlement. The most positive outcomes in terms of the quality of housing and neighbourhoods derive from three main factors—strong tenure security and property rights arrangements, a strong institutional architecture supporting households in their housing efforts, and access to finance.

Self-help housing did not emerge as the most cost-effective form of housing production in terms of total monetary costs. However, the staggered spending schedules and the option to invest when able make it a viable option for poorer households. The relatively high costs of materials and labour in the informal sector point to the need for more stringent regulation of prices. The role of small contractors in this sector emerged as significant, highlighting the need to bring these actors under the ambit of regulation, familiarise them with building rules and regulations, and connect them with opportunities for technical and skill upgrades in building technologies. Better enforcement of building regulation also emerged as an important condition for promoting safety, liveability, and quality of life in these neighbourhoods. These findings suggest that in situations where the Beneficiary-Led Construction (BLC) projects of the ongoing PMAY mission can be implemented at a settlement-wide scale with infrastructural and financial support, the outcomes will be more effective than the individual subsidy approach in producing neighbourhood-level transformations.

Rental Housing

These auto-constructed neighbourhoods provided a large amount of rental housing. Most of it was informal, affecting the tenure security of renting households. In neighbourhoods where owners had a high degree of tenure security, some formal rental contracts were found. The size and quality of the house played a more important role than tenure security in determining rent levels. Amounts and periodicity of rent increases were uneven. The duration of tenancy was, on average, rather long, typically about 7–10 years. In many cases, rental income was the sole source of income for the owners.

Some Observations from the Study

1. Evidence-based policymaking in housing calls for systematic collection and collation of data, across government housing agencies and through standardised methods, on housing demand and supply, the amount of affordable stock provided in different sectors, and the geography of such provisions. Data available with state housing agencies—CMDA, TNHB, TNSCB, and the Tamil Nadu Real Estate Regulatory Authority—must be integrated and made available for intra-departmental reference and research as well as for policymaking and ongoing monitoring. A quarterly summary of the progress of housing construction in general and affordable housing in particular, as evidenced through planning and building permissions, must be computed. Periodic reports similar to the annual *State of the Nation's Housing Report* published in the United States could be produced.
2. Housing agencies must establish a clear threshold for defining affordable housing based on household income and price. Unit size is a misleading and unhelpful metric. The median household income in Chennai should be used to determine and periodically update affordability levels in the city, regulate land and house prices, and target subsidies. Given that most of the housing produced by the private sector and the TNHB in Chennai is currently unaffordable to LIG and EWS buyers,

housing policies should be reconfigured to increase the supply of affordable housing.

3. Incentives such as additional FSI are not directly embraced by market actors to increase supply and reduce prices. The success of such measures depends on factors such as the status of the real estate market, unsold stocks, demand, and wider economic conditions. Incentives and mandates aimed at providing reservations for LIG households or increasing the supply of affordable housing should be accompanied with clear statements of expected outcomes along with metrics and methods to measure them, and should be regularly assessed for their effectiveness.[3]
4. Increasing the supply of serviced land is key to enhancing the supply of affordable housing. As seen in Gujarat's town planning and land pooling schemes, when a grid of roads is laid, more land is released for development as residential layouts emerge with smaller plot sizes. This also facilitates incremental housing projects. Such small housing projects are often closer to the affordable price range and are a major source of rental housing supply.
5. Many small developers, who are not members of large and influential real estate associations (such as the Confederation of Real Estate Developers' Associations of India), feel that government policies and incentives are not supportive of small-scale projects. Although small developers are the major suppliers of affordable housing, they perceive government initiatives, such as additional FSI, as aligned with megaprojects and big developers. Such incentives are not helpful for small properties as they are unable to consume the enhanced FSI for various reasons. Small builders look for concession in areas such as registration charges in the small property segment and efficient approvals without kickbacks to reduce transaction costs. They claim that these measures will have a tangible and direct impact on costs in their segment. In their view, the lower GST rate for affordable housing priced below Rs. 45 lakh is also not helping much as many projects cannot qualify in this slab given the high cost of land in Chennai. Many builders also concede that not

all incentives given to them are passed on to buyers. Hence the question remains as how to target subsidies and other forms of incentives to benefit low-income homebuyers.

6. Earlier state efforts to support autonomous house construction by low-income households through tenure security provisions and loan arrangements resulted in a substantial supply of affordable housing stock within the city. This self-built housing allowed flexible and expansive uses of the unit, and supported the income and livelihoods of residents. Housing policies should pursue this approach of supporting in-situ self-built housing construction wherever feasible. Policies should include measures to upgrade the skills and capacities of local builders and contractors, and to regulate their prices and practices in ways that would safeguard the interests of poor households.

Prospects for Affordable Housing Construction in the Post-Pandemic Scenario

In the pre–Covid-19 situation, the affordable housing market in Chennai, according to industry reports, was booming: 49 per cent of the launches in 2018 were in the 'Rs. 40 lakh and below' category. Private builders echoed this view while emphasising that a major reason for this was saturation in the premium and high-end segments. More and more developers were adding affordable housing projects to their portfolios, although some developers were sceptical of this segment due to lower margins and the lack of institutional support from financing agencies and the government.

However, these prospects appear to be shifting radically due to the pandemic. Developers are now unsure whether the Rs. 30 lakh to Rs. 45 lakh housing segment will pick up soon. In the post–Covid-19 situation, potential buyers in this segment are likely to be the most affected by the economic downturn, salary cuts, and job uncertainties. This segment has also become more vulnerable in terms of accessing credit. There are cases of existing buyers seeking payment deferments. Thus, effective demand for housing in this price segment may be dampened by market conditions.

Access to credit is also likely to be a problem for builders. They claim that banks are reluctant to offer loans to real estate projects, and when they do offer them, they seek additional collateral. To compound these difficulties, collateral assets are not valued for their current market value but for their distress sale value. Given these uncertainties, it seems likely that the housing market will face poor sentiments and low uptake for another six to twelve months. Market recovery will depend also on how individual developers respond to these conditions.

It is critical to recognise that the private housing market is highly fragmented. The majority of developers supplying housing units at the lower price segment operate in the peri-urban areas. They are highly localised players with limited capital and can undertake only small-scale projects. While access to capital and labour are likely to be challenging in the coming months for all builders, small-scale developers will face more severe impacts.

Small builders who retain a labour force of about 25 members are optimistic that they will be able to manage the post-Covid-19 situation. Their difficulty would lie in securing skilled workers such as bar-benders and carpenters, who come from districts adjacent to Chennai, as restrictions on mobility are affecting the workers' return to their worksites.

Large developers who have long relied on construction workers from other states have a different kind of problem. Many have lost their workers during the lockdown period. Some have retained their workers by holding back the retention amount, and are currently facing requests from workers for payments and travel.

The current uncertainties have placed much higher expectations on government agencies such as TNHB and TNSCB to supply affordable housing. The pandemic has also brought home the pressing need to revisit the designs of public housing. Layout design and individual unit plans have thus far focused on achieving the maximum number of units per site. The current crisis has highlighted the need to focus on aspects of well-being and health. Designs that endow housing areas with good public spaces and amenities that can double up as emergency community shelters would have to be encouraged. TNHB and TNSCB may not have in-house capacities and hence procuring well-designed and built housing projects from the market is an option. By playing the role of an influential buyer, the state can shape the affordable market effectively.

Finally, 'Ordinary Buildings'—G+1 or 300-square-foot buildings usually built by households themselves or by small contractors—accounted for the largest stock of affordable housing in the CMA. This segment may continue to constitute the most promising segment of the housing market, both in terms of demand and supply, in the coming months or years. Casual conversations with real estate brokers suggests that even middle-income buyers are revealing a preference for single-unit homes over apartment complexes. Housing policies in the post-pandemic period may need to turn away from large housing projects and pay closer attention to the small-scale affordable housing sector and its needs as this segment may be where investments and construction activity may be concentrated. For this, the question of urban land, affordability, and effective measures to curtail speculation, are critical.

Notes

* This chapter draws on the report (Srivathsan et al. 2020) of our study carried out in 2018–2019 for the Tamil Nadu State Planning Commission.

1. Due to data availability issues, we calculated housing shortage by taking the entire districts of Chennai, Kancheepuram, and Tiruvallur as a proxy for the CMA.
2. However, we faced significant challenges in accessing data on Ordinary Buildings. Approvals for this category are given by local bodies (town panchayats, municipalities, and corporations), which typically fail to aggregate or digitise this data. We succeeded in obtaining approvals data only from the GCC and a few other local bodies, but the absence of comprehensive data on this category remained a significant gap in this study.
3. For innovative measures attempted in other countries to enhance affordability, along with their applicability for Chennai, see our report (Srivathsan et al. 2020).

References

High Level Task Force of Ministry of Housing and Urban Poverty Alleviation, *Report of the High Level Task Force on affordable housing for all*, Government of India, December 2008, available at http://www.naredco.in/pdfs/report-high-level-task.pdf, accessed on 3 November 2021.

KPMG, *Affordable housing—a key growth driver in the real estate sector?* (Report), 2010, available at https://static.wixstatic.com/ugd/a0851b_8a26ebd71b9f4122bbc618b2f318c3c3.pdf, accessed on 3 November 2021.

Ministry of Housing and Urban Poverty Alleviation, *Report of the Technical Group on Urban Housing Shortage (TG-12) (2012–17)*, Government of India, 2012, available at http://nbo.nic.in/pdf/urban-housing-shortage.pdf, accessed on 3 November 2021.

Srivathsan. A, Karen Coelho, Gayathri Pattnam, Sanchana S., and Shalini C., *Dynamics and Determinants of Affordable Housing in Chennai*. Submitted to State Planning Commission, Tamil Nadu, 2020 (Unpublished).

Section VII

Local Governance and Social Development

17

Role of Panchayati Raj Institutions in Dealing with the Covid-19 Crisis

Kripa Ananthpur

The Context

A pandemic, by its very nature, requires a decentralised response to contain and mitigate it. Local governments or panchayats, therefore, have the potential to play a significant role in containing and managing the impact of the pandemic (Chhibber and Verma 2020; Mahapatra 2020). However, in the current scenario, with the exception of a few states where panchayats have played a significant role in managing the pandemic, other states have not realised the full potential of panchayats.

The historic 73rd and 74th constitutional amendments that conferred constitutional status to local governments led to a three-tiered democratic local government structure. In order to make these panchayats into institutions of self-government, the 73rd amendment mandated that the legislature may devolve powers and responsibilities to Panchayati Raj Institutions (PRIs) to enable them to prepare plans and implement schemes for economic development and social justice, including those listed in the 11th Schedule. While the PRIs have been given a role to play in local resource management, they have not been given any concrete powers in disaster management despite being the first responders. The National Disaster Management Act, 2005, makes a passing reference to local authorities but only the zilla panchayat president is given representation in the District Disaster Management Authority (PRIA International Academy and National Institute of Rural Development and Panchayati Raj 2020).

Status of Decentralisation in Tamil Nadu

Generally, decentralisation advocates, while extolling the Kerala and Karnataka models of decentralisation, have viewed Tamil Nadu's efforts at decentralisation critically. This is because the Tamil Nadu model of decentralisation exhibits a sandwich approach where significant power and authority still rest with the district collectors.

However, a comparison between the 2012–2013, 2014–2015, and 2015–2016 reports that rank states based on the level of devolution shows that Tamil Nadu has made a significant improvement in the cumulative devolution index ranking (Table 17.1).

Table 17.1: Comparison of Overall Devolution Ranking of States Across Three Reports (2012–2013, 2014–2015, and 2015–2016)

State	*2012–2013*[a]	*2014–2015*[b]			*2015–2016*	
	Devolution across states	*Devolution in policy*	*Devolution in practice*	*Ranking of states in the aggregate index of policy adjusted against practice*	*Cumulative Devolution Index (Improved Index + Normal Index)*	
					Improved Index (DP_i)	*Normal Index* (DP_a)
Tamil Nadu	**5**	**6**	**15**	**8**	**2**	**4**
Kerala	3	1	1	1	1	1
Karnataka	2	2	3	3	3	5
Rajasthan	4	7	14	7	9	9
Andhra Pradesh	Not covered in this report	14	20	18	8	11
Telangana		13	17	15	7	5

Source: [a] Alok (2013); [b] Unnikrishnan et al. (2015, Chapter 2: 'Ranking of States in Devolution').

In Alok's index of decentralisation, Tamil Nadu ranks 5th overall and 2nd in terms of how closely it follows the mandate of the constitution (Alok 2013). In the 2014-15 and 2015-16 Tata Institute of Social Sciences (TISS) reports, Tamil Nadu's performance shows significant variation between the two periods. The Improved Index (DP_i) ranking for Tamil Nadu in 2015–2016 is 2 (higher than Karnataka) and the Normal Index (DP_a) is 4. While during 2014–2015, Tamil Nadu scored 6 under Devolution in Policy (DP_o) and 15 for Devolution in Practice (DP_r), thus giving it an aggregate index rank (DP_a) of 8 for policy adjusted against practice, in 2015–2016, the scores were 4 (DP_o) and 9 (DP_r), respectively, giving it a DP_a of 4 (Unnikrishnan et al. 2015, 2016). This shows that Tamil Nadu still lags in the Devolution in Practice ranking aspect of the composite index. It also points to the inherent challenges in measuring devolution. At the state policy level, there have not been any significant changes or measures undertaken to improve devolution. Two reasons may be attributed to explain this shift—(a) the increased weightage given to devolution of finances, which pushes Tamil Nadu's rank higher; and (b) the provision of data by state officials. In the 2014–2015 report, Tamil Nadu scored lower ranks due to non-provision of data.

The Devolution Index[1] mainly tends to be an aggregation of the performance ranking of the three Fs devolved to the PRIs—namely, Functions, Finances, and Functionaries. If we unpack the Devolution Index further along these three Fs for Tamil Nadu, we find a wide variation in the performance in these three domains. Tamil Nadu has transferred all 29 subjects to PRIs. In the 2015–2016 report, Tamil Nadu scored 7th rank in Devolution in Policy and 11th rank in Devolution in Practice under devolution of functions (Unnikrishnan et al. 2016, pp. 58–60). This is because many of the functions devolved are supervisory in nature without concrete powers of execution. Village Panchayats (VPs) have the responsibility of providing basic services, such as roads, electricity, public distribution system (PDS), drainage, and sanitation. Even in some of these domains, the technical responsibility rests with the higher tiers. Experience in devolution of finances shows that Tamil Nadu has been performing well consistently. In the 2015–2016 report, Tamil Nadu scored 3rd in Devolution in Policy and 2nd in Devolution in Practice (ibid.). However, much of the funds devolved are tied grants leaving VPs with limited access to untied grants. Although panchayats are empowered to levy a wide range of taxes,[2] in reality, only a few of these taxes are levied. Lack of adequate functionaries directly working under the control of VPs continues to be a problem in Tamil Nadu. The rank for Devolution in Practice for functionaries reflects this by assigning Tamil Nadu a dismal 17th for 2014–2015. Although the figure improves in the 2015–2016 TISS report to 5 (in Policy) and 3 (in Practice), this is misleading as the functionaries that are devolved to work at the VP level are from the line departments and are not under the control of VPs.

In sum, we can say that although Tamil Nadu may not be a laggard state, it is far from being a model state. Tamil Nadu scores high on devolution of funds and functions but not functionaries.

Current Scenario in Tamil Nadu

PRIs, particularly gram or village panchayats, have been at the forefront in handling the Covid-19 crisis in states such as Kerala, Odisha, and Karnataka (Sahoo 2020).The Tamil Nadu Panchayats Act, 1994[3] (item numbers 139–141) provides VPs with exclusive rights, in case of 'dangerous diseases' to take actions, such as closing of public places of entertainment and ensuring that minors suffering from such diseases do not attend schools. In addition, it also gives the panchayat union councils the right to implement compulsory vaccination programmes in such areas. Hence the VPs in Tamil Nadu have the legal mandate to play an important role in containing Covid-19 by enforcing lockdown and quarantine measures.

In Tamil Nadu, panchayat elections, which were to be held in 2016, were held only in December 2019, in two phases, and in only 27 districts. In nine districts[4], panchayat elections were not held at all. A total of 9,624 VPs held elections out of around 12,524 VPs from 314 blocks in the state during the 2019 panchayat elections. In the rest, panchayat secretaries continued to run the VPs at the local level. This has led to two systems of governance operating at the local level. Post pandemic, it would be interesting to assess and compare the effectiveness of these two models of local governance in managing the impacts of the pandemic. Where elections were held, the newly-elected representatives have had to face the mammoth challenge of managing the pandemic within months of taking office. Unfortunately, the media have not reported much on the ways in which local bodies are handling the Covid-19 situation in Tamil Nadu. But preliminary telephonic survey in some districts of rural Tamil Nadu shows that local governments have been actively involved

in tackling pandemic-related issues. In the initial phase, the VPs in Tamil Nadu were involved in handling the following tasks:

- Creating awareness,
- Disinfecting and sanitising of the VPs,
- Ensuring lockdown protocols,
- Ensuring delivery of essential services, and
- Tracking and tracing cases, and enforcing quarantine measures.

In addition, some enterprising VP presidents also took to distributing masks and personal protective equipment, using their own funds. Traditional methods of sanitisation using neem water and turmeric and providing herbal infusions, such as Kabasura Kudineer, to boost immunity have been tried. Panchayats in Tamil Nadu have been closely working with government departments and district administrations in implementing Covid-19–related programmes, such as the PDS, which offers free and subsidised ration to cardholders, and VPs have been monitoring these programmes at the village level. During the pandemic, the Government of Tamil Nadu provided additional ration through the PDS and a direct cash transfer of Rs. 1,000 per household with ration card (*The Hindu Business Line* 2020). VPs have been ensuring effective distribution of these commodities while maintaining social distancing and providing protective gear, such as masks and sanitisers, to the cardholders through self-help groups (SHGs) (Ashok 2020) and home delivery of ration for the most vulnerable groups. In the initial phase, these efforts paid good dividends with very few cases coming from the districts. However, with single-source-related infections and the Koyambedu wholesale market in Chennai emerging as a hotspot, the infection spread to other districts, particularly to rural areas. The situation has been further exacerbated by migrant workers returning from Chennai, other states, and abroad.

Reverse migration to rural areas has put intense pressure on essential services and rural infrastructures at the panchayat level, such as the provision of healthcare facilities—not just Covid-19-related healthcare but also maternal care and childcare, immunisation, and the Integrated Child Development Services scheme's facilities. Families returning with children need access to education and educational materials, subsidised housing, and access to clean water and sanitation. This has put an enormous pressure on scarce panchayat resources.

There have been criticisms that panchayats in Tamil Nadu are acting as implementing agencies of the government rather than as local self-governments and that their potential has been wasted in the fight (Karthik and Sivarajah 2020). In this context, there is a need for a greater role for panchayats in managing both the infection as well as other impacts related to Covid-19. So how should the Government of Tamil Nadu involve VPs in managing this crisis? Panchayats, as governance institutions at the local level, already have mandated roles to play in several critical sectors of the economy under the Tamil Nadu Panchayats Act, 1994. These should be used as entry points by the VPs in their efforts to manage the pandemic in both short and long terms.

Sectoral Interventions by the Panchayats

With all 29 functions under the 11th schedule devolved, some with direct and others with supervisory powers, VPs in Tamil Nadu intersect with several sectors in discharging these functions. In the context of the pandemic, VPs, in addition to providing basic services to the electorate, will have to assume larger responsibilities through sectoral interventions.

Given the massive reverse migration to rural areas in the short term, VPs are under intense pressure to continue to monitor the Covid-19 situation as well as ensure food, housing, and employment for the returning migrants as well as the current population. The government should focus on some short- and long-term measures to ensure that the VPs are able to manage the situation.

Short-Term Strategies

Health and Managing Covid-19

As mentioned earlier, VPs in Tamil Nadu have the mandate to enforce lockdown of public places and to ensure quarantines in case of any new Covid-19 infections arising within the panchayat jurisdiction. VPs should be authorised by the state government to enforce these provisions strictly in the short term.

- VPs should also ensure that people in high-risk category are identified and provided adequate healthcare.
- Programmes dealing with immunisation and antenatal care should proceed uninterrupted.
- In the short term, since access to public healthcare is limited at the VP level, panchayat union councils may be allowed to partner with NGOs working in the health sector and/or private health facilities (that are already registered under the Chief Minister's Comprehensive Health Insurance Scheme) to provide affordable health services to VPs falling within the respective panchayat union council jurisdiction.

Education

The Tamil Nadu government has been providing free laptops to 10th and 12th standard students studying in government and government-aided schools. This, to an extent, has reduced the digital divide in the state.

- VPs need to ensure that students living within the panchayat jurisdiction have access to online schooling by providing space, such as adult education centres or reading rooms, for the poorest of the poor, and also uninterrupted internet connection at these centres.
- VPs will also need to carry out a census of children in the panchayat area to identify dropouts due to reverse migration or economic distress owing to the pandemic and ensure that they are enrolled back in schools.

Employment and Livelihoods Programmes

Employment and Livelihoods Programmes are a critical domain that requires both short-term and long-term strategies. VPs are mandated to provide 100 days of labour on demand under Mahatma Gandhi National Rural Employment Guarantee Scheme (MGNREGS).

During the initial lockdown, the Tamil Nadu government had provided two additional days of wages to all the households registered under MGNREGS.

- In the short term, the demand for MGNREGS has already gone up. VPs need technical help to come out with innovative ideas that ensure social distancing and safety measures while generating employment through MGNREGS. State and central governments should relax the conditionalities attached to MGNREGS.
- The Rural Development and Panchayati Raj department had instructed panchayats in Thanjavur and Thiruvarur to act as employment exchanges by registering agricultural labourers requiring work and providing such labour for farmers requiring wage labour (Ramesh 2020). Such initiatives should be scaled up.
- Tamil Nadu panchayats have the advantage of SHGs created under the Tamil Nadu State Rural Livelihood Mission linked to them. This institutional linkage between the SHGs and the VP allows the VP to use SHG members for initiating common livelihood programmes at the panchayat level. Dairy, tailoring, and cottage industries like papad- and pickle-making are some common livelihood programmes being undertaken by the SHGs which need to be supported by VPs.

Water Management

In April 2020, the Tamil Nadu government sanctioned Rs. 499 crore for the *kudimaramathu* scheme (*The Hindu* 2020), which is aimed at restoring water bodies in rural areas in association with farmers' associations. The power to maintain irrigation works and the execution of kudimaramathu rest with VPs.[5] VPs should be encouraged to take this up on a priority basis as it provides employment in addition to restoring and improving water bodies.

Agriculture and Organising Public Markets

While VPs do not have any direct role to play in agriculture, the panchayat union council has the mandate to undertake tasks like improving agriculture and agricultural stock. The block-level PRIs can initiate strategies to improve the agricultural sector through VPs. VPs currently have been given the responsibility of organising and managing public markets under the Panchayati Raj Act, which can be used as a platform to ensure regular sale of produce during the lockdown period while maintaining social distancing norms.

Food Security

While the government has taken care of the issue of food security through the PDS, this is an area that will require constant monitoring and long-term strategies to ensure that the Sustainable Development Goal (SDG) 2 of zero hunger is not compromised.

- This requires initiatives that build on the philosophy of the midday meal schemes and provide either free or subsidised cooked food to vulnerable groups, with the help of SHGs through community kitchens or adult literacy centres at the village level, especially for the returning migrant families.
- Tamil Nadu government is also implementing ration card portability so that they can be used anywhere in the state. This provision should be activated at the earliest so that the migrants moving within the state can access ration anywhere in the state.

Increasing Tax Collection Capacity at the VP Level

In the present scenario, the already precarious tax collection at the panchayat level is likely to deteriorate further due to the adverse economic impact of the pandemic on the rural economy. In the short term, the state government must provide access to soft budgets to VPs to take care of Covid-19–related activities, such as sanitisation of the panchayat area and provision of food for vulnerable groups.

Local-Level Planning

However, all these suggested interventions will have to be carried out within the ambit of local-level planning to ensure coherence.

- VPs should be given the authority to amend the gram panchayat development plans (GPDPs) to include Covid-19 activities as well and divert the 14th Finance Commission funds to deal with emergency situations. This is especially important as VPs have limited access to untied grants to take care of the sanitisation needs of the panchayats. Since GPDP is a participatory planning exercise, this would be an effective method to assess the current situation at the panchayat level in terms of loss of employment, food security, school dropouts, and so on. This will help not only in planning programmes to tackle the impact of the pandemic but also keeping track of the losses incurred to progress made in SDGs in the last five years.
- The Government of Tamil Nadu had initiated a data-based planning process called Participatory Tracking (P Tracking) for the Village Development Plan in 2017–2018, which was a participatory, household-level census to inform the GPDP. This database had collected information regarding employment and food security at the household level, among other indicators. In the February 2020 budget, the Government of Tamil Nadu institutionalised the P Tracking method as a way of data collection to inform the planning process at the local level. The P Tracking database, along with the Participatory Identification of the Poor (PIP) list—prepared under rural livelihoods programmes, such as the Pudhu Vaazhvu Project—can be used to help identify the poorest of the poor at the community level for intense targeting.

Awareness Creation

The Department of Rural Development and Panchayat Raj should highlight best practices in Covid-19 management as well as those dealing with issues of food security, hunger, and employment

generation, from Tamil Nadu and other states, and disseminate them to all VP members.

Long-Term Strategies

Health and Managing Covid-19

In the long run, there is a need to recruit health functionaries specifically at the VP level.

Given that this is a contentious issue, the Government of Tamil Nadu can explore the possibility of providing a registry of all retired auxiliary nurses, midwives and other health professionals living within the panchayat union council jurisdiction and permit VPs to hire them during the time of health emergencies like epidemics and pandemics.

Local-Level Planning

There is a critical need to energise the third constitutionally-mandated body—the almost defunct District Planning Committees (DPCs)—to come up with a comprehensive plan for revitalising the rural economy by involving all three tiers of PRIs along with urban local bodies in the aftermath of Covid-19 (Aiyar 2020). Currently, DPCs have become notional entities which are often used for political appointments.

- Membership of the DPCs should be revamped to induct experts and subject specialists to help prepare a comprehensive district-level plan. There is a need to bring coherence to the planning process at the district level and to bring the urban and rural priorities within the context of the district and in line with the state's objectives in the aftermath of the pandemic.
- For instance, the special emphasis being placed on skill development by the states and the centre needs a decentralised approach to assess the gaps in skills requirement at the sub-state level in a coordinated manner. Furthermore, with reverse migration, there is a need to take stock of skilled labourers available at the district level. An apex body, such as the DPC, can facilitate, coordinate, and match the needs with the

requirements of both the urban and rural population and link them with suitable employment opportunities.

Increasing Tax Collection Capacity at the VP level

It is important to improve the tax collection capacity of the VPs, with higher number of functionaries and better incentives to collect taxes. This would ensure that VPs have access to untied grants to take care of local exigencies and are not dependent on government funds.

- In line with the literature on behavioural science and tax collection (Weber et al. 2014), we offer a variation that provides social pressure in a manner that is not pejorative. For instance, the house numbers of all the houses in a habitation or ward should be displayed on wall posters along with the status of their tax payment. Juxtaposed with this message will be the poster detailing the cost required for repairing or providing a service in that habitation. Based on behavioural principles related to social identity and salience, this is expected to generate discussion among citizens and subtly compel defaulters into paying their taxes on time to avail the benefit.
- Local SHGs may also be used for tax collection purpose, thus relieving the burden on the VP secretary.

Development Planning

In the backdrop of large-scale reverse migration, it is now essential to critically rethink the model of development adopted by the state.

- Viewing the pandemic as an opportunity, there is a need to think outside the box. The process of development needs to become decentralised and shift its emphasis from urban to rural areas, from metros to small towns, and particularly to sub-district level as that will be the site where jobs will have to be created.
- Under the district administration, both district panchayats and panchayat union councils have the potential to play an

important role in regenerating the rural economy through their standing committees.

Sustainable Development Goals

It is also essential that the state does not lose track of the SDGs. SDG 3, which deals with health, has had a direct impact on other SDGs like Poverty (SDG 1), Hunger (SDG 2), quality of education (SDG 4), and access to clean water and sanitation (SDG 6) (Shah 2020).

- This 'pandemic pause' as Shibli (2020) calls it, has given us time to rethink, review, and revisit our understanding regarding which SDGs to re-prioritise, but this should not be at the cost of critical SDGs like poverty and hunger.
- Local governments will have to play a critical role in ensuring important SDGs like poverty and hunger are mitigated by collective action at the local level, including government and non-governmental actors along with the civil society by continuing to build on the social capital that this pandemic has generated and energised at the local level.

Notes

1. In addition, the TISS reports include IGT (Infrastructure, Governance, and Transparency) and the 3 Fs (Functions, Finances, and Functionaries) in the calculation of the Devolution index.
2. Village panchayats can levy entertainment tax, advertisement tax, tax on agricultural land, and surcharge on additional stamp duty.
3. Chapter VIII: Functions, Powers and Property of Village Panchayats, Panchayat Union Councils and District Panchayats, Tamil Nadu Panchayats Act, 1994.
4. Reorganised districts of Kancheepuram, Chengalpet, Vellore, Tirupattur, Ranipet, Viluppuram, Kallakurichi, Thirunelveli, and Tenkasi.
5. Item 133 under Chapter VIII: Functions, Powers and Property of Village Panchayats, Panchayat Union Councils and District Panchayats, Tamil Nadu Panchayats Act, 1994.

References

Aiyar, M. S., 'The panchayati front: Tap potential of local self-government to fight COVID-19', *The Indian Express*, 6 May 2020, available at https://indianexpress.com/article/opinion/columns/coronavirus-pandemic-panchayati-front-6395715/, accessed on 4 November 2021.

Alok, V. N., *Strengthening of panchayats in India: Comparing devolution across states*, Indian Institute of Public Administration, April 2013, available at https://www.panchayat.gov.in/documents/20126/0/Panchayat_devolution_Index_Report_2012-13%281%29.pdf/a032c0b1-d29d-f521-481d-ad8e5341ab06?t=1554810195314, accessed on 4 November 2021.

Ashok, S., 'Welfare schemes, well-oiled PDS helping Tamil Nadu's poor', *Hindustan Times*, 5 April 2020, available at https://www.hindustantimes.com/india-news/welfare-schemes-well-oiled-pds-helping-tn-poor/story-HgNMVaFI96sEHS71iU5YHO.html, accessed on 4 November 2021.

Chhibber, P. and R. Verma, 'Not just IAS and police, India's Covid-19 fight must use panchayats and municipalities too', *The Print*, 31 March 2020, available at https://theprint.in/opinion/ias-police-india-covid19-fight-panchayats-municipalities/391730/, accessed on 4 November 2021.

Karthik, D. and P. Sivarajah, 'Local bodies a wasted force in grassroots fight against Covid-19', *The Times of India*, 21 April 2020, available at https://timesofindia.indiatimes.com/local-bodies-a-wasted-force-in-grassroots-fight-against-covid/articleshow/75260915.cms, accessed on 4 November 2021.

Mahapatra, R., 'Panchayati raj day: Pandemic and the panchayats', *Down to Earth*, 24 April 2020, available at https://www.downtoearth.org.in/blog/governance/panchayati-raj-day-pandemic-and-the-panchayats-70674, accessed on 4 November 2021.

PRIA International Academy and National Institute of Rural Development and Panchayati Raj, *Role of Panchayati Raj Institutions in Disaster Preparedness and Management–Lessons from Covid-19 Pandemic* (Webinar), 24 April 2020, available at https://pria.org/knowledge_resource/1589187800_Report_of_PRI_webinar_on_24_04_2020.pdf, accessed on 4 November 2021.

Ramesh, N., 'Panchayat offices to turn into employment exchanges', *The New Indian Express*, 2 May 2020, available at https://www.newindianexpress.com/states/tamil-nadu/2020/may/02/panchayat-offices-to-turn-into-employment-exchanges-2138246.html, accessed on 4 November 2021.

Sahoo, N., *Panchayats and pandemic*, Observer Research Foundation, 25 April 2020, available at https://www.orfonline.org/expert-speak/panchayats-pandemic-65185/, accessed on 4 November 2021.

Shah, R., 'In the post Covid-19 era, an opportunity to build back better', *Forbes India*, 5 June 2020, available at https://www.forbesindia.com/article/coronavirus/in-the-post-covid19-era-an-opportunity-to-build-back-better/59899/1, accessed on 4 November 2021.

Shibli, A., 'Sustainable Development Goals: What to salvage from Covid-19', *The Daily Star*, 20 May 2020, available at https://www.thedailystar.net/opinion/open-dialogue/news/sustainable-development-goals-what-salvage-covid-19-1904155, accessed on 4 November 2021.

The Hindu, 'Tamil Nadu govt sanctions Rs. 499 crore for Kudimaramathu scheme', 24 April 2020, available at https://www.thehindu.com/news/national/tamil-nadu/tamil-nadu-govt-sanctions-499-crore-for-kudimaramathu-scheme/article31419515.ece, accessed on 4 November 2021.

The Hindu Business Line, 'Covid-19: TN to provide financial assistance of Rs. 1,000 to all ration card holders', 24 March 2020, available at https://www.thehindubusinessline.com/news/national/covid-19-tn-to-provide-financial-assistance-of-1000-to-all-ration-card-holders/article31149424.ece, accessed on 4 November 2021.

Unnikrishnan, P.V., K. Sita Prabhu, A. Bakshi, M. Bandopadhyaya, S. Dasgupta, G. Abey, S. Iyer, M. K. Jha, P. K. Singh, and J. Sridharan, *Devolution Report 2014-15: How Effective is Devolution Across Indian States, Insights from the Field*, Tata Institute of Social Sciences, April 2015, available at http://doi.org/10.13140/RG.2.2.13669.50402, accessed on 4 November 2021.

Unnikrishnan, P.V., G. Palanithurai, A. Bakshi, G. Sahu, M. Bandopadhyaya, M. K. Jha, N. Deori, P. K. Singh, S. Iyer, and K. Sita Prabhu, *Devolution report 2015–16: Where Local Democracy and Devolution in India is Heading Towards?*, Tata Institute of Social Sciences, April 2016, available at https://www.panchayat.gov.in/documents/20126/0/devolution2015-16.pdf, accessed on 4 November 2021.

Weber, T. O., J. Fooken, and B. Herrmann, *Behavioural economics and taxation* (Taxation Papers Working Paper N.41-2014), European Commission, 2014, available at https://ec.europa.eu/taxation_customs/system/files/2016-09/taxation_paper_41.pdf, accessed on 4 November 2021.

18

Covid-19 Pandemic and Social Protection in Tamil Nadu

Need to Strengthen a Life-Cycle Approach

Gayathri Balagopal and M. Vijayabaskar

The pandemic and measures undertaken to arrest its spread have thrown into sharp relief the importance of social protection. While the pandemic made visible the importance of public healthcare systems, efforts to contain its spread through lockdown highlighted the insecurities and vulnerabilities of the bulk of the country's workforce.

Tamil Nadu has a long history of commitment to social protection combined with strong economic performance. Using an approach that combines dimensions of promotion, prevention, and protection (Guhan 1994) across different stages of a person's life cycle, social protection measures have played an important role in reducing absolute poverty and inequality in the state.[1]

The pandemic has demonstrated how extreme shocks can not only undermine existing systems of protection but can also have long-term implications for sustaining and expanding human development. Disruptions in access to education, health, and livelihoods are superimposed on pre-existing vulnerabilities. In this context, this chapter evaluates the existing social protection system in Tamil Nadu from a life-cycle perspective, highlights possible impacts of Covid-19 on social protection, and identifies possible interventions to strengthen it both as a response to the Covid-19 crisis and as a long-term measure to achieve Sustainable Development Goals.

Figure 18.1 depicts existing social protection schemes at different stages of the life-cycle in Tamil Nadu.

Figure 18.1: Life-Cycle Stages of Social Protection in Tamil Nadu

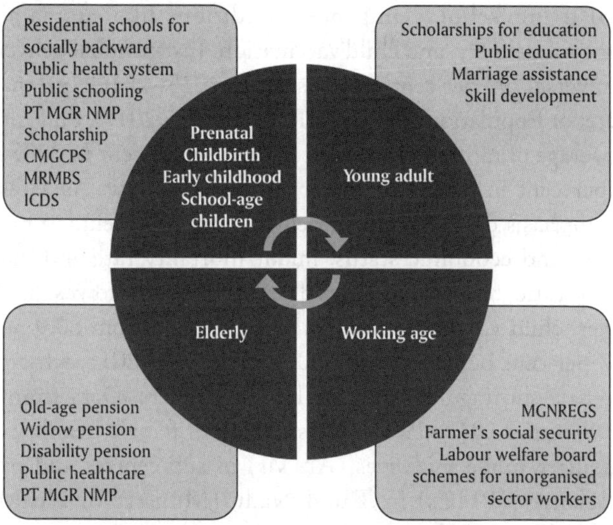

Note: CMCHIS: Chief Minister's Comprehensive Health Insurance Scheme; CMGCPS: Chief Minister's Girl Child Protection Scheme; ICDS: Integrated Child Development Services; MRMBS: Muthulakshmi Reddy Maternity Benefit Scheme; PDS: Public Distribution System; PT MGR NMP: Puratchi Thalaivar M. G. Ramachandran Nutritious Meal Programme; SC: Scheduled Castes; ST: Scheduled Tribes.

Source: Adapted from Planning Commission (2014).

We first discuss social protection systems at each stage of the life cycle (e.g., prenatal and school age) and then examine systems which cut across the life cycle (e.g., health and sanitation and food security). Each section also discusses the possible impacts of Covid-19. We conclude by suggesting short-term and long-term measures to address the gaps.

Protection During Prenatal and Early Childhood

Tamil Nadu has various social protection schemes during prenatal and early childhood. During pregnancy, the state provides universal health services, but maternity benefits are targeted and conditional. The Muthulakshmi Reddy Maternity Benefit Scheme (MRMBS) started by the state government in 1987 comprises cash and in-kind transfers that are given to women who belong to below poverty line (BPL) households and meet conditions like antenatal care, institutional delivery, and child vaccination. Institutional delivery was near universal (99 per cent) in the state in 2015–2016 (International Institute for Population Sciences [IIPS] and ICF 2017). Full antenatal care coverage of mothers increased from 27.5 per cent in 2005–2006 to 45 per cent in 2015–2016 but still remains low. As a result of policy emphasis on institutional delivery, improvements in maternal education and economic status, infant mortality rate and maternal mortality ratio have declined and are among the lowest in India. However, child vaccination has shown a decline from 80.9 per cent to 69.7 per cent between 2005–2006 and 2015–2016, which could be due to a shortage of frontline health workers. Data from *Rural Health Statistics 2018–19* show a shortfall of female health workers and auxiliary nurse midwives (ANMs) in sub-centres and primary health centres (PHCs) in Tamil Nadu (Ministry of Health and Family Welfare 2019).

Tamil Nadu introduced the Cradle Baby Scheme in 1996 and the Chief Minister's Girl Child Protection Scheme (CMGCPS) in 2001–2002 to address the problem of female infanticide and sex-selective abortion. While there was improvement in child sex ratio between 2001 and 2011, there are districts like Ariyalur (897), Cuddalore (896), Dharmapuri (913), Namakkal (914), and Perambalur (913), in which child sex ratios are lower than the national average.

The Integrated Child Development Services scheme was initiated by the central government as an important stakeholder in child development with the objective of improving the nutritional and health status of children in the age group 0–6 years through a package of services such as supplementary nutrition, immunisation, health check-up, referral services, preschool education (PSE), and health education campaigns. In Tamil Nadu, 58.5 per cent of children between 0 and 71 months received supplementary food, 46 per cent received vaccinations, and 56.4 per cent received health check-up from anganwadi centres (AWCs) in 2015–2016 (IIPS and ICF

2017). Furthermore, 58.5 per cent of children in the age group 0–59 months were weighed at AWCs, and 82.6 per cent of mothers whose children were weighed received counselling on food practices. In addition, 50.4 per cent of children between 36 and 71 months received PSE through AWCs. The utilisation of AWCs was highest among scheduled caste (SC) children than among other social groups. In 2018–2019, nearly 13.8 lakh children attended PSE in AWCs, nearly 29 lakh children received supplementary nutrition, and 37.9 lakh children availed vaccination, weight monitoring, and health check-ups at AWCs in Tamil Nadu (Social Welfare and Nutritious Meal Programme Department 2019).

Impact of Covid-19 on Early Childhood

Child Vaccination

The pandemic has diverted the health workforce to Covid-19-related activities, which could further drive down child vaccination.

Sex Ratio

As a result of Covid-19 livelihood shocks, girl children face potentially higher risk of being eliminated by female infanticide and sex-selective abortion.

Anganwadi Services

With the closure of AWCs during the pandemic, routine services provided through these centres have been disrupted. The state government has ordered that home rations should be distributed to all the children enrolled at AWCs. But PSE, counselling of mothers, anthropometric measurement of children, and child vaccination have been stalled. Children's health and early childhood interventions have, therefore, been adversely affected by Covid-19.

Protection During School Age and Adolescence

One of Tamil Nadu's best-known social protection schemes for school children, the Puratchi Thalaivar M. G. Ramachandran Nutritious

Meal Programme (PT MGR NMP), started in 1982, promotes school enrolment, attendance, and nutrition. The government provides stationery to all children in government and government-aided schools, and cash incentives to certain categories. Since 2011–2012, the state government has sanctioned laptops to all students in higher secondary classes in government and government-aided schools. To prevent dropout among girls, the government introduced free-of-cost sanitary napkin scheme in government schools in 2011. Every adolescent girl (10–19 years) who attends school and is out-of-school in rural areas is provided 18 packs of sanitary napkins (six pads per pack) in a year. These schemes coupled with well-developed school infrastructure have resulted in a massive drop in the incidence of child labour. Gross enrolment ratio (GER) was higher among girls than boys in primary, upper primary, secondary, and higher secondary stages of schooling in 2016–2017 in the state (National Institute of Educational Planning and Administration [NIEPA] 2018). Information shows that state intervention has resulted in a more inclusive system, with girls, SCs and scheduled tribes having high GER in relative terms. However, nearly one-fourth of children with special needs (CWSN) were out-of-school in the state, which suggests that there might be transportation, infrastructural, and social barriers.

Impact of Covid-19 on School-age Population

Educational Interruption

A major adverse impact of Covid-19 is school closure and the resultant disruption in education. Table 18.1 displays the enrolment of children in different stages of education, which also reflects the number of children affected by school closure. Nearly 131 lakh children's school education has been affected by the pandemic. In 2016–2017, nearly 1.5 lakh CWSN were enrolled in schools in Tamil Nadu (NIEPA 2018). Due to Covid-19, these children have not been able to attend school. The government has made provisions for home-based physiotherapy services and mobile van with therapy services for special children, while following safety precautions (Department of Welfare of the Differently Abled 2020).

Table 18.1: Number of Boys and Girls whose Education will be Disrupted, by Stage of School Education in Tamil Nadu, 2016–2017 (Actual Numbers)

Stage of School Education	*Boys*	*Girls*	*Total*
Primary	29,04,963	27,41,015	56,45,978
Upper primary	17,13,470	16,89,444	34,62,914
Secondary	11,45,668	11,11,038	22,56,706
Higher secondary	8,56,004	9,63,924	18,19,928
Total	66,80,105	65,05,421	1,31,85,526

Source: NIEPA (2018).

Digital Divide

Children in government and government-aided schools in higher secondary classes have laptops, but access to the internet is not widespread. Unless this is addressed, online classes may aggravate social divides in access to education, as only 18.1 per cent of households have a computer and 19.6 per cent of households have internet access in Tamil Nadu (National Statistical Office 2019a). However, data from the National Family Health Survey (NFHS-4) shows that 94.7 per cent of households in the state own a television (IIPS and ICF 2017), which could be a means to broadcast lessons. Otherwise, the digital divide combined with livelihood shocks among parents could push children into the workforce.

Limited Access to School Incentives

While cash transfers may have not been affected, the closure of schools has prevented access to in-kind transfers like midday meal and sanitary napkins for children studying in government and government-aided schools. In 2018–2019, nearly 49.8 lakh children benefited from midday meal in school. These children have been affected by closure of schools.

Protection to Working-age Population

The state has been a pioneer in constituting social welfare boards with a protective focus for workers in the unorganised sector, for both the self-employed and the casually employed. The aim is to protect against employment injury, death, disability, maternity, and old age.

The state has 17 schemes under the Unorganised Workers Welfare Board for the informal workforce in the state, apart from other welfare boards for workers in specific sectors. Additional cash benefits have been provided to workers during the pandemic period through the welfare boards. There are, however, gaps in both the extent of coverage and the extent of provisioning, and this has implications for informal workers, who are vulnerable to income shocks. In 2018–2019, among the employed, the share of casual workers was 31.5 per cent, of regular employees was 34.6 per cent, and of self-employed was 33.9 per cent in Tamil Nadu (National Statistical Office 2020). This pattern reinforces the need for a stronger social protection net, as nearly all those employed as casual labour did not have a written contract and are mostly ineligible for any social security benefit. Even among regular employees, 78.7 per cent did not have a written job contract, 53.5 per cent were not eligible for paid leave, and 46.7 per cent did not have social security benefits in Tamil Nadu (ibid. 2020).

Impact of Covid-19 on Working-age Population

Livelihood Shock

According to the International Labour Organization (ILO), 82 per cent of informal workers in low- and middle-income countries were expected to experience a decline in their earnings in the first month of the Covid-19 crisis, and 74 per cent of them were expected to experience a rise in relative poverty rates in the absence of any income replacement scheme (ILO 2020a). As a result of the lockdown during the pandemic, workers had not been allowed to go to their place of work except for those who were employed in the health sector and essential services industries. Even when the lockdown was being lifted in a staggered manner, certain sectors remain closed, as those were high-risk categories.

While the information technology sector is amenable to work from home, this is not an option for those in manufacturing, construction, and several services. Data from the Centre for Monitoring Indian Economy shows that monthly unemployment rate in 2020 in Tamil Nadu witnessed a sharp rise from 6.4 per cent in March to 49.3 per cent in April, followed by a decline to 33 per cent in May (Centre for quarantined. If the elderly are reverse quarantined, they are expected to experience severe deprivations, as they lose income from their labour, and their children who would have been out-of-work during the lockdown would not be in a position to support them. Prior to Covid-19, 83.1 per cent of the elderly in rural areas and 79.5 per cent in urban areas received economic support from their children (National Sample Survey Office 2016). The pandemic-induced economic shock could have exposed the elderly to abuse from family members.

Health and Sanitation Protection

Tamil Nadu has one of the better performing public health systems in the country. Consultations and medicines are provided free-of-cost at the point of delivery, and diagnostics are charged at highly subsidised rates. The state's population relied heavily on public health facilities for outpatient (54 per cent) and hospitalised treatment (49.9 per cent) in 2017–2018 (National Statistical Office 2019b). However, data from *Rural Health Statistics 2018–19* show that the public health system faces understaffing of ANMs, specialist doctors, radiographers, and laboratory technicians in PHCs and community health centres (CHCs), and doctors in district hospitals and sub-district hospitals (Ministry of Health and Family Welfare 2019).

In 2018, while 99.8 per cent of households in Tamil Nadu had an improved source of drinking water, 68.3 per cent of households did not treat water before drinking (National Statistical Office 2019c). Besides, while only 15.9 per cent of households in the state had piped water supplied into the dwelling, 34.5 per cent had to depend on public taps for access to drinking water. Only 27.3 per cent of households washed their hands with soap and water before a meal. Furthermore, only 67.6 per cent of households had access to latrines for exclusive use of their household, and 21.5 per cent of households did not have access to a latrine. In households that had latrines, only 60.3 per cent had water and soap. This shows that without universal provision of piped water supply into houses it would be difficult to adhere to Covid-19 norms for physical distancing, as people have

Monitoring Indian Economy 2020). Thus, vulnerable workers acute livelihood shocks, which would have resulted in drastic f consumption. Due to many informal workers not being regis under the state government's welfare boards, they would not received cash benefits to tide over the shock.

Informal Workers and Risk of Virus Transmission at Workplace

Once the lockdown was eased, workers who might show symptom Covid-19 but are not entitled to paid leave would prefer to conti working, which could then result in transmission of the virus.

Protection During Old Age

The Government of Tamil Nadu has social transfers and soc services, which function as a form of protective social security or safe net. The old-age pension scheme for the BPL elderly, introduc by Tamil Nadu in 1962, is an unconditional cash transfer ar currently stands at Rs. 1,000 per month. In 2018–2019, 12.5 lak elderly people benefited from the Indira Gandhi National Old Ag Pension Scheme, and 9.4 lakh widows benefited from national an state widow pension schemes (Social Welfare and Nutritious Me Programme Department 2019). Yet, a large share of the 75 lakl elderly population is not covered under social security pensions Among the major states, Tamil Nadu has the second-highest shar (10.4 per cent) of the elderly population in India, after Kerala There is also an overlap between ageing, widowhood, morbidity, anc disability among the elderly, especially women.

Impact of Covid-19 on Elderly Population

Temporary Removal from Workforce

Due to a lack of universal pension for the elderly and poor access to occupational pension, 43.7 per cent of the elderly population are working in the state (State Planning Commission 2017). As per guidelines issued by the Ministry of Health and Family Welfare, the elderly population were supposed to remain at home or be reverse to collect water from common sources. Furthermore, hand-wash hygiene is suboptimal in the state.

Impact of Covid-19 on Health Services

Disruption of Routine Health Services

Clearly, shortages in human resources can disrupt the routine functioning of public health services, like child vaccination, during the pandemic. Nearly one in four children missed their scheduled vaccination during the pandemic in Tamil Nadu (Narayan 2020). This disruption adversely impacts the poor who depend on publicly-provided services. Covid-19 might not be the last pandemic that the country will witness. Besides, given the possibilities of outbreaks like dengue, chikungunya, H1N1 annually, these shortages will expose the population to a lack of healthcare and expenditure shocks arising from use of private health services. Declining revenues because of disruptions in economic activity will also adversely impact investments in sanitation and public health.

Food Security: Universal and Non-Cash Transfers

While there are suggestions at the all-India level for cash transfers to replace provision of food, events (such as the pandemic) that disrupt supplies highlight the importance of making food available to the vulnerable. Tamil Nadu has one of the best public distribution systems (PDS) in the country. The state's universal PDS contributed to reduction of the poverty gap index (using the Tendulkar line) by 61.3 per cent in 2011–2012 (Drèze and Khera 2013).

Impact of Covid-19 on Access to Foodgrains

Protection Against Food Shocks

As the pandemic has left a large number of workers in the informal economy without an income, universal PDS in the state is likely to have protected them against food insecurity. Issues of access to the PDS by inter- and intra-state migrant workers have also been pointed out.

Suggestions

The pandemic has, therefore, reinforced the importance of universal floors and the pitfalls of targeting. Apart from well-recognised errors of exclusions, and issues with using a definite measure to divide the poor from the non-poor, a major factor that is seldom recognised is that the non-poor may easily fall below the poverty line due to livelihood shocks, as the ongoing pandemic tellingly illustrates. 'Expected' poverty, that is, the extent to which people are vulnerable to fall into poverty, therefore, should become a yardstick.

There are also several examples worldwide about how national governments have sought to provide social protection for workers, particularly in the informal economy, during this pandemic (ILO 2020b). In India, the bulk of the expenditure and interventions are being undertaken by state governments. However, as M. Govinda Rao points out, there has been a reduction in the autonomy of state governments to mobilise resources and a shortfall in transfer of resources by the union government to state governments (Rao 2020). Since social protection is primarily the prerogative of state governments, the resource crunch has repercussions in this area. Furthermore, conditions for borrowing are likely to erode the autonomy to innovate in response to regional conditions.

We now turn to more specific interventions.

Maternity Benefits

For the duration of the pandemic, the state can consider relaxing the conditions associated with the MRMBS and instead transfer the entire cash and in-kind benefit to beneficiaries as soon as pregnancy is detected. After the pandemic subsides, the state must consider transferring the first instalment as soon as pregnancy is detected so that the mother and foetus will get optimum nutrition in the first trimester.

Girl-Child Protection

In 2018–2019, there were only 37,014 beneficiaries under the CMGCPS (Social Welfare and Nutritious Meal Programme

Department 2019). As there is a high risk of sex-selective abortion of females during Covid-19, this scheme has to be expanded in Ariyalur, Cuddalore, Dharmapuri, Namakkal, and Perambalur districts by focussing on blocks which perform poorly on the Gender Inequality Index.

Access to Education and Nutrition

As educational institutions remain closed, if the state has to adopt online teaching, the government must ensure that all children can access online classes. Online classes must be tailored for CWSN. Although all students in higher secondary stage in government schools and government-aided schools have access to the free laptop scheme, students in other classes do not have access. In addition, access to the internet is relatively low in the state. There must be no digital divide based on caste, place of residence, or disability. As an immediate crisis response to school closure and learning interruption, online classes should first be offered to students in higher secondary classes, and then efforts should be made to identify household access to laptops, tablets, and television. As most households in the state have television, classes for upper primary and secondary school students can perhaps be provided through this medium. The local governments can be entrusted with provision of midday meal rations along with stationery, soaps, and sanitary pads to school children during the course of the pandemic. Improving learning outcomes in the medium term too is critical for sustaining human development.

Labour Welfare and Income Security

The ILO has argued that 'as there is little time to design new schemes, successful programmes should be prioritised and scaled up, such as cash transfers, child allowances and programmes used for shelter and food relief' (ILO 2010a, p. 11). In the short run, there is a clear need to enrol more workers, including intra-state and inter-state migrants, in the welfare boards and also to disseminate information among members on the benefits of being a registered member. Using Census of India population projections for 2018 (Office of the

Registrar General & Census Commissioner 2006) and share of casual workers in 2018–2019 from the National Statistical Office, based on rough estimates, there were nearly 90 lakh casual workers in the state. In 2018–2019, there were only 4.4 lakh beneficiaries under the unorganised workers welfare board (Kafeel 2019). Clearly, even before Covid-19, coverage under unorganised worker welfare was just five per cent. The immediate actionable solution is to expand coverage to at least one-third and gradually include a larger share once the state's revenue improves. To be ready for emergencies like Covid-19, occupational safety and health plans, which follow guidelines issued by the health department, have to be implemented in the industrial and service sectors. All workers should be screened at the worksite, should wear masks, and use sanitisers or soap. In rural areas, the government should expand access to the Mahatma Gandhi National Rural Employment Guarantee Scheme and provide work based on demand.

Access to Social Security Pensions

The central government and health experts have advised reverse quarantining of the elderly during the pandemic, which means that elderly will need to be kept out of the workforce temporarily. Although their children continue to provide the bulk of the economic support, it is clear that the state has to step up efforts to include larger sections of the elderly and widows under the ambit of social protection, as their adult children themselves would have experienced income shocks. Using the data collected by Tamil Nadu Women's Development Corporation, the government must extend the pension scheme to the elderly, especially women, who face multiple deprivations.

Staffing of the Public Health System

The state has faced barriers in achieving universal coverage on antenatal care and child vaccination, partly due to supply-side constraints, such as shortfalls in human resources. Shortfalls have to be addressed immediately to prevent disruptions to routine maternal and child health benefits as well as to improve the public health infrastructure. For instance, prior to the pandemic, in 2018–2019 in Tamil Nadu, there was a shortfall of 306 ANMs in PHCs, 181 doctors in PHCs, 1,407 specialist doctors in CHCs, 308 radiographers in CHCs, 581 pharmacists in PHCs, 1,235 lab technicians in PHCs, 713 nursing staff at CHCs, 362 doctors in district hospitals, and 692 doctors in sub-district hospitals (Ministry of Health and Family Welfare 2019). During the pandemic, the government recruited 1,508 lab technicians in government hospitals, 1,323 nurses, and 530 doctors. The immediate task is to fill the shortfall of doctors, specialist doctors, radiographers, ANMs, and pharmacists.

Sanitation

Investment in sanitation is known to prevent diseases among children and adults. Contaminated water, inadequate availability of water in the household and open defecation can lead to adverse consequences for child health, like stunting and wasting. Urgent attention has to be paid to ensure that households get access to piped water supply into their homes and to encourage behavioural change regarding handwashing. The expansion of public works to provide piped water supply will also provide employment. The government must provide soaps and sanitisers along with the relief kit.

From Disaster Relief to Disaster Protection Systems

At present, 'natural' disasters like floods, cyclones, and pandemics are seen as one-off external shocks to the economy and the livelihoods of the vulnerable. But given that such shocks and extreme climate events are recurring, mitigation measures can no longer conceive of such events as rare. For example, the state has witnessed two major floods, three cyclones, and a major drought in the five years preceding the pandemic. It therefore calls for better disaster management systems that emphasise preventive measures. The effects of such shocks on livelihoods are also shaped by urban and agrarian ecologies and the quality of growth. Social protection can, therefore, no longer be imagined independent of the process of development itself.

Acknowledgements

This note draws significantly from the authors' report *Vulnerability, State and Social Protection in Tamil Nadu: A Life Cycle Perspective* (2018). The study was funded by UNICEF. The authors thank Akila Radhakrishnan (UNICEF).

Notes

1. In Guhan's words, promotional measures 'aim to improve endowments, exchange entitlements, real incomes and social consumption', preventive measures 'seek more directly to avert deprivation in specific ways' and protective (also referred to as safety net) measures are 'yet more specific in their objective of guaranteeing relief from deprivation' (Guhan 1994, p. 38).

References

Centre for Monitoring Indian Economy, *Unemployment rate in India*, 2020, available at https://unemploymentinindia.cmie.com/, accessed on 5 November 2021.

Department of Welfare of the Differently Abled, *Detailed report of action taken during Covid-19 lockdown period 2020*, Government of Tamil Nadu, 2020.

Drèze, J. and R. Khera, 'Rural Poverty and the Public Distribution System', *Economic & Political Weekly*, 48(45/46), November 2013, pp. 55–60, available at https://www.epw.in/journal/2013/45-46/special-articles/rural-poverty-and-public-distribution-system.html, accessed on 5 November 2021.

Guhan, S., 'Social security options for developing countries', *International Labour Review*, 133(1), 1994, pp. 35–53, available at https://heinonline.org/HOL/LandingPage?handle=hein.journals/intlr133&div=11&id=&page=, accessed on 5 November 2021.

International Institute for Population Sciences (IIPS) and ICF, *National family health survey (NFHS-4) 2015–16: India*, International Institute for Population Sciences, 2017, available at http://rchiips.org/nfhs/NFHS-4Reports/India.pdf, accessed on 5 November 2021.

International Labour Organization (ILO), *COVID-19 and the world of work* (3rd ed.) (ILO Monitor), 29 April 2020a, available at https://www.ilo.org/wcmsp5/groups/public/@dgreports/@dcomm/documents/briefingnote/wcms_743146.pdf, accessed on 5 November 2021.

______, *Social protection responses to the COVID-19 pandemic in developing countries: Strengthening resilience by building universal social protection* (ILO Brief), May 2020b, available at https://www.ilo.org/wcmsp5/groups/public/---ed_protect/---soc_sec/documents/publication/wcms_744612.pdf, accessed on 5 November 2021.

Kafeel, N., *Policy note 2019–2020 (Demand Note 32)*, Labour and Employment Department, Government of Tamil Nadu, available at http://cms.tn.gov.in/sites/default/files/documents/labemp_e_pn_2019_20.pdf, accessed on 5 November 2021.

Ministry of Health and Family Welfare, *Rural Health Statistics 2018–19*, Government of India, 2019, available at https://main.mohfw.gov.in/sites/default/files/Final%20RHS%202018-19_0.pdf, accessed on 5 November 2021.

Narayan, P., 'Vaccination rate dips in Tamil Nadu, threat of infections up', *Times of India*, 9 May 2020, available at https://timesofindia.indiatimes.com/city/chennai/vaccination-rate-dips-in-tn-threat-of-infections-up/articleshow/75637005.cms, accessed on 5 November 2021.

National Institute of Educational Planning and Administration (NIEPA), *School Education in India: U-DISE Flash Statistics 2016–17*, 2018, available at http://udise.in/Downloads/Publications/Documents/Flash_Statistics_on_School_Education-2016-17.pdf, accessed on 5 November 2021.

National Sample Survey Office, *Health in India: NSS 71st round (January–June 2014)* (Report No. 574), Ministry of Statistics and Programme Implementation, Government of India, April 2016, available at http://mospi.nic.in/sites/default/files/publication_reports/nss_rep574.pdf, accessed on 5 November 2021.

National Statistical Office, *Key indicators of household social consumption on education in India: NSS 75th round (July 2017–June 2018)*, Ministry of Statistics and Programme Implementation, Government of India, November 2019a, available at http://mospi.nic.in/sites/default/files/publication_reports/KI_Education_75th_Final.pdf, accessed on 5 November 2021.

National Statistical Office, *Key indicators of social consumption in India: Health, NSS 75th round (July 2017–June 2018)*, Ministry of Statistics and Programme Implementation, Government of India, November 2019b, available at http://mospi.nic.in/sites/default/files/publication_reports/KI_Health_75th_Final.pdf, accessed on 5 November 2021.

———, *Drinking water, sanitation, hygiene and housing condition in India, NSS 76th round (July–December 2018) (Report No. 584)*, Ministry of Statistics and Programme Implementation, Government of India, 2019c, available at http://mospi.nic.in/sites/default/files/NSS7612dws/Report_584_final.pdf, accessed on 5 November 2021.

———, *Annual report, Periodic labour force survey (PLFS), 2018–19*, Ministry of Statistics and Programme Implementation, Government of India, June 2020, available at http://mospi.nic.in/sites/default/files/publication_reports/Annual_Report_PLFS_2018_19_HL.pdf, accessed on 5 November 2021.

Office of the Registrar General & Census Commissioner, India, *Census of India, Population Projections for India and States, 2001-2026*, Ministry of Home Affairs, Government of India, 2006, available at http://statehealthsocietybihar.org/survey_reports/Population_Projection_Report_2006.pdf , accessed on 15 March 2022.

Planning Commission, *National Social Protection Strategy (NSPS) of Bangladesh*, Government of the People's Republic of Bangladesh, 26 January 2014, available at http://socialprotection.gov.bd/wp-content/uploads/2016/08/NSPS.pdf, accessed on 5 November 2021.

Rao, M. G. 'States' Loss of Fiscal Autonomy in a Centralised Federal System', *The India Forum*, 5 June 2020, available at https://www.theindiaforum.in/article/states-loss-fiscal-autonomy-centralised-federal-system, accessed on 5 November 2021.

Social Welfare and Nutritious Meal Programme Department, *Performance budget 2019–2020*, Government of Tamil Nadu, 2019, available at http://cms.tn.gov.in/sites/default/files/documents/swnmp_e_pb_2019_2020.pdf, accessed on 5 November 2021.

State Planning Commission, *Tamil Nadu Human Development Report 2017*, Government of Tamil Nadu and Academic Foundation, 2017, available at http://www.spc.tn.gov.in/tnhdr2017.html, accessed on 5 November 2021.

19

Food Security in the Covid-19 Era

Umanath Malaiarasan

Natural disasters and calamities have greatly impacted the human race in multiple ways in the past, causing colossal loss of life and property, collapse of societal functions, stress, economic crisis, and environmental degradation, though the misery inflicted by such catastrophes throughout the ages have not have been equally felt by all sections of society. Needless to say, the poor and the disadvantaged—rather than the rich—continue to bear the brunt of calamities, like climate change, that the world is confronted with, and the resultant economic and food crises that follow (Balasubramanian 2018).

At present, the Covid-19 outbreak and the consequent lockdown have crippled socio-economic activities, depriving poor people of their livelihood and cultural space. The global economy has taken a severe beating following the onset of the pandemic and the attendant stringent containment measures for six to seven months in the United States, the European Union, India, China, and elsewhere. This has had a debilitating effect on the labour force, especially those in the unorganised sector, drawn mostly from marginalised sections of society. These vulnerable communities have been drastically affected in terms of loss of employment, loss of income, and a lack of adequate food consumption.

Lockdown and the Most Vulnerable

In India, the more-than-three-month-long nationwide curfew intended to contain the pandemic brought to a standstill all social and economic activities. Not only children and the elderly, all working people remained homebound. There was an exodus from the cities by migrants, who marched in thousands towards their native villages, with little or inadequate cash reserves in their hands. It is still not certain whether they will all return to the cities even after the pandemic is over. While it is true that the extended lockdown has helped in arresting the furious spread of the virus to a certain extent, it has disrupted the livelihood of ordinary and daily-wage workers in rural as well as urban regions.

Workers in the informal sector are mostly daily-wage earners, who are less likely to have formal work arrangements, decent working conditions, and adequate social security. Furthermore, since they remain voiceless and without any effective representation by trade unions or similar organisations, they are the most vulnerable to economic shocks arising out of the Covid-19 pandemic. Let alone job security, they do not have any kind of statutory benefits, such as insurance cover and provident fund from the employers, and may not have lump-sum personal savings. For instance, migrants account for more than 70 per cent of the workforce engaged in non-agricultural sectors, and mostly they do not have any written job contract. Worse, 55 per cent of them are not eligible for paid leave while 50 per cent do not have any social security benefits (Ministry of Statistics and Programme Implementation 2019). The informal sector in the country employs 415 million workers, which is about 90 per cent of the total workforce (Jha 2016). It covers millions of small and marginal farmers, agricultural labourers, construction and road workers, shepherds, fisher folk, weavers and artisans, forest gatherers, workers in manufacturing (factories and workshops), housemaids, street vendors, transport workers, hairdressers, and waste collectors (Chen 2020). Once the lockdown was announced, all these workers have been rendered unemployed, which has resulted in a complete loss of income, leading to reduction in affordability and accessibility of food items. Estimates indicate that the income of such workers decreased by 22 per cent in the first month of the pandemic spread, resulting in increased poverty rate from 22 per cent to 36 per cent (International Labour Organization 2020; Kim et al. 2020).

Studies indicate that the working class, the poor, and the marginalised communities would be the hardest hit by Covid-19

(Evelyn 2020; Galea 2020). Ringing alarm bells, the United Nations World Food Programme (WFP) has also warned that the number of people facing food crises across world could double by the end of 2020. A study (Sabarwal et al. n.d.) had given a disturbing forecast that any economic crisis could claim 2.4 lakh infant deaths in developing countries. This pandemic has not left women and children untouched. Women and children in poorer families are more likely to suffer from lack of food and malnutrition, as the containment steps are expected to result in less care for children and women, given the necessity to divert resources towards health-related concerns and the emergency response both at a household and at national levels (Wenham et al. 2020). Similar problems have been reported during previous epidemics, including the Ebola outbreak in West Africa (Korkoya and Wreh 2015; Sochas et al. 2017). It was also noted that women are the major contributors to the total family income in the households of the poorest of poor.

Covid-19, Food Supply Chain, and Dietary Pattern

Coming close on the heels of an economic slowdown, the pandemic and the continuing lockdown in many states have caused a food crisis. On the supply side, there is a collapse of the food supply chain right from the local market to the international trade arena. For instance, farmers and traders are unable to move food products from the farmlands to the ultimate consumer in view of the many obstacles, including barriers on movement of labour and vehicles even at local and regional levels. Along with restrictions on movement, the limited demand for food items from households, hotels, and restaurants have dampened the current harvest season as well as the sowing or planting operations for the upcoming cropping season.

Given this grim reality, agricultural activities have shrunk as farmers are not ready to burn their fingers. As an immediate consequence of this, we might witness a shortage in the regular supply of food products in terms of variety and quantity, which might turn acute in the post–Covid-19 period. As almost all countries are affected by Covid-19, there are already difficulties in the import of food products (Glauber 2020; Seleiman et al. 2020), especially pulses and edible oils in India. According to the Solvent Extractors' Association of India, the total edible oil imports in April 2020 decreased about 34 per cent when compared to last year's import in the same month. It is worth noting that these two are major food items, rich in protein and fat respectively, and account for a large chunk of India's imports. Hence, the curbs at present on the movement, both at local and international levels, have led to a disruption of the entire food supply chain in the country—from production to processing, packaging, transporting, marketing—giving rise to higher food prices, inaccessibility, and inadequate consumption of healthy food products. During such a climate of volatility and uncertainty, there is every possibility of stockpiling and hoarding of essential and durable food commodities, particularly pulses, in anticipation of higher prices, short supply, and unavailability in the days ahead. This would distort market dynamics, causing hyperinflation in the food sector. To understand the magnitude of this problem, let us take the price fluctuation of rice, the staple diet in South Asia. Retail price of rice rose by 10 per cent to 20 per cent on an average in January–April, 2020 in India, Pakistan, and Sri Lanka. Significantly, international rice price too shot up by 16 per cent against the 2019 average, while wheat price went up slightly (by about 2 per cent) as of end-May, 2020 (Kim et al. 2020).

As far as India is concerned, street vendors and small retailers are the primary source of supplying fruits and vegetables to poor people. Since the business of these two bottom-most categories of traders has been the worst affected by the lockdown, the sales of fruits and vegetables was expected to come down considerably, which in turn was expected to substantially reduce the intake of multivitamins and micronutrients by poor people.

On the consumption side, the Covid-19 shutdown witnessed a sharp fall in the purchasing power of the poor, resulting either in a reduction in the size and number of meals or in foregoing food for the whole day. There was a danger that if the situation became worse, people might even consume wild foods, immature crops, seed stocks, and items which are not part of their normal diet. We have seen such consumption across states in the past. Now, due to loss of income and disruption in the food supply chain, nutritious foods (such as vegetables and fruits), livestock products (like milk, meat, and eggs), and fish products have either become inaccessible or expensive, and consequently the poor tend to buy less and less of such food. Similarly, when staple food items, such as rice, wheat, and pulses, become more expensive, people are more likely to reduce consumption of these essential commodities without any option of substituting them. Moreover, with schools remaining closed, millions of poor school children were deprived of free mid-day meals provided by the government, on which they relied for their basic nutrition. If access to food gets snapped, a natural corollary would be an increase in child mortality, which will have a devastating effect (Roberton et al. 2020). Ultimately, a decline in the quality of diet increases problems associated with malnutrition.

Malnutrition and Covid-19

A healthy diet has a profound effect on the immune system, greatly reducing disease susceptibility (Naja and Hamadeh 2020). Inadequate intake of iron, zinc, and vitamins A, C, E, B_6, and B_{12} leads to deterioration in the functioning of the immune system (Gleeson et al. 2004), increasing the risk of getting infected. Food insecurity results in chronic undernutrition, which makes children vulnerable to infectious diseases, causing maternal anaemia in pregnant women, obesity, and the development of non-communicable diseases, including Type 2 diabetes (Food and Agriculture Organization of the United Nations 2019) and in due course turning them into a fertile hunting ground for Covid-19 and leaving them with poor prognosis (Watanabe et al. 2020). Insufficient nutrient intake would result in less immunity and a higher risk of Covid-19 in the short run and weaker health, reduced well-being, and inequity in the long run, indicative of higher levels of poverty. Hence, ensuring availability of adequate food and affordability to purchase nutrient rich food items is important not only for enhancing people's healthy diet and strengthening the immune system for long life but also, as an immediate goal, to ward off epidemics like Covid-19.

Although India has made significant progress in reducing poverty, food insecurity, and malnutrition over the past four decades, the country continues to grapple with a high level of malnutrition among the population, resulting in underweight, stunting, wasting, and anaemia. According to a 2015 report of the Food and Agriculture Organization, 5 per cent of pregnant women are anaemic (iron deficient), around 33 per cent of women have low body mass index, and a substantial number of children under age 5 years are stunted (38 per cent), wasted (21 per cent), and underweight (35.7 per cent) (Food and Agriculture Organization of the United Nations et al. 2015). Research findings reveal that the vast majority of people with micronutrient deficiencies live in low-income, South Asian countries, including India (Mark et al. 2016). A recent survey on micronutrient intake in select states of India showed that the proportion of preschool children who did not meet at least 50 per cent of the Indian Recommended Dietary Allowance (RDA) for calcium, vitamin A, riboflavin, and vitamin C ranged from 51 per cent to 82 per cent, while the corresponding figure for adolescents was 52 per cent to 85 per cent (National Nutrition Monitoring Bureau 2012). The intake of micronutrients, such as iron, vitamin A, riboflavin, vitamin C, and folic acid was less than 50 per cent of RDA in 51 per cent to 83 per cent of pregnant women (International Institute for Population Sciences [IIPS] and ICF 2017). Another study (Atkin 2016) clearly indicated that migrant households in India consume fewer calories per person, when compared to non-migrant households in the same village.

While India is already struggling with significant poverty, inequality, and poor nutrition, a further economic crisis brought about by the Covid-19 pandemic is likely to be disastrous, resulting in the denial of access to a diverse and nutritious diet among informal sector workers (Roberton et al. 2020). We can see subjectively the cumulative effect of the pandemic combined with existing malnutrition problems. Thus, this pandemic would prove to be a major hurdle in the way of achieving the Sustainable Development Goal 2 of reduced poverty, hunger, and malnutrition in India by 2030.

Food Security Measures

Before Covid-19, for over four decades, a number of measures were taken to eliminate the problems of food and nutrient insecurity, by increasing production, accessibility, and affordability. Such interventions included the Green Revolution and its associated technologies, advancements and developments in irrigation, and the introduction of various social security programmes, like Targeted Public Distribution System (TPDS), Integrated Child Development Services (ICDS), Balwadis childcare centres, Tamil Nadu's Mid-day Meal Scheme (PT MGR NMP), Pradhan Mantri Matru Vandana Yojana, and POSHAN Abhiyaan, aimed at improving the health and nutritional status of vulnerable sections. The recent National Food Security Act, 2013, too, ensures accessibility of major food items (5 kg per person per month) at a highly subsidised price (rice at Rs. 3 per kg, wheat at Rs. 2 per kg and coarse cereals at Rs. 1 per kg), covering around 75 per cent of the rural and 50 per cent of the urban population. Some states follow their own policy in this respect. For instance, Tamil Nadu has adopted universal public distribution system (UPDS) and provides free rice to all households, irrespective of socio-economic status.

Amidst Covid-19, the union government took several steps to address the sudden food crisis that arose due to the outbreak, with the prime focus on the millions of people engaged in the informal sector. According to reports, more than 37,900 relief camps were set up for migrant workers, serving food to more than 16 million people. In all, about 1.65 million workers have been accommodated and fed so far. In addition, 5 kg of rice and wheat and 1 kg of dal were supplied. Thus about Rs. 2.3 trillion and 75 million tonnes of cereals were allocated additionally to various food security schemes such as TPDS, midday meals, and ICDS (Parajuli 2020).

Apart from the union government, state governments have followed their own food security measures as an immediate response to the virus scare. For instance, the Government of Tamil Nadu extended a cash dole of Rs. 1,000 each to every ration-cardholder, besides supplying free rice, dal, oil, and sugar free to all eligible households. The Government of Kerala provided a food basket containing rice, wheat, sugar, salt, edible oil, pulses, spices, and non-food items (such as soap and sanitisers). The Government of Delhi supplied 1.5 times more ration to families entitled under the Public Distribution System (PDS).

Moreover, some states offer cooked meals at highly subsidised prices through canteens (Tamil Nadu's 'Amma Canteen', Rajasthan's 'Anna Poorna Rasoi', and Delhi's 'Aam Aadmi Canteen'), which sustained the vulnerable, including migrants, unskilled labourers, and poor students, even during the lockdown. Tamil Nadu's Amma Canteen, launched in 2013 and run by women's self-help groups, is a pioneer in this regard. At an Amma Canteen, one can get Idly at Rs. 1 and a variety of rice (curd rice, tamarind rice, or sambar rice) at Rs. 3–Rs. 5. Providing breakfast, lunch, and dinner every day throughout the year, except on specified holidays, these canteens remain the lifeline for those who are outside the ration card system and other social security programmes as well as migrants who are unable to avail of PDS food material.

Despite significant efforts by both union and state governments to ensure availability and accessibility of food items, many outreach programmes have not been implemented, or have been implemented poorly, due to implementation difficulties during the lockdown. For instance, as all schools remain closed amidst the pandemic, providing midday meals for poor children under ICDS has been disrupted and stopped in most places, and worsened undernutrition among children. Further, simply providing food grains does not ensure nutrition, especially for children, women, and pregnant and lactating mothers. They need food items which are rich in micronutrients and vitamins for a nutritious and healthy diet. Almost all food security programmes include cereals, such as rice and wheat, but most of the nutrient-rich food items are not covered under any PDS programme. Specifically, the role of pulses, millets, and other coarse grains is either meagre or completely absent in most of the food security programmes under the PDS. Similar is the case of fruits, vegetables, and other food items. Hitherto, there has been no policy option for the distribution of fish and livestock products, such as meat and milk products, through the PDS. Hence, the supply chain for many food products not covered in the PDS might be the most vulnerable to the lockdown, raising questions of nutrition insecurity and malnutrition problems.

Apart from these, the current PDS has been criticised for problems in its implementation. First, the current PDS benefits only local people, ignoring migrant workers. Recently, even before the outbreak of the pandemic, some initiatives, such as the 'One Nation, One Card' (ONOC) programme, had been introduced by the union government to tackle the issue of food insecurity among migrants. However, ONOC has been confronted with a few bottlenecks at the level of implementation, like managerial problems with respect to the states' role and rights in PDS distribution in the event of adopting this system. Previously, there was no specific programme concerning food and nutritional security of family members of unorganised and migrant workers. Second, identifying the exact beneficiary for availing any food security programme under PDS is an important issue. Until now, the beneficiaries (e.g., the number of family members) were identified based on the 2011 population census. Considering the increase in population since then, there is a possibility of having leftout a large chunk of the poor, who need government assistance in relief efforts like food supply during the pandemic (Drèze 2020; Sengupta and Jha 2020). Already, some states like Tamil Nadu have creditably adopted UPDS in supplying food grains. Third, the current PDS has been responsible for huge wastage of food grains while stocking, transporting, and so on. All these are expected to remain and aggravate the problems of undernourishment, malnutrition, and poverty in the country.

Conclusion and Policy Measures

Food production, trade, commerce, and the supply chain are in a precarious situation, with the economy hurtling down due to Covid-19 containment measures. These have had adverse consequences on the dietary pattern and nutrient intake of the people. If proper precautionary measures are not undertaken to address the issues of food and nutrient security associated with the Covid-19 pandemic, there would be a spill-over effect on poverty, inequality, education, health services, and production assets of the poor in the aftermath period of the pandemic, which will threaten the achievement of Sustainable Development Goals by 2030. Therefore, it is time to strengthen our food supply system through appropriate policy measures, to protect disadvantaged people, not only during the pandemic crisis, but at all times.

Short-Term Measures

1. Monitoring the proper functioning of labour and food markets is important to identify a crisis as and when it occurs as well as to ascertain the victims of the crisis and the needy. The labour and food markets are considered to be the key factors impinging upon livelihood, poverty level, food security, nutrition, and health of the vast citizenry, specifically, migrants and daily-wage earners.
2. The sudden lockdown created a huge mismatch between supply and demand for food materials, specifically for perishables. The prices of vegetables varied across markets, and within two to three days, prices of perishables oscillated drastically. This was because of a lack of proper distribution arrangements during the distress situation, that is, the frequent closing of permanent markets and opening of new market places in cities as well as villages. This affected producers and consumers. To avoid such pitfalls in distribution, we need an immediate forum comprising all stakeholders, including farmers, traders, street vendors, and marketing agencies supplying food items at the municipal or panchayat level. NGOs and volunteers can be entrusted to estimate food availability and demand for a region and a family. Accordingly, a food basket containing cereals, pulses, edible oil, milk products, fruits and vegetables, salt, bread, and other nutritional and health-related products should be distributed to every family, irrespective of socio-economic status, regularly (at intervals) during the entire period of the pandemic and containment, so that the full efficiency of containment measures can be achieved by keeping people in their homes (rather than roaming around the streets of the city searching for their basic needs). Such a mechanism would support the government's efforts and that of the civil society in achieving food security.
3. Until the pandemic is over, the scope and scale of existing schemes like 'Amma Canteen' should be enlarged in terms of number and size as per the data available about the users and migrants around a specific distance from existing canteens to effectively address the incidence of hunger. Care should be taken to ensure the quality of the food provided at these canteens.

4. Extending required support to agricultural and food processing industries is an urgent need. This can include providing additional credit support, postponing the repayment of monthly instalments without any additional interest rate, debt relief, proper clearance of insurance amount, increasing the subsidies on electricity, fuel, fertilisers and other farm inputs, increasing support prices for farm products, and supporting infrastructural arrangements like cold storages.
5. To overcome the problem of unemployment, existing development programmes, such as the Mahatma Gandhi National Rural Employment Guarantee (MGNREG) Scheme, should be accelerated during the distress situation by increasing the number of working days per person and increasing the wage rate by at least 50 per cent. The present MGNREG scheme supports only one member in a family; it should be increased to two to three members per family, during the lockdown period. The government can also identify and implement new development projects by involving MGNREG workers in rural and urban regions.

Long-Term Measures

1. Given the lacunae in the present system, a structured support system, right from food production to distribution, should be created to ensure availability, accessibility, and affordability of essential and nutritious food commodities to all members of the society at all times.
2. As most development and industrial activities are centred around urban regions, the rural hinterland, which continues to be backward, will not be able to provide enough employment opportunities to migrant workers who have returned to their villages due to the pandemic. Hence, supporting and establishing micro, small, and medium enterprises in villages or semi-urban areas would be an engine of growth by generating employment opportunities and subsequently arresting migration in the long run.

3. A separate statutory authority or institution should be formed to monitor, regulate, and account for the welfare of migrants and workers in the unorganised sector.
4. Migrant workers should be provided accessibility to PDS products at their workplaces.
5. It is important to supply nutrient-rich food commodities, such as finger millet, pearl millet, sorghum and other minor millets, through the PDS to reduce micronutrient deficiencies. This will help not only poor consumers but also small and marginal farmers to profitably market their produce at the right time for a fair price. In this regard, we need appropriate policy options.
6. All the food commodities supplied through the PDS should conform to quality and hygiene standards.
7. Digitalisation, online portals, and e-marketing and e-platforms in agricultural and food sector may help policymakers to easily manage the supply chain and food distribution across the country.
8. Since pandemics like Covid-19 cripple international trade—export and import of agricultural commodities—the country needs to recast its trade policies to safeguard the welfare of farmers, producers, and consumers. For instance, there should be lower tariffs and taxes on select imported food items, such as pulses and edible oils, to ensure adequate availability and price stability in the domestic market. Export-supportive infrastructure and logistics should be kept undisturbed by Covid-19, as India is a trade-surplus country in rice, meat, milk products, tea, honey, and horticultural products.
9. As of June 2020, the impact of the Covid-19 pandemic and the lockdown (on the socio-economic system) has been largely felt only by experience, and not in clear, numerical terms. Therefore, it is imperative to develop a big data and analytical system to ascertain the actual negative impact of the pandemic on the employment pattern, food supply chain, food and nutrition–related health issues, and livelihoods of local and migrant workers, in order to revive the economy and redeem it from the devastation caused by the pandemic.

References

Atkin, D., 'The Caloric Costs of Culture: Evidence from Indian Migrants', *American Economic Review*, 106(4), April 2016, pp. 1144–1181, available at http://doi.org/10.1257/aer.20140297, accessed on 5 November 2021.

Balasubramanian, M., 'Climate change, famine, and low-income communities challenge Sustainable Development Goals', *The Lancet Planetary Health*, 2(10), October 2018, pp. E421–E422, available at https://doi.org/10.1016/S2542-5196(18)30212-2, accessed on 5 November 2021.

Chen, M., 'To die from hunger or the virus. An all too real dilemma for the poor in India and (elsewhere)', *United Nations University (UNU)-WIDER*, April 2020, available at https://www.wider.unu.edu/publication/die-hunger-or-virus, accessed on 5 November 2021.

Drèze, J., 'Excess stocks of the Food Corporation of India must be released to the poor', *The Indian Express*, 9 April 2020, available at https://indianexpress.com/article/opinion/columns/coronavirus-lockdown-food-for-poor-migrants-mass-exodus-jean-dreze-6353790/, accessed on 5 November 2021.

Evelyn, K.,"'It's a racial justice issue': Black Americans are dying in greater numbers from Covid-19", *The Guardian*, 8 April 2020, available at https://www.theguardian.com/world/2020/apr/08/its-a-racial-justice-issue-black-americans-are-dying-in-greater-numbers-from-covid-19, accessed on 5 November 2021.

Food and Agriculture Organization of the United Nations, *The State of Food Security and Nutrition in the World 2019*, 2019, available at http://www.fao.org/3/ca5162en/ca5162en.pdf, accessed on 5 November 2021.

______, International Fund for Agricultural Development and World Food Programme, *The state of food insecurity in the world 2015. Meeting the 2015 international hunger targets: Taking stock of uneven progress*, Food and Agriculture Organization, 2015, available at http://www.fao.org/3/a-i4646e.pdf, accessed on 5 November 2021.

Galea, S., 'The Poor and Marginalized will be the Hardest Hit by Coronavirus', *Scientific American*, 9 March 2020, available at https://blogs.scientificamerican.com/observations/the-poor-and-marginalized-will-be-the-hardest-hit-by-coronavirus/, accessed on 5 November 2021.

Glauber, J., D. Laborde, W. Martin, and R. Vos, 'COVID-19: Trade restrictions are worst possible response to safeguard food security', *International Food Policy Research Institute*, 27 March 2020, available at https://www.ifpri.org/blog/covid-19-trade-restrictions-are-worst-possible-response-safeguard-food-security, accessed on 5 November 2021.

Gleeson, M., D. C. Nieman, and B. K. Pedersen, 'Exercise, nutrition and immune function', *Journal of Sports Sciences*, 22(1), January 2004, pp. 115–125, available at https://doi.org/10.1080/02640410310001 40590, accessed on 5 November 2021.

International Labour Organization (ILO), *COVID-19 and the world of work. (Third edition) Updated estimates and analysis* (ILO Monitor), 29 April 2020, available at https://www.ilo.org/wcmsp5/groups/public/@dgreports/@dcomm/documents/briefingnote/wcms_743146.pdf, accessed on 5 November 2021.

Jha, P., *Labour in Contemporary India*, Oxford University Press, 2016.

Kim, K., S. Kim, and C-Y. Park, *Food Security in Asia and the Pacific amid the COVID-19 pandemic* (ADB Briefs No. 139), Asian Development Bank, June 2020, available at http://doi.org/10.22617/BRF200176-2, accessed on 5 November 2021.

Korkoyah, D. T., Jr., and F. F. Wreh, *Ebola Impact Revealed: An assessment of the differing impact of the outbreak on the women and men in Liberia* (Report), UN Women, Oxfam International, Liberia Ministry of Gender and Development, Liberia Institute of Statistics and Geo-Information Services, and Liberia WASH Consortium, 1 July 2015, available at http://hdl.handle.net/10546/581371, accessed on 5 November 2021.

Mark, H. E., L A. Houghton, R. S. Gibson, E. Monterrosa, and L. Kraemer, 'Estimating dietary micronutrient supply and the prevalence of inadequate intakes from national food balance sheets in the South Asia region', *Asia Pacific Journal of Clinical Nutrition*, 25(2), 6 January 2016, pp. 368–376, available at http://dx.doi.org/10.6133%2fap jcn.2016.25.2.11, accessed on 5 November 2021.

International Institute for Population Sciences (IIPS) and ICF, National Family Health Survey (NFHS-4), 2015–16: India, 2017, available at http://rchiips.org/NFHS/NFHS-4Reports/India.pdf, accessed on 5 November 2021.

Ministry of Statistics and Programme Implementation, *Periodic labour force survey (July 2017–June 2018)*. Government of India, 2019, available at http://www.mospi.gov.in/sites/default/files/publication_reports/Annual%20Report,%20PLFS%202017-18_31052019.pdf, accessed on 10 July 2020.

Naja, F., and R. Hamadeh, 'Nutrition amid the COVID-19 pandemic: A multi-level framework for action', *European Journal of Clinical Nutrition*, 74(8), 20 April 2020, pp. 1117–1121, available at https://doi.org/10.1038/s41430-020-0634-3, accessed on 5 November 2021.

National Nutrition Monitoring Bureau, *Diet and Nutritional Status of Rural Population, Prevalence of Hypertension & Diabetes among Adults and Infants & Young Child Feeding Practices —Report of Third Repeat Survey* (NNMB Technical Report No. 26), National Institute of Nutrition, Indian Council of Medical Research, 2012, available at https://www.nin.res.in/downloads/NNMB_Third_Repeat_Rural_Survey%20%20%20Technicl_Report_26%20(1).pdf, accessed on 5 November 2021.

Parajuli, B., 'How India Can Improve Its Food Security After the Pandemic Passes', *The Wire*, 18 May 2020, available at https://thewire.in/agriculture/how-india-can-improve-its-food-security-after-the-pandemic-passes, accessed on 5 November 2021.

Roberton, T., E. D. Carter, V. B. Chou, A. R. Stegmuller, B. D. Jackson, Y. Tam, T. Sawadogo-Lewis, and N. Walker, 'Early estimates of the indirect effects of the COVID-19 pandemic on maternal and child mortality in low-income and middle-income countries: a modelling study', *The Lancet Global Health*, 8(7),1 July 2020, E901–E908, available at https://doi.org/10.1016/S2214-109X(20)30229-1, accessed on 5 November 2021.

Sabarwal, S., N. Sinha, and M. Buvinic, *The Global Financial Crisis: Assessing Vulnerability for Women and Children*, n.d., available at http://econ.tu.ac.th/class/archan/RANGSUN/EC%20460/EC%20460%20Readings/Global%20Issues/Global%20Financial%20Crisis%202007-2009/Academic%20Works%20By%20Instituion/IBRD/Global%20FinCrisis-%20Assessing%20Vulnerabikity%20for%20Women%20and%20Ch.pdf, accessed on 5 November 2021.

Sengupta, S., and M. K. Jha, 'Social Policy, COVID-19 and Impoverished Migrants: Challenges and Prospects in Locked Down India', *The International Journal of Community and Social Development*, 2(2), 26 June 2020, pp. 152–172, available at https://doi.org/10.1177/2516602620933715, accessed on 5 November 2021.

Seleiman, M. F., S. Selim, B. A. Alhammad, B. M. Alharbi, F. C. and Juliatti, 'Will novel coronavirus (Covid-19) pandemic impact agriculture, food security and animal sectors?' *Bioscience Journal*, 36(4), 25 May 2020, pp. 1315–1326, available at https://doi.org/10.14393/BJ-v36n4a2020-54560, accessed on 5 November 2021.

Sochas, L., A. A. Channon, and S. Nam, 'Counting indirect crisis-related deaths in the context of a low-resilience health system: The case of maternal and neonatal health during the Ebola epidemic in Sierra Leone', *Health Policy and Planning*, 32(3), 11 November 2017, pp. 32–39, available at https://doi.org/10.1093/heapol/czx108, accessed on 5 November 2021.

Watanabe, M., R. Risi, D. Tuccinardi, et al., 'Obesity and SARS-CoV-2: A population to safeguard', *Diabetes/Metabolism Research and Reviews*, 36(7), 21 April 2020, pp. 3325, available at https://doi.org/10.1002/dmrr.3325, accessed on 5 November 2021.

Wenham, C., J. Smith, and R. Morgan, 'COVID-19: The gendered impacts of the outbreak', *The Lancet*, 395(10227), 14 March 2020, pp. 846–848, available at https://doi.org/10.1016/S0140-6736(20)30526-2, accessed on 5 November 2021.

Notes on the Contributors

S. Anandhi is Professor, Madras Institute of Development Studies (MIDS), Chennai.

Kripa Ananthpur is Associate Professor, MIDS, Chennai.

P. G. Babu is Director, MIDS, Chennai and Professor, Indira Gandhi Institute of Development Research (IGIDR), Mumbai (on leave).

Gayathri Balagopal is an independent researcher and consultant, based in Chennai.

Shesadri Banerjee is Economist, Monetary Policy Department, Reserve Bank of India (RBI).

Maarten Bavinck is Visiting Professor, UiT The Arctic University of Norway.

Karen Coelho is Associate Professor, MIDS, Chennai.

E. Deepa is an independent researcher, based in Chennai.

P. Durairasu is former Principal Chief Conservator of Forests and Head of Forest Force, Government of Tamil Nadu, Chennai.

A. Ganesh-Kumar is Professor, IGIDR, Mumbai.

K. Jafar is Assistant Professor, MIDS, Chennai.

A. Kalaiyarasan is Assistant Professor, MIDS, Chennai.

Chandan Kumar is Visiting Faculty, Russell Square International College, Mumbai.

Vikas Kumar is Associate Professor, Azim Premji University, Bengaluru.

Umanath Malaiarasan is Assistant Professor, MIDS, Chennai.

Ajit Menon is Professor, MIDS, Chennai.

Krishanu Pradhan is Assistant Professor, Pingla Thana Mahavidyalaya, West Bengal.

Poonam Singh is Assistant Professor, National Institute of Industrial Engineering, Mumbai.

K. Sivasubramaniyan is Professor (Retired), MIDS, Chennai.

A. Srivathsan is Executive Director, Center for Research on Architecture and Urbanism, CEPT University, Ahmedabad.

C. Veeramani is Professor, IGIDR, Mumbai.

L. Venkatachalam is RBI Chair Professor, MIDS, Chennai.

A. R. Venkatachalapathy is Professor, MIDS, Chennai.

M. Vijayabaskar is Professor, MIDS, Chennai.

Index